More on the Gentle Art of

Verbal Self-Defense

MORE ON THE GENTLE ART OF
VERBAL SELF-DEFENSE

Suzette Haden Elgin, Ph.D.

PRENTICE
HALL
PRESS

New York   London   Toronto   Sydney   Tokyo   Singapore

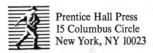

Prentice Hall Press
15 Columbus Circle
New York, NY 10023

Copyright © 1983 by Prentice-Hall, Inc.

Originally published by Prentice-Hall, Inc.

PRENTICE HALL PRESS and colophons are registered trademarks of Simon & Schuster Inc.

Library of Congress Cataloging-in-Publication Data

Elgin, Suzette Haden.
  More on the gentle art of verbal self-defense.

  Continues: The gentle art of verbal self-defense.
  1980.

  Bibliography: p.
  Includes index.
  1. Verbal self-defense.   2. Interpersonal communication.
  3. Conflict (Psychology).   4. Verbal behavior.
  I. Title.
BF637.V47E433   1983   153.7   82-24145
ISBN 0-13-602665-6

Manufactured in the United States of America

17   16   15   14   13   12

Contents

Contents

Contents

Preface

This book develops further the system of self-defense against verbal abuse presented in *The Gentle Art of Verbal Self-Defense* (Prentice-Hall, 1980). If you haven't read that book and can't conveniently get a copy, you will still be able to use this intermediate book; the basic terms and concepts you might need for that purpose are explained in the Appendix beginning on page 266.

My grateful thanks go to Virginia Satir, to John Grinder, to George Miller, and to the many other scholars and researchers whose work laid the foundations on which mine is based. I am grateful to my students and my clients, who have offered me so many useful comments and suggestions over the years. Thanks are due to the readers of the first book in this series, whose letters helped me greatly in the preparation of the present book. And special thanks go to Elizabeth Chater, to Kristine Wenkle, to Rebecca Haden, and to my long-suffering household.

You are certain to have questions about the material in this book that I have failed to answer, either because I don't know the answer or because the question didn't occur to me. If you'll write to me (Ozark Center for Language Studies, Route 4, Box 192-E, Huntsville, Arkansas 72740), I will do my best to send you an answer or to suggest where one might be found. If you are interested in Verbal Self-Defense training, or in becoming an official VSD trainer, please contact me directly.

Suzette Haden Elgin, Ph.D.

More on the Gentle Art of

Verbal Self-Defense

1
Introduction

"Sticks and stones'll break my bones, but *words*'ll never hurt me!" Do you believe that? Many of the foremost thinkers of our time believe it. They believe it so strongly that they write books about it and teach courses in it and base entire theories on it.

You probably first heard the "sticks and stones" incantation somewhere between three and six years of age. It came in handy in situations where half a dozen kids were dancing in a circle around some other kid, jeering any one of a whole list of deadly child insults. "Teacher's pet!" "Sissy!" "Four-eyes!" "Hillbilly!"— these will do for examples, in case you've forgotten.

And whether you were the victim in the center or one of the tormentors in the outer circle, you knew that the incantation was nothing but a ritual. It was just like asking "How are you?" when you didn't care one bit how the other person was. Or saying "Thank you very much" for a present that turned out to be a package of underwear instead of the thing you'd asked for and longed for. When you found yourself in the middle of that circle you shouted "Sticks and stones" because it was do that or cry, and crying was the worst thing you could possibly do. When you were on the outside and you heard "Sticks and stones," you appreciated the fact that your victim could play by the rules. But you didn't for one instant believe that the words being shouted didn't hurt like blazes.

Children have a fine set of reliable intuitions about language that have not yet been entirely destroyed by the pernicious language environment they live in. Fooling the very young ones is so hard that we say "They can see right through you." Children, even today's television children, still know "Sticks and stones" for the foolishness that it is. But grown-ups in this century have been taught to ignore such intuitions, and they are paying dearly for that. We are all paying.

The grown-up version of "Sticks and stones" appears in a lot of fancy formulations. We can boil them all down to common-sense terms rather easily; all claim that this is what happens in the real world:

1. Somebody says something to you.
2. You say to yourself, "That hurt me."
3. *You are wrong*. It wasn't what they said that hurt you. It was what you said to yourself.
4. Other people can't hurt you with their words—only you can hurt you.
5. All you have to do to put an end to being hurt is stop saying dumb things to yourself.

Now there is a *little* thread of truth in there. It's true that you can torture yourself very effectively if you put your back into it. You can go over and over the hurtful words. You can make yourself a kind of tape recording in your head, so that it's easy to replay the whole scene. You can reinforce the hurt and wear it into your memory the way you'd learn the lines of a play. You can spend whole chunks of your time doing this and hurt yourself a lot. But that's a different process from an honest reaction of pain to verbal abuse. And nothing can change the fact that the first hurt, the hurt that got you started in your effort to drive yourself berserk, was *somebody else's language behavior.*

The way that people all around me were suffering because they were victims of verbal abuse bothered me so much that I wrote a book explaining a set of basic techniques they could use to defend themselves. That was *The Gentle Art of Verbal Self-Defense,* the first book in this series. Because that book was the written equivalent of an emergency room, I behaved as if I could take it for granted that "Words'll never hurt you" was nonsense. Getting across the techniques of verbal self-defense mattered far more to me than making theoretical arguments. Now, however, I can take time to fill in the blanks and argue against the "Sticks and stones" myth. I can take time to argue that the list on page 2 is a distortion of the truth, and that what happens in the real world is this.

1. Somebody says something to you.
2. You feel pain, because of what they said.
3. You feel obligated *not* to feel pain because you have heard the grown-up version of "Sticks and stones."
4. Because you can't live up to that obligation, you feel guilty and ashamed, and that causes you even more pain.
5. This keeps happening; you keep hurting.

Let me say it for you, loud and clear, so that there can be no possible misunderstanding:

WORDS CAN HURT YOU

Other people's words can hurt you. You bet they can. And although "words" is a useful summary for what goes on, it's not just words. It's all language behavior, including silence, which is the withholding of words. It's body language. It's the way people look at you, the way they hold their bodies when you're around, the tone of their voices when they speak, the way they either let you come near or draw away from you, the expressions on their faces, and whether they bother to change their clothes for you.

And yet that myth represented by the first list is *most* respectable. Some of my best friends believe it devoutly. Books are written about it by great scholars and scientists, as well as by nonscholarly authors of "self-help" manuals. Courses are taught in it at our universities and professional schools. Whole institutes are created and funded to devote themselves to spreading the word around. If I'm right, and if the children are right, and if language can be just as brutally hurtful as any stick or stone, then how come all these important people disagree with me?

We'll spend some time looking at that question, because so much of the harm done to people owes its effects to another myth: *If rich and powerful and important people believe it, it must be true*. That idea kept everybody believing that the world was flat for many centuries. Rich and powerful and important doctors dissected corpses and then went straight on to deliver babies without washing their hands—because they believed that infections were caused by such things as how wicked the patient had been lately and what kind of miasmas lay over the swamps that year—and they caused a mountain of deaths. Rich and powerful and important people declared solemnly, in the most exclusive places, that airplanes could not possibly fly. In the 1800s, rich and powerful and important people proposed that the United States Patent Office should be closed down because everything had already been invented. *Sometimes, rich and powerful and important people believe things that are wrong.* We'll come back to this, but it would be well to keep it in mind.

Then there's the interesting question, "What's in it for me?" Usually, when you can be made to believe something, there is a reason for that. What's in the myth about the harmlessness of other people's words that makes it so appealing? Think about it. What does it have to mean? How about this?

If other people can't hurt me with *their* language, then I can't hurt anybody else with *my* language. If they think they've been hurt by my words, that's their problem, and it just shows how mixed up they are—it's not *my* fault.

This tidily relieves you of all responsibility for your language behavior, verbal and nonverbal. And it gives you a license to do all the harm you like, while blaming it on the people you hurt! That *is* magic!

This is a fertile breeding ground for all violence, by the way, because it feeds a total callousness toward others. The only way you can make it work for you, you see, is by learning to be very very good at ignoring the language of other people. The better you are at turning off their language input, the better the myth will work on your behalf. It's a short step from that to turning off all input and managing such handy tricks as blaming the poor for their poverty, blaming the sick for their illnesses, and blaming every misfortune from cradle to grave on the person it happens to. (It is usual, if you believe in the myth, to insist that things don't "happen" to people at all.) But all the time you believe you are remaining indifferent to the words and body language of others, your own body and mind are betraying you.

You have to process all that language input. You can't let garbage pile up in your house—you have to either take it out and burn or bury it, or pay somebody to do that for you, or run it through a garbage disposal unit. If you don't, pretty soon *you* will be buried in the garbage. And as language comes at you, you have to do something with *it,* too.

The way that human beings process language is perhaps not what you always thought it was. For example, you don't listen to a sentence all the way to the end, go back and determine what all the words in it mean, and then put that together and extract a meaning for the whole sentence. You couldn't possibly do that, because while you were trying it you would miss the next sentence, and you would grow more and more hopelessly behind.

Instead, every time somebody begins a sentence in your hearing, you immediately begin guessing which of the theoretically infinite sets of sentences possible in your language it is. You do that by using your real-world knowledge about your language, about the situation, and about the speaker to reduce that infinite set to a small and manageable one. You do that by running possible sentences from the reduced set through your head until you find one that matches what you are hearing. If you are polite, you let the speaker finish the sentence even though you know how it's going to end—or you may be one of those individuals who constantly finishes other people's sentences for them, perhaps because you don't think they finish them fast enough.

There isn't time for you to run every possible sentence through your head. If you tried that, you'd still be working on the very first sentence you ever heard, and you wouldn't be through with it when you died. You use knowledge you already have to restrict the possible sentences to a small number, and as soon as you come up with a sentence that has the same meaning as the one you're hearing, you drop that and listen to the next one. You do exactly the same thing when you read, except that the input is written down instead of spoken aloud.

You can't help doing this, any more than you can help breathing or keep your heart from beating. Nature has wisely put a sort of filter into the system for us, so that we are able to tune out a certain amount of the input to our eyes and ears; if that filter breaks down, *we* break down, just like an overloaded electric circuit. But beyond that natural limitation, we have no choice. You can't just "choose" not to smell a skunk, no matter how much you'd like to. You can't choose not to process language coming at you either.

The minute you start processing it, you have stopped being able to ignore it. You are taking an active part in that sentence being said to you, because that's the way a human being works.

And that's not all. The entire time someone is talking, that person is going through a complicated set of body movements that are matched (synchronized) with his or her speech; that is perhaps not surprising. But you may not realize that as you *listen* to somebody talk you are also going through a set of body movements that are matched to those of the speaker. The delay between the other person's speech and your movements is at most fifty milliseconds. You don't know you're doing that, and you can't keep from it without really exerting yourself. It takes a fancy camera, with stop action that will slow movements down to fractions of seconds and freeze them for examination, to make this pattern show up. Babies do it from the moment of birth, moving in unison with the speech they hear. When you slow down the films of conversation to the point where you can see this, it's like watching people in a dance. Again, you are participating—actively participating—in the language you hear. Indifference is impossible. Ignoring the language in your environment is impossible if you are able to hear it.

But if you don't know you're doing it, what does it matter? If you don't know you have heart disease or high blood pressure or cancer, does it matter? You don't know that your blood is flowing through your veins, you aren't aware of that—does that mean it doesn't matter? You aren't aware of the activities of your pancreas or your medulla oblongata—you may not even know you have such things inside you. Does that mean that it doesn't matter? On the contrary, it all matters so much that unless these things you are unaware of are working properly you are likely to die.

The psychiatrist who makes solemn pronouncements about how crucial it is to bring the garbage piling up in your mind to the surface where it can be dealt with should not be surprised when that process doesn't help much. Psychiatrists and other mental health workers today have to struggle along in a foolish framework of contradictions. The "Words can't hurt you" myth requires the victim constantly to suppress the real pain caused by language and pretend that it doesn't exist. This denial of reality causes constant stress, just as if you were required to keep your eyes tightly shut at all times while pretending that you could see perfectly well.

The poor mental health professional has to tell you that other people's words can't hurt you, only you can hurt you—and at the same time encourage you to scrabble around in your head and drag out the words that couldn't hurt you but did, so you can talk about them. This is an impossible situation. About all he or she can do is fall back on hazy remarks about how the reason you are sick is because you let other people's words hurt you—which, of course, makes it your fault and makes you feel guilty.

In such a situation, what can you do? Well, because the adviser's words can't hurt you (but they do), you bury deep in yourself both the hurtful words and the fact that you couldn't keep them from hurting. That means that the physician, counselor, minister, or social worker is *putting new garbage in just as fast as he or she is taking old garbage out*. No wonder it doesn't work very well! It doesn't take anything but common sense to see that this is going to be of use only when the garbage that comes out is so much worse than the garbage going in that almost any exchange is an improvement. (This is why it's often harder to help a person who is only depressed or upset than to help someone who is much more sick mentally.)

It's also not surprising that the rate of mental and emotional illness is so high in the helping professions. These people are actively participating, all day long (and sometimes all night as well), in other people's pain—and pretending staunchly that it doesn't hurt. You'd get sick, too, if you had to do that for a living.

Human beings can't live with constant stress. You can adapt to it sometimes. You can cope with it for a while if you get a break from it every now and then. But if it never stops, something has to give.

The "Words can't hurt you" myth creates too much stress for anyone to bear. Somewhere deep inside you the child that you used to be knows it is a lie. You have to work hard to keep that child quiet. You have to process language behavior that

8

causes you pain and bury the pain. And then you have to bury the *knowledge* that you buried the pain, because only people who are *sick* let other people's language hurt them, remember? Something is the matter with you if you let other people's words hurt you, and you *should* be able to stop that—which means you're a failure, and that hurts. So you throw that down in the basement of your mind with all the rest of the garbage. And then one day the basement is so full it won't hold any more at all, and things start leaking out under the bottom of the basement door. This book is about how to keep all that from happening.

SUPPLEMENTARY QUOTATIONS

It is my opinion that what actually happens to people is not as important in producing illness as what they *think* happened is. In other words, if something bad happens, you don't *have* to get sick if you can avoid getting miserable about the situation.

Remember, I called all diseases "behaviors," in other words, things that people do [Ellerbroek, 1978a, pp. 95, 120].

The world is perfect, each of us is all-powerful, shame and guilt are merely arbitrary notions, truth is identical to belief, suffering is merely the result of imperfect consciousness—how like manna all this must seem to hungry souls. For if we are each totally responsible for our fate, then all the others in the world are responsible for *their* fate, and, if that is so, why should we worry about them? [Marin, 1975, pp. 46–47].

To follow the currently fashionable idea that people have total control over their lives and should therefore take responsible action in them too often leads people to exercise "terminal control"—the only kind they have in many instances—so, unable to enrich their marriages they dissolve them, unable to improve their jobs they quit them, unable to reform their relationships they terminate them and, tragically, unable to better their lives they sometimes end them. [J. Miller, 1977, p. 35].

SUGGESTED READINGS

CLARK, V. P., et al., eds. *Language: Introductory Readings*, third edition. New York: St. Martin's Press, 1981. (A fine anthology of brief articles about language and linguistics, for the most part nontechnical. Good background material for students of verbal self-defense.)

COLE, R. A. "Navigating the Slippery Stream of Speech." *Psychology Today*, April 1979, pp. 77–87. (A nontechnical discussion of the processing of oral speech and the role of context.)

ELLERBROEK, W. C. "Language, Emotion and Disease." *Omni*, November 1978, pp. 93–95, 120. (See quotations above.)

MARIN, P. "The New Narcissism." *Harper's*, October 1975, pp. 45–56. (See quotations above.)

MILLER, G. A. *The Psychology of Communication*. New York: Basic Books, Inc., 1975. (Includes a good nontechnical discussion of language processing, with experimental evidence.)

MILLER, J. "A Message Center for Mental Health ..." *Human Behavior*, July 1977, pp. 25–36. (See quotation above.)

PELLETIER, K. R. "Mind as Healer, Mind as Slayer." *Psychology Today*, February 1977, pp. 35–40, 82–83. (See quotation above.)

PERT, A. "The Body's Own Tranquilizers." *Psychology Today*, September 1981, p. 100. (A brief discussion of the endorphins, as they affect the perception of pain and as mechanisms for handling stress.)

RESTAK, R. "The Brain Makes Its Own Narcotics!" *Saturday Review*, March 5, 1977, pp. 7–11. (Another good brief article on the chemicals produced by the human brain, and their receptors.)

SONTAG, S. *Illness as Metaphor*. New York: Vintage Books, 1979. (A discussion of the difference between historical perceptions of illness and our contemporary ones. Highly recommended.)

2
Back to the Basics

"Conversation in the United States is a competitive exercise in which the first person to draw a breath is declared the listener [Nathan Miller, quoted in Bolton, 1979, p. 4]."

CONVERSATION DEFINED

Do you know how to carry on a conversation? Can you do it with ease and skill? Do you, in fact, know what a conversation *is?* There are many situations in which one person talks and then some other person talks—are all of them properly described as conversations?

Like the flatness of the earth as seen from a Kansas back porch, these questions may seem too obvious for discussion. But conversation is as complicated as a football game and often involves higher stakes. And like a football game, unless you do it by the rules it doesn't count. Conversation is not just "people talking," and the facts about conversation are far from obvious. All the following sequences represent people talking, but not one of them counts as a conversation.

EXAMPLE ONE

X: You *know* I don't like hotdogs!

Y: Well, the concerto has an oboe in it.

X: Nobody knows what the square root of minus one is anymore.

Y: Particular demographics have significant parameters with factual equivalents, so to speak.

EXAMPLE TWO

X: Well, here we are! Finally, a chance to talk!

Y: At last! What'll we talk about?

X: I don't know. What do you want to talk about?

Y: Oh, I don't care. You know me—whatever you'd like is okay with me.

X: No, really, *you* decide . . .

EXAMPLE THREE

X: Last Tuesday morning—I know it was Tuesday because I always do the Backberry account on Tuesday, and let me tell you, you don't forget the Backberry account, not if you know what's good for you, so I always know it's Tuesday, see—last Tuesday morning I'd no more than gone out the front door when I saw that big old dog of my sister's sitting right out on—

Y: Hey, Joe—

X: —my front porch like it owned it, you know? And I said to myself, I said, if she thinks I'm gonna feed that darned old dog of hers just because she's too cheap to give it—

Y: Joe?

X: —its breakfast, she can just think again, I mean I wasn't born yesterday, and so I says to Ellen go get me that water pistol I brought home for the kid last night, and I went . . .

EXAMPLE FOUR

X: Young man, I am sick and tired of telling you to pick up this room! *Sick and tired.* All day long I work my fingers to the bone so you can have things nice, don't I? *Don't I?*

Y: Yes, ma'am.

X: And what do I get for it? What do I get, I ask you? I get your dirty socks under the bed and your dirty shirts under the dresser and your old dead frogs all over the bookcase and dust mice in the corner. . . .filth, that's what I get! Don't I?

Y: Yes, ma'am.

Conversation (*not* represented by any of those examples) used to be a popular activity. It was something you could be skilled at and admired for. Women had their "afternoons," for the specific purpose of taking part in conversation. People sat out on their front porches late into the night engaging in conversation for no other reason than because they liked doing that.

Nowadays, conversation as such appears to be almost entirely the property of the very rich, who are idle because they can afford to be, and the very poor, who are idle because they can't afford not to be. In between those extremes you may talk, when the talk is for a practical purpose, but you don't carry on conversation. People watch television instead. In at least half the houses I've visited over the past ten years, even while people were talking to one another the television was talking right along with us. It never seemed to occur to the owners that they could turn it off. And because conversation has become less and less common as a human activity, the basic facts about it have been to a great extent forgotten.[1]

THE PERFECT CONVERSATION

Conversation, like all other language behavior, is not random. If it were, you wouldn't be able to recognize the foregoing examples as nonconversations. But you may not be aware of the

---

[1]Recently linguists have begun to study human conversation in the same way geologists study rock formations. In some cases they could have saved themselves much trouble by going to the conversation manuals published routinely in the 1800s.

rules you are following when you "converse," and some examination of the process is therefore in order. Here is the pattern for a hypothetical perfect conversation; to keep it as free of complications as possible, we'll just call the speakers X and Y and Z.

1. X chooses himself or herself as first speaker and introduces a *topic*.
2. X talks about the topic for two or three sentences.
3. X chooses Y to be second speaker, letting Y know that by giving a clear set of cues.
4. Y accepts the *turn* to speak.
5. Y develops X's topic further, for one to three sentences.
6. Y selects Z to be next speaker, and provides the necessary cues for transfer of the turn.
7. Z accepts the turn.
8. Z develops X's topic for one to three sentences.
9. Z selects the next speaker, providing the necessary cues for transfer of the turn.
10. This continues until the topic has been thoroughly developed or the speakers have all run out of time, with roughly equal time to speak and equal number of turns going to each speaker.
11. Finally, one of the speakers chooses himself or herself to be last speaker and concludes the topic introduced originally by X.

We can immediately see two crucial elements here in the perfect conversation—the *turn,* and the *topic.* Somebody has to talk first, somebody has to respond to the first speaker, and the turns have to go around the group equitably. Somebody has to introduce a topic for the conversation to be about; somebody has to support or attack or otherwise develop that topic; everybody has to do his or her part.

Which is more important, turn or topic? The question can't be answered, because the two are so interdependent. It does you no good to be an expert at getting and keeping turns if you can't introduce and maintain successful topics. And no topic, no matter how fine, will be of any use if you aren't able to get turns and keep them long enough to make that topic succeed.

Look at Example One on page 12. Here the problem is that no topic is ever selected. Each person, so far as we can tell, is talking on a separate topic, and there is no interaction. (Toddlers behave like this, each one carrying on a private monologue alongside the others, in what looks like perfect contentment. So do some married couples, amazingly enough.) Turns are being taken, in the sense that only one person is talking at a time, but there is no reason for the sequence of turns. You could scramble them in any order you liked and it would make no difference.

In Example Two we have two people each trying desperately *not* to be the one who introduces the topic. They are both afraid that what they have to say won't be pleasing to the other person or will cause anger, and they're never going to get anywhere. Unlike Example One, here there is some system to the sequence of turns. For example, you couldn't rearrange them like this:

X: At last! What'll we talk about?
Y: Well, here we are!

But the fact that one utterance follows vaguely from a preceding one, showing that the speakers do know the rules for turn-taking, is no help. Without a topic, conversation is impossible.

In Example Three, a topic has been established. The language used is going to be about Joe's sister's dog. But no conversation is taking place, because the first speaker is not about to give up the turn to anybody else. Pretty soon, unless these two people are trapped in a stalled elevator, Joe is going to find himself all alone talking to his thumb. And all who know Joe and are familiar with his language habits are going to have an extra rule in their own systems that goes like this: "Avoid Joe."

Finally, in Example Four a topic is established in no uncertain terms and turns are being taken according to a clear system. When X asks a question and pauses, Y takes a turn long enough to say "Yes, ma'am." But that order is being imposed by force, and still, even with both topic and turns, there is no interaction. If the child made no response at all, it wouldn't change anything. If X just shook her fist and stamped both feet, it would convey much the same information. This is not a conversation, it's a lecture, and a punitive lecture at that. Example Four shows clearly that the establishment of a sequence of turns and the introduction of a topic are what scientists call "necessary but not sufficient conditions." Without them, you have no conversation, but having them does not *guarantee* conversation. There must also be control of these two elements.

CONTROL OF CONVERSATION

In my first book on verbal self-defense, I concentrated almost entirely on the skill of responding to the utterances of other people, especially people attacking you verbally. I wanted to make it clear that you could listen to those utterances and tell which ones were verbal attacks. And I wanted to show you how to respond to verbal attacks in a nonviolent way, without being forced to resort either to counterattacks or to a sacrifice of your own dignity and self-respect. I felt safe assuming that such attacks would happen in your language environment and that you needed to learn how to deal with them, and I still feel that way. But in this book I want to move on to a level of skill not limited to responses, and that means learning something about how to control conversation.

Just being able to grab the turns is not enough; any child can do that, or anybody with a sufficiently loud voice and sufficiently bad manners. And it's not enough just to introduce topics—you must also be able to make them succeed. Consider this bit of research: "Topics introduced by men succeeded 96 percent of the time, while topics introduced by women succeeded only 36 percent of the time (even though, overall, women initiated 62 percent of the topics in the conversations) [Parlee, 1979, p. 56]." Studies of this kind originally led linguists and researchers to believe that there was something inherently inequal in the linguistic dominance relations between males and females. But that was a misconception, and the point of such studies is not directly tied to gender except coincidentally.

The point is that the failure/success ratios reported in the research, and the attitudes described, are not unique to conversations between men and women. They are the typical profile for any conversation between two individuals in which one is markedly more dominant than the other—you could substitute "physicians" or "professors" or "executives" for "men," and then substitute "patients" or "students" or "employees" for "women," without doing much violence to either the statistics or the sentiments expressed. The control of conversation in this country is ordinarily found in the hands (or mouths) of dominant individuals, who a great deal of the time happen also to be males. It is time that those being dominated, whatever their gender, learned to do something about that.

This makes it necessary for me to digress just a bit. Some of you may be uneasy about all this talk of control and domination. If you had wanted to control things, you're thinking, you would have bought one of those best-sellers that tells you how to trample the most people underfoot the most quickly and permanently. I understand your concern. I feel the same way about all those articles in the literature of the service professions lately on how to control the "manipulative" patient or client or applicant.

The crucial problem here lies, as it so often does, in the vocabulary we are using. The terms *dominance* and *control* bring to mind the pecking order in the chicken yard, and head apes or top wolves enforcing their boss status with fang, claw, and muscle. That is a misunderstanding.

Let's eliminate, once and for all, the following idea: *There exists some completely neutral way to carry on language interactions.* If that were true, your concern would be valid, but it isn't. There is no such thing as neutral language interaction.

Imagine someone so irrationally dedicated to the concepts of equality and democracy that he or she found it unfair that some numbers are bigger than other numbers. You'd have to point out to this fanatic that "fair" has nothing to *do* with numbers. The number two is going to be bigger than number one, and six is going to be bigger than two, and so on to infinity, because *that is the nature of numbers*. And in just the same way, no matter how much you may admire the abstract concept of an absolutely neutral conversation with no one in control, it can never happen—and it has no more to do with fairness than the fact that eighteen is a bigger number than three.

Consider the simplest element of any conversation—somebody has to talk first. Without a first speaker, you have only silence. You may not want to be first speaker; you may prefer to leave that role to somebody else. But *that isn't neutral*. That is a choice you have made, an active choice to refrain from speaking first, and it represents an effort on your part to control the conversation, whether you like it or not. Each time there is an opportunity for the turn to be passed along to you, you have to choose to accept that turn or refuse it—again, your effort to control the conversation. Each time you yourself speak, you are going to have to decide whether to keep the turn or pass it on; if you decide to pass it on, you are going to have to decide whom to pass it on *to;* if you keep it, you are going to have to choose either to help the introduced topic succeed or contribute to making it fail. The two speakers in Example Two on page 12 may both be under the impression that they aren't trying to dominate the conversation, but they are mistaken. When they decide that somebody else must establish the topic, and insist on that turn after turn, they are only trying to establish control for themselves without taking any risks.

Nothing can happen in conversation until the dominance relations are established, but dominance relations in conversation are like dominance relations in number. They imply no moral judgments.

Because you have to take part in this system of control or refrain from all conversation forevermore, surely you would rather know what you are doing and know how to do it well. Which brings us back to our topic.

TURNS:
Getting them, keeping them, and passing them along

When I ask people to suggest a rule for turn-taking, I almost always get this answer: Get the *first* turn. As it happens, getting the first turn is not important at all.

There will be situations in which you can see that nobody else wants to speak first, and you might then do it yourself as a favor to the others or simply to avoid wasting time. People who refuse to look at you or at each other even for a few seconds are telling you as clearly as they can that they either don't feel able to talk first or aren't willing to. In such cases, if you feel the same way they do you might as well all go home. If not, you would be doing everyone a favor by speaking up and getting the show on the road.

But there will usually be at least one person in any group who is eager, or even determined, to talk first. And your best strategy is to let any such people get whatever they are so anxious to say over with. If you force the issue and make them wait to talk (assuming that you have the power to do so) they will not be listening to you but will be rehearsing their own speech in their heads and watching you for the first chance to leap in and get the turn away from you. This makes your own speech a waste of time and effort. Even in a group of only two—you and the determined other person—your own message will have a far better chance of being understood if you let the other person take the first turn. They may have something they are so anxious to say that they really feel it cannot wait—let them say it and get it over with. Some people may feel that they must talk first because they systematically use talking first as a way to demonstrate how important and powerful they are. If so, let them make their demonstration and be done with it, particularly because you know it is meaningless. Your concern, ordinarily, will not be with getting first turn, or any other specific turn. It will be with knowing how to get the turn *when you want it*, at any point in a particular conversation. Here, we have a few rules to help us along.

RULE ONE

Turns are passed on at an <u>optional</u> *pause or at the end of a sentence—wait for one of those.*

Pauses occur naturally at some places in sentences, and a speaker who doesn't put them in sounds strange. A speaker will have to pause at the place indicated by the comma in "I drove to the bank to pick up my sister, but then I went on over to your place." That sort of pause, required by the sound system of the language, is not something the speaker has any choice about and is not a signal of willingness to give up the turn. Little kids know this, but can't rely on other little kids to follow the rule; so they try to get around it by talking at blistering speed with *no pauses ever no matter what*. Their goal is to leave no *chance* for anyone to grab at a pause and take the turn. The result sounds like a child talking and is not becoming in an adult.

If you take the turn at an obligatory pause inside a sentence, you aren't playing by the rules—you're interrupting. Wait for an optional pause, one that the speaker does not have to make, or for the end of a sentence before you try to get the turn. It is much more difficult for a person to object that you've interrupted if you observe this rule.

If you happen to be the one with the turn and you want to ensure that someone won't take it from you at the end of a sentence, set up what you say so that they'll obviously be interrupting you if they do. Like this: "Now, I have three points that I want to make, and then I'd like to hear your ideas on the subject. First, (Point One). Second, (Point Two). Finally, (Point Three)." Anyone who moves in on you before the sentence presenting your third point is finished can legitimately be charged with interrupting and can't get off the hook by saying "Oh, I thought you were through." When you are waiting to get the turn and the other speaker has set up a kind of verbal agenda like this, respect it; you've been told where to anticipate the first pause that will mean "Now I am ready for someone else to talk"; you should wait for it.

RULE TWO

To get a speaker to provide you with a cue to take the turn, establish eye contact with him or her and frown just a little. (If the speaker is from a cultural group that considers direct eye contact rude, do this _very_ fast; with an Anglo speaker, particularly one accustomed to a dominant role, you may have to hold the eye contact almost to the point of a stare.) _Don't smile or murmur "mmhmm"_—both of those are "Go on talking" cues.

RULE THREE

If the speaker selects you to take the turn (assuming there are more than two present), you're fine. If you want the turn but the speaker selects someone else, you may "borrow" the turn from the person selected—but then you must pay it back at the first transfer point.

Speakers will indicate that you are their choice to get the turn by looking directly at you and smiling, perhaps by leaning toward you slightly or making hand gestures toward you. If they are anxious to maintain a dominant role, they may address you by name or offer a direct invitation, such as, "Bill, did you want to say something?" (An invitation like this carries with it the message that the speaker has the right to determine who talks

21

when and intends to enforce that right—don't use such utterances if that's not the message you want to get across.) A direct question that is appropriate is not that sort of message; if you are the only one present who knows anything about the cello, and the speaker says, "Bill, how much does a cello weigh, usually?" that is an ordinary question rather than a power declaration and should be so interpreted.

When the speaker gives the cue for the turn to someone else, but there are good reasons why you should have it instead, you may want to borrow it. You do that by saying something like this:

- "Bill, before you say anything about that I wonder if I could make one minor point?"
- "Bill, before you answer that question there's something that I feel ought to be said."
- "Bill, would you mind very much if I just said something briefly here before you respond to that?"

Notice what you are doing when you structure your utterance in this way. By speaking directly to the selected person and mentioning his or her name, you are acknowledging that you know who has been selected for the turn. By putting in a sequence such as "before you answer" or "before you respond" you are pointing out that what *you* want to say is only to precede what he or she was going to say—that is, you are making it clear that you are borrowing the turn and promising to give it back. You are asking for postponement, not surrender of privilege.

This is rarely a polite thing to do. Doing it without an excellent reason is plain bad manners. When there *is* a good reason, however, and it must be done, doing it this way is far better than a naked interruption. If you see that Bill has been selected for the turn and you simply ignore that and start talking, that is an interruption. Bill may be willing to excuse you for borrowing his turn—if you do it as suggested above, say what you have to say quickly and concisely, and then pass the turn to him immediately with a "Thanks, Bill, I appreciate that; now, it was your turn to talk." He *won't* forgive you for interrupting. I assume it's obvious that you don't borrow a turn by saying that you wonder if you could make "just half a dozen points." It also should be obvious that you don't forget whom you borrowed the turn from. If Bill (when you speak to him) looks as though he doesn't intend to *let* you borrow, break off eye contact at once and go on as though you hadn't understood that. If you do this properly, it will mean that the only way Bill can refuse the loan is by interrupting *you*. If that happens, and it is clear that he really is determined not to let you speak, let it go; this is exactly like trying to take the first turn when someone else is determined to have it, and it's a waste of your energy. It's not Bill who looks foolish in the following sequence, it's you.

> *You:* Bill, before you say anything about that I wonder if I could make just one point?
> *Bill:* No—I'm sorry, you couldn't.
> *You:* Bill, I really do feel that what I have to say is important here.
> *Bill:* Sorry. I don't.
> *You:* Bill, I think you ought to let me get in just a few brief words here—
> *Bill:* Look, it's my turn to talk, and I intend to talk. Is that clear?

The longer you go on like this, the more ridiculous you will appear; and if you manage to make Bill so disgusted that he gives in and lets you talk, you can be sure that nobody will have the slightest respect for what you say. Not by that point. This is not a winnable exchange.

RULE FOUR

If the speaker offers an obvious cue indicating willingness to give up the turn but doesn't select anybody to take it, choose yourself by referring directly to the speaker.

23

You do this in one of two ways, depending on the relative status you have with the speaker. If you are substantially outranked, refer to the speaker in the third person, and address what you say to the other(s) present. If your ranks are approximately equal or if you outrank the other person, refer to him or her by direct address. Here is an example of each.

- *When you are outranked:* "What Doctor X says is true. And I would like to add my support to her statement by pointing out that ..."
- *Otherwise:* "Doctor X, you're absolutely right. And I'd like to add my support to your statement by ..."

RULE FIVE

To <u>avoid</u> taking a turn, do none of the above. Avoid eye contact at any point when it's clear that a chance to transfer turns is coming up. Take a note, look at notes already taken, or find something else that you can reasonably look at. And if the speaker tries to force you to take the turn by addressing you directly, just take it long enough to pass it on.

Avoiding eye contact by staring at the floor or the ceiling or reading a newspaper is rotten strategy. There are always things you can legitimately pretend to need to look at—if you're desperate, drop something and look for what you dropped. But don't let people think you're refusing eye contact only to avoid the turn. Better to be thought rude because you don't wait until after the conversation is over to look for the pencil you dropped than to be thought rude for deliberately refusing to look at the speaker.

If you can't avoid the turn but don't want it, accept it and pass it on

- "I only wish I had something useful to say on the subject, but I don't. Jane, help me out, would you?"

- "What I know about the issue we're discussing would fit on the head of a pin—I'd rather hear what Jane has to say on the subject."
- "I don't think this is a good time for me to try to take that up, frankly. Jane, how about you doing the honors?"
- "Fortunately, we have someone here who is qualified to talk about that. Professor X, would you oblige?"

The absolutely informal equivalent of such pass-alongs is the reliable "Jane, *you* tell them." And you will have to consider the situation and the speakers present to decide what level of formality is appropriate. But you don't have to take the turn if you don't want it, not in a conversation, not even when the conversation is part of a more formal situation, such as a small committee meeting. Passing on the turn every time you get it may mean you won't be asked to the next meeting, but it is always an option open to you. The important thing is to *follow the rule and choose the next speaker.* That is, you can't get away with just "I don't want to talk" or "Ask somebody else." Get rid of the turn according to rule, and you can usually count on the person you handed it to to move right in there and leave you home free. Most people are delighted to be chosen.

Duration of Turns and Conversation

There's no formal rule about how many turns are possible in a given conversation or how long a given turn may be. But speakers are aware of an *informal* system and will observe roughly the following "rules of thumb":

1. One person talks at a time.
2. The speaker has the right to decide who gets next turn.
3. When a topic has been covered, the conversation is over unless a new topic is introduced.

4. No one turn lasts more than three sentences unless it is divided in advance into sets of no more than three sentences each. ("I would like to make three points at this time. First . . .")

5. No person takes more than three offered turns in a row if there are others present. That is, in a sequence such as *X:Y:X:Y:X:Y*, *Y* should use part of the last turn to select a speaker other than *X* or *Y*.

6. Everyone is offered at least one turn, unless some people have made it extremely clear that they do not want a turn—in which case their wishes should be respected.

The number three in that set of rules is, of course, chosen as the *average* number, and turns will range from two to as many as five sentences, depending on many outside factors, such as sentence length. If you aren't certain what's appropriate, three will always be a safe choice.

Neglecting to observe the final rule can have serious consequences. I once sat through a very long conversation in a group of seven people, all of them conversing by the rules. Each time someone selected me for a turn, I used it to pass it directly to someone else. After several hours of this, the dominant speaker decided that it would be a good idea to make an issue of the matter and insisted that I speak. The strategy was an old familiar one: "Everyone else has really pitched in and tried to help resolve this issue. Do you think you're so special that you can be excused from doing your part?"

I explained, carefully, that if I were forced to speak nobody would be at all pleased with what I had to say. This was more courtesy than the dominant speaker deserved, but I am a courteous person. My warning was ignored, however, and the request for me to "share my perceptions" was escalated, at which point I was no longer under any obligation to be polite. I then obliged the dominant speaker to the best of my ability. This involved a demonstration that the entire session had been one of the silliest experiences I'd ever had the misfortune to be included in, with specific points of evidence to support my position. And it ruined an otherwise successful meeting for everyone present.

I think it is safe to say that you should *never* force people to participate in a conversation when they've made it clear that they don't want to, not even if you are firmly convinced that it is "for their own good." (This is as true when you are a parent or teacher and the reluctant speaker is a child as it is in any other situation, by the way.) Don't force it, unless you are willing to risk a communications disaster, especially if there are ample signals to let you know that the person who isn't talking is a skilled communicator. The time and place to find out why that's happening is after the interaction is over, and in private.

Now, the $64,000 question. What do you do in the following all-too-familiar situation? Someone has the turn, and what that someone is doing with it is a torment to everyone present. The speaker is boring, is abusive, or refuses to follow the rules for turn-taking. Everyone is miserable. And you are not in a sufficiently intimate situation to allow anybody just to bring it to an end with something roughly like "Bill, shut up, please. For all our sakes." What do you do, assuming that nobody else appears willing to deal with the matter?

This is a case where you do interrupt. Be very sure that it *is* this case; be certain that the only way to save the conversation is to take the turn away from Bill against his will. And then quit fiddling around, and *do* it—as gently, and as quickly, as possible, like this:

> I know we'd all like to hear the rest of what Bill has to say, but it's time we moved on to the problem of where the toxic waste containers will be buried. My understanding of the situation is this. . . .

If Bill keeps talking, *you* keep talking. Louder. And longer. Only endurance will get you through this. And do not, under any circumstances, make eye contact with Bill. Your point is that Bill is now both inaudible and invisible; you don't make that point by looking at him.

If you are ordinarily accustomed to a subordinate role in language interactions, you'll find this a scary thing to do. If you're a woman, you will probably feel guilty doing it. Neither your fear nor your guilt is any excuse for not doing it when it has to be done—ignore both, and deal with them later, at your own convenience.

TOPICS:
Introducing them
and making them succeed

It does you no good at all to be skillful at getting turns and holding onto them if you have no topic to introduce, or if you can't maintain your topic (or a topic already introduced by a previous speaker). We began this chapter with a hypothetical perfect conversation; let's take a look at its opposite. Let's look at a whole set of possible responses to someone's attempt to introduce a topic and get a conversation started, in which not even one member of the set will help that topic succeed.

Topic Proposed
- "You know, I'm disgusted with Congress."

Responses
- "Did you pick up the mail?" (ignoring the topic)
- "I am, too. Did you pick up the mail?" (changing topics)
- "Nobody wants to talk about how you feel about Congress. Did you pick up the mail?" (abusive put-down)
- "I'm sure you are, but there are *important* things to talk about. Did you pick up the mail?" (patronizing put-down)
- "So what?" (hostile challenge)
- (Silence) (hostile nonresponse)

28

Another possibility is the full-speed-ahead interruption, like this

- "You know, I'm disgusted with—"
- "Did you pick up the mail?"

And finally, there is the negotiation for another topic, like this:

- "I know you are; and I'd like to talk to you about that. But right now I'm so mad about what happened at work today that I can't think about anything else. You want to talk about *that* for a while?"

When I run through this set in seminars and classes, people ordinarily show one of two emotions. They become excited and want me to understand that every single time they try to talk about anything that matters to them they get one of these responses back, and they are sick to death of it. Or they become very angry and inform me in no uncertain terms that they just by damn do not put *up* with that kind of thing and that's all there is *to* it. Occasionally people just sit there and grin, which means that this is how they handle other people's topics and they are getting a kick out of seeing how much everybody else is bothered by the list. They enjoy using those responses, you see, and not only are they aware of it, they're proud of it. These are your standard "Fastest Mouth in the West" people, and there's no point in wasting your attention on them. I let them sit there and grin and consider it a charitable donation.

Those pathetic statistics about women introducing 62 percent of all topics and seeing all but 36 percent of them fail, while men can claim a 96 percent success rate, are relevant at this point. We can be sure that we have those statistics to deal with because they are characteristic of conversations between persons differing markedly in power, in which the subordinate person does most of the work—proposing topics for others to support or shoot down—while the dominant person just rides along deciding which proposals live and which die. Because women by and large are in subordinate roles in our society, any set of statistics on communication involving large numbers of men and women will turn out that way.

That doesn't mean it represents what is right or "natural." But it will not go away just because it has been noticed. Powerful people tend to enjoy power and be unwilling to give it up without a struggle, and they have more resources to struggle with than subordinate people. Whether you are being dominated because you are a woman, because you are younger (or older), because you make less money, or for some other reason entirely—unless you prefer to be dominated, you had better make up your mind to take some specific action to change the situation. The people dominating you are unlikely to do that work for you.

Remember that in verbal self-defense one of your primary techniques is to use your attacker's strength for your defense. The stronger your opponent is, the more strength there is available for you to take advantage of and turn to your own purposes.

Look at the following interaction, which takes place at an ordinary breakfast table.

INTERACTION ONE

> *Wife:* Do you realize that the slump in the housing market is so bad that most people don't even bother to *think* about buying a house? It must be awful for people just starting out, not knowing if it's ever going to get any better.
>
> *Husband:* Will you please explain to me why this salt shaker never works?
>
> *Wife:* Oh, isn't it working? I'm sorry. It was working when I used it.

HUSBAND has ignored WIFE's attempt to launch a topic. She is invisible and inaudible, and *he* is going to talk about that salt shaker. Whereupon, WIFE abandons her topic instantly and *supports* his topic. They are now going to have a conversation about the salt shaker until HUSBAND decides he wants to talk about something else.

We can switch the genders here, if the wife is the dominant speaker—it will work just as well and be just as rotten as an example of conversation if the man proposes the housing market as topic and the woman goes roaring past with the winning salt shaker. Both arrangements are possible; both are common. (And in many marriages there is an unwritten agreement that in public it will be the man who wins, but at home it will be the woman. In such cases you need to know whether this particular "division of labor" represents the man agreeing that at home he will *let* the woman win, in which case he is still the dominant member of the pair even when he loses.)

Eligible Topics

It's important to point out here that the topic introduced by the wife is an *eligible* topic, so far as we can tell. It's a subject of general interest, it's not obscene or inflammatory, and there's no reason to consider it taboo. This matters, since sometimes a topic has to be shot down in a hurry because it should never have been brought up. We are all familiar with such topics and can remember painful examples from our own experience. The time your mother was visiting you and your daughter decided to discuss sexual practices you knew her grandmother would *not* wish to discuss. The time your boss came to dinner and your spouse—not realizing that because of a serious row at a labor-management meeting the very *word* "raise" was temporarily inflammatory—decided to take up the topic of the larger salary you should have been earning. In such situations, the topic disappears down a conversational rabbit hole, and the quicker the better. We will exclude such miscalculations from our discussion.

Adults are usually tolerant when children bring up topics that aren't eligible, because they realize that this is the result both of the child's very different viewpoint about the world and of lack of experience in conversation. We show the same tolerance toward the very old, not because they are inexperienced but because one of the privileges of advanced age is rule breaking, to a reasonable point. But usually we expect that all topics proposed will be eligible in at least a broad sense.

There may be times when you have good reason to raise a topic that is not eligible. You may be determined to air an issue that you know quite well nobody present wants to have aired, for your own excellent reasons. You may feel that the only appropriate strategy in some particular situation is to shock the others present, in which case an eligible topic is not suited for your needs. But of this you can be sure—the more ineligible a topic is, the harder it will be for you to make it succeed. Let's begin, therefore, by assuming that (like the wife in the previous interaction) you have chosen a topic that should be fully eligible. Now, how do you make it succeed?

Reinforcement
with Body Language

The simplest way to reinforce a topic is with body language, if that option is open to you. If you are close enough to the person ignoring your topic or failing to support it, and if that person is not someone utterly beyond your sphere in status, use a firm and immediate *touch*. Assume that you are the wife and you've brought up the housing market problem. Your husband says, "Will you please explain to me why this salt shaker never works?"

Lean toward him, put your hand firmly on his arm, establish eye contact if possible—but in no case let go, even if he refuses to look at you and doggedly stares at the salt shaker—and repeat what you said in the first place. Don't say "Listen to me!"

or "Didn't you hear me? Have you gone deaf?" or "You never listen to me when I talk!" or any of those other things that may seem to you to be indicated. Think—if you start that, what is going to happen? He has thrown out his line about the salt shaker. You say, "Why don't you ever pay any attention to me when I talk to you?" Do you then have any reason to expect him to talk about the housing market? You are at that point two conversational turns removed from the housing market, and it is probably lost forever. Your husband will say something like this.

> *Husband:* Why don't I ever pay attention to *you?* Come *on* ... why don't you ever pay attention to *me?* I asked you what was the matter with this salt shaker—have you gone deaf? I do need to get to work sometime this morning, you know, and I'd just as soon eat some breakfast first if you don't have any objection."

> Then . . .

> *Wife:* Good grief, why would I have any objection to your eating breakfast?

> *Husband:* I don't know why, and that's exactly my point. You don't have any logical reason to booby-trap the salt shaker every morning, so why do you do it?

The conversation will never get back to your topic, but the salt shaker topic (which is ridiculous, as topics go) has succeeded handsomely and is likely to appear in the next half dozen turns, along with the topic of your general unsatisfactoriness as a person.

Instead of going along with this, lay your hand firmly on his arm and repeat your opener. It doesn't have to be word for word, but it should be approximately what you said originally. Touching during conversation is a dominance gesture in American mainstream society. The powerful feel free to put their arms around their subordinates' shoulders, to pat their hands or knees, to give them a "playful" punch with the fist or a dig in the ribs.² When you, the wife, reinforce your topic by a firm, unemotional use of touch, your husband may well be sufficiently struck by your behavior to give you his attention.

The *choice* of body language is important, however, because it isn't always going to be a spouse whose attention you're after. The firm but gentle hand laid on someone's wrist and forearm, with your thumb against the inner side of the arm, is exactly the right amount of contact in casual situations. It is enough like the way a nurse takes someone's pulse to be both nonthreatening and nonsexual, but it clearly demands attention. *Hold* the gesture, because moving your fingers over the other person's arm or stroking the arm has sexual overtones. Touch the forearm rather than the hand, because hand patting is a "poor little you" gesture. Touch the forearm rather than the shoulder, because shoulder touching is seen as a kind of grabbing. Touch the forearm rather than the cheek, because cheek touching is a very intimate gesture. And once you have the attention you requested—for example, once full eye contact is established or something is said along the lines of "I'm sorry, what were you saying?"—terminate the touch immediately.

Nothing but experience will make it possible for you to know when you can do this and when you can't.³ In the course of that experience you are bound to make mistakes—learn from them. In Computer Mode⁴ you don't touch people, which is one of the reasons that mode is the safest; be very careful about touching anyone who seems determined to stay in Computer Mode.⁴ Touching someone who is busy Blaming may get you in

²Women who react to the quick pat from male superiors by claiming sexual harassment are quite right to protest, but the male who claims that he had no idea you'd take it that way is probably not lying. He's a boor, but he's likely to be telling the truth, because women have been submitting to such gestures from dominant males for so long that the males have come to see them as only ritual.

³Do not, under any circumstances, touch someone from a culture you are not completely familiar with. The consequences of cross-cultural touching are neither trivial nor amusing—they can be disastrous.

⁴For a brief explanation of the term *Computer Mode* and the others in this paragraph see the Appendix; Chapter 3 will discuss the various modes in detail.

trouble, since a Blamer may escalate the touch. For example, the husband in the previous interaction might react to your touch by roughly shaking off your hand and saying, "Keep your hands off me!" (If this happens, you have problems larger than just making your topic succeed, and this is not the place to go into them.) Placaters don't just touch, they pat, stroke, and *hang* on people, and such touching is offensive, as are the unpredictable touching behaviors of the Distracter. The firm but gentle hand on another's forearm, for only so long as is necessary to secure attention, is a Leveler gesture. It says, "I would very much like for you to listen to what I'm saying, please." And nothing more. Just a polite "please," not "Oh, *please, please,* I beg of you!"

How much of a status difference can you risk trying to span with this gesture? More than you might think. If you are the newest checkout clerk in the supermarket and the person you propose to touch is the male chief executive of the supermarket chain visiting your store on an inspection tour of the sales district, that is too big a gap. If you are a student and the other person is the president of your university, that's too big a gap. But you can probably count on your own instincts to give you reliable information in such extreme cases. The rule you are following is simple: If the person you propose to touch is someone that you could carry on a nonritual language interaction with informally, you may try the hand-on-forearm gesture. Here is an example of a ritual interaction, for comparison.

INTERACTION TWO

Company President: Well, so you're our newest clerk!

      You: Yes, sir.

      CP: I hope you'll be happy with Glorious Foods, Miss—(eyebrow goes up, and he leans toward you slightly)

      You: Smith, sir. I'm sure I will be.

      CP: That's the spirit, young lady!

You: Thank you, sir.
CP: Not at all, not at all!

In that sort of interaction you would only touch the man if you needed to let him know that his pants were on fire. (And in that case you'd have to, because if you just said "Sir, your pants are on fire," he would tell you what a great sense of humor you had and move right along, flaming away.) This is not a conversation.

Verbal Reinforcement
When Body Language Can't Be Used

If you are in a meeting with a number of people and the one whose attention you need is clear down at the other end of the table, the strategy of touch is not going to be available to you. For example, assume there are nine of you in a committee meeting to discuss this year's budget.

INTERACTION THREE
X: All right—does anybody have something to discuss?
You: Yes. *I* do. I think we ought to take a good look at the memo that came up from sales yesterday about the problems they're having. They clearly do not understand how a line item budget works.
X: How about you, Bill? Anything on your mind this morning that can't wait?

Does this happen? All the time. Can you do anything useful about it? Yes. Your line goes like this.

You: I'm sure Bill will agree with me that the most urgent matter before us is the Sales Department's confusion about working with a line item budget.

X, who has put you down smartly with the first response to your proposed topic, may now realize that you won't play that game and invite you to continue. Alternatively, X may invite Bill to comment on the line-item-budget question. At which point, you must decide if you can count on Bill to carry the ball. If so, relax; your topic is launched. If not, you'll have to borrow Bill's turn. Watch:

> *You:* I'm sure Bill will agree with me that the most urgent matter before us is the Sales Department's confusion about working with a line item budget.
>
> *X:* Well, Bill? Do you think sales is confused about line items?
>
> *You:* Bill, before you respond to that I'd like to make just one brief point. The Sales Department is getting more copier paper by ordering a new *copier*, because there's just so much paper per machine and they keep running out. That works, but there are better ways to handle a supply problem.

If you do this, remember—you don't look at Bill for more than an instant when you ask to borrow; you look at X. Make your point, quickly as promised, and then turn to Bill to signal that you're giving back the turn he surrendered.

Some people have to be taught a lesson; subtle techniques are wasted on them. Someone with whom you have to talk frequently, and who has established a *habit* of never letting your topics succeed, may require stronger measures. The technique sometimes taught in assertiveness workshops and communications seminars under the name "Broken Record" is one such measure. It's no fun at all; it goes like this:

INTERACTION FOUR

> *John:* You know, I really don't think I can pass that test we're having Thursday. I don't understand what it's supposed to cover. Do you think anybody in the class knows what's going on?
>
> *Bill:* Hey, you see that bird over there? I bet that's a hawk!
>
> *John:* You know, I really don't think I can pass that test we're having Thursday.

Bill: You don't *see* hawks around here! Turkey buzzards, maybe, but not hawks. Wonder what he's doing?

John: You know, I really don't think I can pass that test we're having Thursday.

Bill: That's the third time you've said that! What, you think I'm asleep or something?

Now John has Bill's attention, and he can repeat his statement that he doesn't understand what the test is supposed to cover and ask for Bill's opinion.

This is a boring and laborious technique. It should be used only with someone you have to talk to frequently. It should be used only with someone who has essentially forced you into it by consistently and repeatedly ignoring your topics. It may take a lot more than the three repetitions illustrated above to get the other person's ear. And you may have to go through the whole process a dozen times before that other person at last realizes that you really and truly do not intend to allow him or her to dominate you verbally by shooting down every topic you propose.

Please don't waste your time or your energy doing this unless all these conditions are met. If you only have to talk to Bill twice a year, it's absurd for you to bother. Let those who have to deal with Bill the Topic-Killer on a constant basis work it out, unless the issue raised in your topic is a genuine emergency matter. Then, of course, you will have to deal with it yourself.

Unsuccessful Topics

If you are someone whose topics never seem to succeed, no matter whom you are talking to, you have a different kind of problem. You will need to do some serious self-investigation, rather than just learning a technique or two for occasional confrontations. There are three possible explanations to consider.

1. Everyone you talk to is rude, domineering, and completely lacking in consideration for other people.
2. Every topic you propose is so unpleasant or so boring that nobody can bear to discuss it.
3. You are one of those people whose language behavior is an open, though usually unconscious, invitation to be bullied.

The first explanation is possible, but farfetched. If that's it, you need to find new associates, not new language patterns, and if you can't do that you are going to be subject to constant stress. You need expert help—get some. The other two explanations are far more likely to be what's really going on, and you need to take a serious look at them one at a time.

First, is what you say simply too unpleasant or too boring to qualify as a topic? As unobtrusively as you can, write down each topic that you try to launch over the course of several days. All you need to do is scribble a word or two on a scrap of paper. If you can't get away with doing it on the spot, do it as soon as possible. If you miss a few because two hours went by before you could record them and by that time you'd forgotten them, it doesn't matter. (If you cannot remember any of them unless you write them down right away, you've answered the question— only if all your topics were deadly would this happen.)

When you have a respectable number of items on your list, sit down and look it over. If you've been honest, it won't look like this:

- Bay of Pigs disaster
- why turtles don't use speech
- anorexia nervosa organic after all
- gold standard
- New Jerusalem Bible translation
- most dangerous chemical by-product

Nobody raises only topics of that kind except with a script to talk from, as on "talk shows." Somewhere in there the speaker would have had "lost my toothbrush," "out of aspirin," and "rotten weather." But the lists below are not so rare:

The All-One-Topic List of Topics
- the time I had my appendix out
- pain in throat
- blister, right foot, third toe
- Harry's hernia
- indigestion
- doctor's appointment
- fever blister

The No-Topic List of Topics
- potholder too thin
- out of orange juice
- coffee too weak
- windy
- coffee too strong again
- not windy
- flu going around, maybe

The All-Taboo List of Topics
- Sally's bowel operation
- what the dog threw up
- how Larry looked in his casket
- how radiation sickness starts
- my diarrhea
- why your religion is ridiculous
- what Marie made me promise not to tell

Nobody believes that his or her list is going to look like any one of those three. But I am not exaggerating. Somewhere in those lists, just as in the first one, there would also be "lost my toothbrush," "car won't start," and perhaps "why turtles don't use speech." But people I have worked with who complained that they could never get anybody to pay attention to what they talked about have one and all presented me with lists that are essentially just like those three examples. They are astonished to see their own lists, but they then understand why their topics fail.

If you always talk about the same thing—even if that one thing is a genuinely interesting and acceptable subject when it isn't run into the ground—people will stop listening to you. If everything you talk about is equivalent in interest to a three-day-old tuna noodle casserole, as in the no-topic list, people will keep changing the subject to protect themselves. And if you can't think of any topics that don't make your listeners feel sick, disgusted, angry, or abused, they will ignore you because they can't bear not to.

The chances are excellent that if you are given to any of these habits in your choice of topics you have been doing it for so long that you've become completely unaware of it. Only when that list is written down and staring you in the face will you see that your problem is not in the way you talk but in what you talk about. By all means, take the time to find out if this is the source of your problem. And if it is, work on eliminating it, even if it means that for months you have to make yourself *advance* lists of topics the way elegant young ladies used to do before an important social occasion. Of *course* you will sound stilted and artificial for a while. Better that than going on as you are—and in time the artificialness will go away. Conversation breeds conversation, and you will acquire new topics that genuinely interest both you and other people as you go along.

Suppose your topic list isn't like those three, but shows an ordinary mix of interesting subjects and the occasional "lost my toothbrush." Then you are probably one of those "Please Kick Me, I Like/Deserve It" verbal victims. The cure for that is to study verbal self-defense and put its principles into practice; by using this book , you can get rid of your victim profile.

Now we can move on beyond the basics to some verbal self-defense skills that you can use after you get *into* a conversation.

SUPPLEMENTARY QUOTATIONS

Have you ever felt one down in a conversation without knowing exactly why? Felt the other person was doing something that made you feel uncomfortable even though it wasn't anything he or she actually said? If so, you may have been the victim of what some social scientists call conversational politics—the violation of normal "rules" of conversation in order to assert power [Parlee, 1979, p. 48].

Language is like a game, we are often told; but if so, it is a game with soft rules: not like chess, played on a board of abstract geometry, but rather like golf, to be played on this actual course or that [Vendler, 1980, p. 209].

SUGGESTED READINGS

ADDEO, E. G., and R. E. BURGER. *EgoSpeak: Why No One Listens to You*. New York: Bantam Books, Inc., 1973. (Very useful because of its graphic presentation of the middle-class Anglo male's perception of the world and its reflection in language. The discussion of language in the workplace in Chapter 3 is invaluable for learning what sort of verbal games you should expect to encounter there.)

BOGARD, M. R. *The Manager's Style Book: Communication Skills to Improve Your Performance*. Englewood Cliffs, NJ: Prentice-Hall, Inc., 1979. (Valuable for exactly the same reasons as Addeo and Burger's book—as a thorough presentation of the world of business communication as seen by the Anglo male, upper-class and top management this time.)

BOLTON, R. *People Skills: How to Assert Yourself, Listen to Others, and Resolve Conflicts*. Englewood Cliffs, NJ: Prentice-Hall, Inc., 1979. (The most thorough book I know on basic communications skills—so detailed that it can be irritating to the advanced student, but ideal for the person with no previous knowledge of the subject.)

HUNSAKER, P. L., and A. J. ALLESSANDRA. *The Art of Managing People*. Englewood Cliffs, NJ: Prentice-Hall, Inc., 1980. (Although directed at managers, useful to any student of verbal self-defense. Fine sections on body language, on the use of time and space in communication, and on intonation. Highly recommended.)

KOTKER, Z. "The 'Feminine' Behavior of Powerless People." *Savvy*, March 1980, pp. 36–42. (A good discussion of the subordinate-equals- "feminine" research, with special attention to the workplace.)

PARLEE, M. B. "Conversational Politics." *Psychology Today*, May 1979, pp. 48–56. (See quotation above.)

PHILIPS, S. U. "Sex Differences and Language." *Annual Review of Anthropology* No. 9 (1980), pp. 523–44. (A thorough and non-technical survey of the research on gender differences as reflected in communication, both verbal and nonverbal.)

SACKS, H., et al. "A simplest systematics for the organization of turn-taking for conversation." *Language* 50, No. 4 (December 1974), pp. 696–735. (A scholarly discussion of the subject, but not overpoweringly technical. Many good examples from real conversation.)

VENDLER, Z. Review of *Pragmatics* by Peter Cole. (New York: Academic Press, 1978). *Language* 56, No. 1 (January 1980), pp. 209–11. (See quotation above.)

3
Using
the Satir Modes

Virginia Satir is a world-famous therapist specializing in family therapy. During her years of experience with clients, she has developed a system for classifying language behavior under stress that is extremely useful as part of the framework of verbal self-defense. Her five communication categories, which we will call the Satir Modes, are Blamer, Placater, Computer, Distracter, and Leveler.

Satir was interested in these verbal behavior patterns for their use in therapy. Our interest is in the way they can be used to identify the communication patterns of people in everyday life, which means that we are approaching them somewhat differently.

IDENTIFYING
THE SATIR MODES

THE BLAMER

The Blamer uses language with open and obvious hostility. Blamers are determined in their language to make certain that responsibility for anything that goes wrong, or anything that might go wrong, is placed on somebody else's shoulders. And they prefer to make that responsibility permanent. Blamers use language as a way to clear themselves of all such responsibility, no matter how trivial.

Typical Blaming utterances are these:

- "*Why* do you always spoil the whole day for everybody?"
- "*Why* can't you ever consider anybody else's feeling but your own?"
- "I will *never* understand why you always act like this."
- "You *never* think about what *I* might want to do, or how other people might feel—you don't care about anybody but yourself."

You might think that Blaming would always mean shouting and swearing and "carrying on," but it doesn't. Sentences like those above are as likely to be uttered in a cold, grim, tight-lipped manner as they are to be shouted, depending on the person who uses them. Furthermore, they frequently are part of the language repertoire of people who deliver them with sickly sweetness, tacking *darling* on one end and *sweetheart* on the other, like this:

- "Sweetheart, the way you always completely ignore the feelings of everybody around you just *amazes* me. .... Don't you think you ought to consider other people at least *once* in a while, darling?"

45

It's not hard to spot a Blamer who *is* shouting and threatening and tossing off insults. Such Blaming is language used as the cave-dwelling prehistoric human is said to have used a club, and you can't miss behavior like that. It's not all that serious, either, unless you are trapped in a situation that doesn't allow you to defend yourself and from which you can't easily escape. Unless they have helpless victims on hand, your average habitual Blamers quickly end up lonely and bitter, talking to the bare walls. Nobody will listen to such stuff for long unless they literally have no choice.

Far more dangerous is the Blamer who is not so obvious, because you won't automatically ignore what such a person says to you. A major clue to Blamer Mode is the constant use of words such as *always, never, only, everybody, anybody, ever, not even once,* and so on. Listen carefully—is the person you are talking with behaving as if every sentence were part of a permanent covenant etched in granite? If so, you may be dealing with a Blamer, and you should be wary.

The body language of a Blamer can be recognized fairly easily. Watch for clenched fists, gritted teeth, knotted eyebrows, stiff choppy gestures, and a posture that makes the person seem to be looming over you. Everything about Blamer Mode is threatening, angry, and punishing; it is the easiest of all modes to spot and the most useless to adopt for yourself.

THE PLACATER

The Placater is also concerned about placing blame, but has a very different approach from the Blamer's. The Placater, like the Blamer, wants responsibility placed elsewhere. But the Placater doesn't care where it's placed, just so long as he or she doesn't have to take it on. The Placater also differs from the Blamer in using language as a way to deny responsibility not just for bad things but for good things as well. Where the Blamer is an obvious verbal bully, the Placater is an equally obvious verbal victim, a kind of wiggling cocker spaniel puppy of language.

Here are some typical Placater utterances:

- "Oh, you know me, *I* don't care! Whatever you want to do is okay with me, *you* know that!"
- "Oh, *you* decide! It doesn't matter to me at all."
- "Of course I don't mind staying home with the kids, I *love* to stay with the kids! And I didn't really want to go with you people anyway, I was just pretending so you wouldn't feel bad . . . you go on and have a good time, I'll be fine."
- "Did I make you mad? I'll bet I did, didn't I? You know, it's a wonder you ever talk to me at all, the way I keep putting my foot in my stupid mouth! I'm so sorry . . . just forget all about what I said. What do *I* know about it, anyway?"

Nonverbally, the Placater appears uneasy and worried, even when the major issue under discussion is so trivial that it's hard to imagine anyone being concerned about it. The Placater is trying desperately to be nice, to please everybody at all times, and never to rock even the littlest boat. Watch for wide eyes, frequent blinking, smiles that aren't called for, lip biting, and a sort of constant intense leaning toward other people. It's hard for many Placaters to hold still.

And do not underestimate the dangerousness of Placater Mode—it can sucker you into traps you never anticipated. There is nothing helpless about the classic Scarlett O'Hara type, and anybody who is identified to you in advance as a "poor little thing" should be given close attention until you are sure you know what you are dealing with.

THE COMPUTER

The Computer is very different from the Blamer and the Placater. Where the Blamer projects obvious anger and the Placater projects obvious anxious concern and fear, the Computer uses language as far as possible to *hide* emotion rather than to project it. Blamer language places all responsibility on others who are clearly identified; Placater language denies all responsibility but is careful not to place it on anyone or anything else either; Computer language places all responsibility firmly on abstractions. "Star Trek's" Mr. Spock was an excellent example of a Computer (except when his human side betrayed him); the "perfect butler" is also a perfect Computer.

Computers talk like this:

- "Undoubtedly there is a reasonable explanation for all this."
- "It's clear that there is no cause for anyone to be concerned."
- "One (or *A person*) would hesitate to express an opinion with regard to that situation."
- "Perhaps it might be possible to determine that at a later date, but for the moment any sort of statement would be premature.

A Computer's body language is as close to no body language at all as is possible. Facial expressions are carefully kept to the bare minimum necessary to indicate that the Computer is not asleep or dead, with the most extreme example being a sort of faint distaste; no movement is made that isn't absolutely unavoidable. And although the examples above all use a highly educated vocabulary, the "strong, silent type" of the cowboy movie also relies on Computer Mode. Crucial to Computer Mode is the elimination of all references to *I* and of as many references to identifiable others as can be managed—a strong tendency to *Yup* and *Nope* will go a long way toward achieving that pair of goals.

THE DISTRACTER

The Distracter uses all three Satir Modes described above, but never settles on one long enough for anybody to notice. Verbally and nonverbally, the Distracter cycles rapidly through the Blamer, Placater, and Computer Modes in a way that gives an impression of total disorganization, silliness, and even panic. Just about the only thing you are unlikely to encounter in Distracter Mode is silence—the Distracter appears to feel obliged to say or do *something*, no matter how inappropriate.

Here's a Distracter talking:

- "I always believe that if you have something to say you ought to *say* it and not beat around the bush, don't you think so? I mean, not that I *care*, you understand, if somebody wants to be a hypocrite that's their business. ... Oh, not *you*, though, I didn't mean *you* are hypocritical! Goodness, I don't judge other people's behavior! But there are certain principles of conduct that are basic to civilized conversation and of which one must remain aware. But of course you aren't listening to me. You never do. No, really, you never have any interest in what *I* might have to say. Oh, you might have some interest, it's hard for me to tell, you know? Though maybe that's a little too strong—oh, I don't know *what* I mean, *you* know how I am!"

This kind of thing, accompanied by the same kind of wild swing from one style of body language to another, can pass right through tiresome and become intolerable. It doesn't take long, either.

THE LEVELER
Now, if we take out these four modes of communicative behavior, we have one left over—the Leveler. You can't set up a list of characteristics for Leveler Mode as you can for the other four, because it changes to fit the situation and the context. One way to define Leveler Mode is by the absence of any of the defining characteristics of Blaming, Placating, Computing, and Distracting. And that will prove useful. But there is something else that goes with Leveling, and to understand it you need to consider all three channels for the production of language.

One channel is the actual words spoken or written or signed, the elements we traditionally think of as language and refer to as communication. A second is the nonverbal channel; it includes gestures and facial expressions, postures of the body, and the like. For sign language users it would include all body language that was not specifically a part of the vocabulary of sign. And then there is something that young people used to call "vibrations." This is a third channel, made up of the feelings that the speaker or writer or signer experiences—perhaps below the level of conscious awareness—at the same time that the rest of the communication is going on. The first two can be directly observed; the third is something we lack a vocabulary for, and if there is a way to observe it, it cannot be easily explained—we say that we "feel" it rather than hear it or see it.

Ideally, all three channels match—this is called *congruence*. Ideally, there is no conflict between what someone feels, what that same someone says or signs or writes, and what is conveyed by his or her body language; it all has the same meaning. And that is the primary characteristic of Leveling.

I am using the word *ideal* here in a formal sense, to describe the communication of a chunk of information as fully as it is *possible* to communicate it. Leveling may be very unpleasant. A person who feels hatred for you, speaks to you of that hatred, and uses body language that matches both speech and feelings, is Leveling. That is ideal communication in the formal sense, but you may not enjoy it much.

Leveling, true Leveling, has one characteristic that you should keep in mind: *You can rely on it*. That has its good points, even when you don't like its content, because you know where you stand. And it is because of this that the use of Leveler Mode by phonies—people who can make you *believe* that their language can be trusted to correspond to their feelings—is the most dangerous of all kinds of communication. There are ways to spot a phony Leveler, and we'll come back to them in later chapters.

A person who is skilled at communication can move easily from one Satir Mode to another, choosing the one that is best for the particular situation and time. (This is not like the Distracter, who uses the different Satir Modes almost randomly without making reasoned choices.) Probably we all have a Satir Mode that we prefer to use, one in which we feel safest and most comfortable. All of us use one mode more expertly than the others and have a tendency to choose that mode when we are under stress and need to be free to concentrate on other things than the characteristics of our language behavior. But it is not ordinarily the case that we are unable to move beyond that single mode.[1]

When you spend a great deal of time with someone, you will find it easy to identify his or her preferred Satir Mode, and it is well worth your time to do so. You will also want to identify your *own* preference; to do this, you will have to listen to yourself more carefully than you may be accustomed to doing. Don't jump to the conclusion that you "know" you prefer Computer, or Placater, or whatever. Listen to the things you say over the course of a week; get someone else to help you observe your language if necessary, *then* decide.

There are long-term strategies for interacting with people who prefer one Satir Mode to another, and they will be discussed throughout this book. For the moment, let's turn our attention to some short-term strategies.

RESPONDING
TO THE SATIR MODES

When You Are Dominant

Identifying a particular speech with a particular category is not difficult. All the patterns are familiar, and you probably can name half a dozen persons in your own circle who are clearly

---

[1]This is one of the ways in which Satir's use of the modes differs from ours. She often had to concern herself with the problems of a person who was *locked in* to one particular mode and could use the others only very badly, if at all. And she had to deal with an extreme degree of mismatch between the inner channel of feeling and the two outer channels. She would expect the Blamers she encountered in therapy, for all their forceful outer image, to often be people terrified that no one respected them. Such problems are the proper concern of expert therapists and go beyond the scope of this book. For a more extensive discussion of Satir Modes in therapy, see the suggested readings at the end of this chapter.

51

typical of each (with the possible excepton of Leveling.) But after you have made that identification, what do you do next?

First, if you don't know *what* to do, *go to Computer Mode and maintain it*. This is an emergency technique, to be used while you make up your mind. The safest stance and the one least likely to get you into hot water is Computer Mode—that is why some people prefer it. Computers take no risks, and they are willing to accept the fact that the penalty for taking no risks may be that very little information is exchanged. When in doubt, use Computer Mode.

Second, except when you are certain that the language coming at you is in Leveler Mode, don't *match* Satir Modes. To answer a Blamer utterance with another Blamer utterance just means two clubs swinging at the same time. Placating back at a Placater is about as productive as discussing things with your cat—perhaps less so. The very idea of two or more Distracters trying to communicate with one another inspires pity. And although you may respond to Computer Mode with Computer Mode because you are using the emergency rule and don't know what else to do, when all communication stays in that mode nothing much is going to happen—what does happen will happen *very* slowly. (That is why committee meetings, which are often conducted entirely in Computer Mode by everyone present, usually accomplish so little and take so long to do even that.) The only example of matched Satir Modes that is truly effective for the communication of information is Leveling for Leveling.

Third, avoid the Distracter Mode completely if you can. You will find yourself in situations where one of the other four modes is the best choice, and obviously so. But I know only one situation in which Distracting is a useful language strategy. If, and only if, you find yourself in a situation in which the very best thing you could do is make yourself look like a complete idiot, there are few quicker or easier ways to accomplish that than to use Distracter Mode. Such situations are fortunately rare.

Now let's look at a hypothetical conversation, with the goal of analyzing it for use of Satir Modes.

INTERACTION FIVE

(You are at home with your ten-year-old daughter. She has asked you to let her go to Girl Scout camp with some of her friends, and you have told her she can't go.)

> *Child:* You don't care *any*thing about me! You *never* let me do anything I want to do, you only think about what *you* want! I'll *never* forgive you for this, not *ever!*

Notice—this child has only spoken three short sentences, but she has managed to work into them all of these words: two *anythings*; two *nevers* and a *not ever*; one *only*. She has used heavy stress on three of these words—that is, you hear them pronounced more loudly and with higher pitch than she would ordinarily have pronounced them. It should not be necessary for the child also to shake her fist at you; she is unquestionably using Blamer Mode.

You want to answer your daughter in a way that will support your original statement, that she cannot go to Girl Scout camp. You also want to keep this interaction from turning into a fight. What do you do now? Here's a Blamer response:

> *Parent:* I'm sick and tired of always having to argue with you about every decision I make, and I'm not going to put up with it this time. I'm the grown-up, you're the child—do you think you can manage to understand that? And I, the grown-up, am telling you once and for all that you, the child, are *not* going to Girl Scout camp! Period! Not only that, if you say *one more word* on the subject, you are *never* going to go to Girl Scout camp!

This may make you feel important and powerful. Your daughter may even have it coming, particularly if you know she is aware that you'd like to let her go to camp and can't because of something beyond your control, such as a lack of the money to pay for it. She is trying to bully you, after all, and you're entitled to defend yourself. But if you do it this way, you have failed completely in your second communication goal—not letting the interaction turn into a fight. You're bigger and stronger and probably louder, and you have a larger vocabulary. You also control such power tokens as money and privilege. Chances are good that you can win by Blaming. So what? There's nothing honorable or admirable about this kind of victory. When you've proved that you can bully your child better than your child can bully you, what does that get you? There is probably a better way. Here's a Placater trying:

> *Parent:* Honey, you know I don't have anything against letting you go to camp with your friends! You know me better than that, sweetheart, don't you? I didn't mean to make you think I didn't care anything about you. ... I don't know what I *said* that made you feel that way! I must not be in very good shape this morning if I can't express myself any better than *that!* You know I wouldn't want you to be unhappy, honey ... why would I want *that,* for heaven's sakes?

This parent is working hard to avoid a fight, that's obvious. It's not obvious that what's being said will back up the decision not to let the child go to camp, however. The most likely response is this one:

> *Child:* If you really *mean* that, you'll let me go.

Now you can start all over, from square one, with the child still in full control of the language environment.

Computer, then? Here's a Computer response, in two versions—one formal and one informal:

> *Parent:* There are undoubtedly parents of whom it can be said, with some degree of accuracy, that their refusal to allow their children to attend a summer camp represents evidence that they feel no concern or affection for those children. There are parents of whom it can be said that such an action is evidence of their selfishness. Such

parents might well be concerned with the question of whether their behavior can be forgiven by their children. However, it is not the case that this situation represents an example of that kind, and further discussion of the matter would not be productive. The subject is, therefore, closed.

Parent: There are parents that you can say—and not be far wrong—they won't let their kids go to summer camp 'cause they don't care anything about their kids. There are parents that you can say they act that way 'cause they're plain selfish. People like that, they'd do well to worry about whether their kids'll forgive them or not. But this isn't like that, and there's no point in talking about it any longer. Let's just let it go.

All right. Compared with either the Blamer or Placater response, this is much better. Your child is not well equipped to come back at you and continue the discussion in Computer Mode, which demonstrates that you are the boss here without making it necessary for you to stoop to insults and threats. You are most definitely not fighting with your child, and it will be clear to her, if you stick to this stance, that any fighting she does she will have to do all by herself without your help. Your original statement that she cannot go to camp has been strongly reinforced. And by keeping the interaction in Computer Mode you have avoided the question of whether *you* personally care about *her* personally. All your talk has been of hypothetical parents and hypothetical children and their hypothetical behavior. By all means, if you are not comfortable Leveling with your child in this situation, handle it in this way, in Computer Mode. You have granted the child a certain amount of dignity; you have agreed that her opinions are valid for some parents and for some children. You have not told her that her statements are stupid or childish or irrational—just that they don't happen to apply to this specific situation. You haven't threatened her, as you would have if you had used Blamer Mode. And you haven't invited her to keep on with the confrontation as you would have if you'd tried Placating. You have not ignored her—notice that each item she raised in her opening Blamer move has been mentioned by you and responded to. This is important; it means that you have *let her topic succeed*.

The only hazard to the Computer response is the one it always has—very little communication has taken place. You have really done nothing, in terms of information, but repeat what you said in the first place and acknowledge the limited validity of her response. If the point of the whole interaction was not actually forcing you to let the child go to camp, but testing you on this question of whether you *care* or not, your daughter is not much better off than she was before she tried this out.

If every such attempt is met with the same sort of response, she will eventually stop trying. You then risk having a child who concludes—on the basis of the only evidence available to her—that you are essentially *without* emotion toward her. It's not that you dislike her, it's that you really don't have any feelings one way or the other. (This is far from being the worst possible situation, by the way. It is better than having the child feel either that you can't stand her or that she is being strangled with possessive and unreasonable love.)

If you have reason to believe that what's really happening is in fact that your child is using the camp issue as a way of asking you how you feel about her, then Computer Mode is not the best one, though it is still better than Blamer, Placater, or Distracter. In this situation, if you can do it honestly, you should Level with your daughter and respond to what she is really asking you, like this:

> *Parent:* I love you very much. I want you to know that. Scout camp or no Scout camp—and it has to be no Scout camp this time—you really matter to me.

This is taking risks, you see. Unlike the Computer response, this is laying everything out in the open where it can be stomped on, if that happens to be the way the child feels about it. Maybe you have read the signals wrong, and you aren't being tested after all. Maybe she's just too unhappy to do anything but hit out at you, which is a different problem altogether. When you Level like this, you have to do it with the full knowledge that the response may very well be like the following bit of destruction:

> *Child:* Oh, really? Well then, you've got a problem, because I don't care if you love me or not.

If you can't handle that, don't risk it. You may want to give some serious thought to *why* you can't handle it, but don't risk it. Because once this exchange has taken place you will have trouble forgetting about it, and you're likely to bring it up when you lose your temper. Like this: "As I recall, you don't give a damn whether I love you or not, so why are you talking to me?" It will come between you and your daughter, even if she was only striking out at you in frustration and didn't really mean what she said. If she meant it—which is a definite possibility—you will have landed yourself some real trouble, and you may not want to do that.

Finally, just to show you why Distracter Mode is basically the dregs of communication, here's what a Distracter response in Interaction Five would be like.

> *Parent:* Oh, I don't know what to say to you! I *never* know what to say to you! Why can't you act like other children once in a while, will you tell me that? I don't *care* if you go to camp or not ... *you* know me, what do *I* care? Honey, you know it doesn't make any difference to me what you do, so long as you're happy. However, there exist situations in which a variety of otherwise attractive options are simply not feasible—a reasonable person keeps that firmly in mind. But I don't know. ... *Why* do you always put me on the spot like this?

I don't think this requires any comment. If you're not sure I'm right, read it aloud and listen to yourself.

When You Are Outranked

In Interaction Five you were the person who had control of most of the power. You were bigger, more verbally sophisticated, and had the ability to reward or punish in direct and observable ways. Your situation at work may be almost exactly the same—if, for example, you are a physician and you must respond to a Blaming utterance from a patient—or if you are an executive and are confronted by Blaming language from a member of your staff.

But let's assume, for purposes of discussion, that it's not like that, and that at work you find yourself on the lower end of the power scale.

INTERACTION SIX

(You have just asked your employer to let you have your vacation two weeks earlier than scheduled, so that you can take advantage of a travel special that isn't available at the later date.)

> *You:* Would you have any objection to that?
> *Employer:* Unfortunately, it isn't possible.

This is short and sweet, even for openers, but notice how it is structured. One way to avoid any expression of emotion, and thus to defuse a confrontation, is to keep all reference to *I* and *you* out of your utterances. The word *unfortunately* has no *I* in it; it says, abstractly, "It is unfortunate that ..." You, the employee, are not referred to directly; neither is the employer. It is the Fates, or the government, or the economic situation— something "out there" and not subject to either your control or your employer's—that is being held responsible for the refusal. What do you do? Remember that Distracter Mode is out absolutely. This is not a situation in which you would accomplish anything by trying to look ridiculous.

How about this? "I *knew* that's what you'd say! That's the way you *always* are, any time I ask you for anything!" Hear the heavy stresses? Hear the "always" and the "anything"? You're right, this is Blaming. It says, "You're saying no, and you're responsible for that no, and you always say no, and it's because you personally are unreasonable and mean." If you get back a Blamer "Oh, don't be ridiculous—do you *always* have to behave in that idiotic way?" it will tell you one of two things. Either your employer doesn't feel it's worth bothering to try to communicate with you effectively, which means you have a problem; or your employer is going to match you Blaming utterance for Blaming utterance and there's going to be a fight, which still means you have a problem.

Using Blamer Mode with a person in a superior dominance position, with someone who has the power to reward or punish you in concrete real-world ways, is always a dangerous move. True, your employer opened with a Computer move and you are following the basic principle of not matching Satir Modes. But Blaming is a poor choice. That leaves Placating, Computing, and Leveling—which do you use?

Here's a Placating response:

Employee: Oh, well. ... It doesn't matter. I didn't really care whether I got to go on that cruise or not.

Now that's pathetic. If you didn't care, pray tell, why did you take up your boss's valuable time asking? Placating, a great deal of the time, is a way of saying "Please pick on me, I thrive on abuse," and if what that gets you *is* abuse you should not be surprised.

Because your employer spoke to you in Computer Mode and you want to avoid matching Satir Modes, it begins to look as if your only possible choice is to Level. At which point, *stop.*

What are you doing? Why are you doing it? And is it a long-term strategy or just an isolated incident? What are you up against?

There is the situation in which you intend to establish a precedent. You have no intention of being a troublesome employee; on the other hand, you don't intend to be pushed around. You may not have any large emotional investment in the

59

particular vacation period you've asked for—like the child for whom Girl Scout camp was not the real issue. This may simply be your first move in a planned strategy of making it clear to your employer that you are to be respected; the vacation request is then just a means you've chosen to make that point with. If that's so, now that you've been turned down, you have to make a quick decision. Is this specific disagreement one you can afford to push as a way of establishing your precedent, without taking risks that are out of proportion to the possible gain?

It's right here that many people who are taken with the idea of learning to be "assertive" get into trouble. You are absolutely right, no matter what the job market is like, to make it clear to your employer(s) that you aren't someone who can be indiscriminately used as a doormat. That is a proper decision. Doormats have no job security and will be instantly dumped when an even more pliable doormat turns up on the scene.

But the item you choose as a way of stating your position *must* be one that can be argued about without loss of face on either side. It must not be so insignificant that it makes you look silly. (A typical example is the major confrontation over who is going to get the desk by the window.)[2] On the other hand, your *first* move of this kind should not be over an issue that is so laced with emotional poison that there is no way it can be resolved without a fight—for instance, it should not be about your refusal to tolerate smokers in the office with you *if your boss is a smoker.* It should not be about something that you know has just been a major issue with your employer in a labor-management hassle. On a long-term basis you may want to deal with precisely those

[2]Michael Korda and many other power brokers disagree with me on this, because of all the evidence that a windowed office is a mark of high status. I understand their reasoning. However, people who have power in *spite* of the lack of a window (or executive desk or any other physical symbol of that sort) have achieved a status that is not tied to the objects that surround them. If you allow yourself to depend on objects and artifacts to ensure your status, you're at the mercy of anyone with sufficient power to make changes in those objects. Such status trains you to be lazy and object-dependent. A major argument to obtain something that will only weaken you is a foolish move—if your status is real, you will be *offered* the object without having to argue for it. (And you may then decide whether you wish to achieve even more status by refusing it.)

issues, but that should not be where you start. First you establish the precedent, *then* you apply it to matters of importance.

There is a wonderful story in Ivan and Carol Doig's book *News: A Consumer's Guide* (Prentice-Hall, 1972). They tell of the monk who asked his superior if he could smoke while he was praying and was told, "Certainly not." Another monk, who had been listening, asked if he could pray while he was smoking, and was given not only permission but encouragement. They had asked the *same question*, but the issues they raised in the structuring of the question were very different. Presumably there is almost nothing a monk could do that would not be made better if he prayed while he did it; and the wise monk shaped his request to fit that principle, knowing in advance that it was a principle his superior would subscribe to.

If you know, therefore, that your employer is not rigidly committed on the subject of vacation schedules, and that vacation schedules are neutral ground with room for maneuvering, you might want to try Leveling, like this:

> *Employer:* Unfortunately, it isn't possible.
>
> *Employee:* I'm not sure that's true. .... There are four people who are familiar with the work I'm doing, and two people who don't mind changing places with me on the schedule. There shouldn't be any problem.

That's Leveling. You feel that it's no big issue for you to be allowed to change your vacation time, you've said so, and you've explained why without any sort of emotionalism. Presumably you've paid careful attention to your body language and have spoken in a neutral tone, sitting in a relaxed but alert position, making sure you were using no threatening gestures or facial expressions. Everything matches. Now your employer says, "Perhaps there shouldn't be a problem; nevertheless, it simply is not possible. Not this time." What is your next move?

Remember, this was a situation in which you didn't actually care about the vacation schedule. Don't lose track of that just because someone has said *no* to you twice. Your employer has come back at you again in Computer Mode, repeating what was said originally, which means that an attempt is being made to avoid a fight. The "Not this time" on the end, however, moves *out* of Computer Mode just a little and refers to this specific situation instead of an abstract principle. Your employer is saying, "I can't give in on this, but I understand that my refusal can't just be automatic. I agree that you have the right to ask me again another time." Your employer is Leveling, just barely.

If your vacation schedule were a matter of serious importance to you, you might want to continue in Leveler Mode—you would then ask that the precise reasons for refusing you be stated and discussed. If you don't really care and establishment of a principle was your true goal, you should probably back off. "Not this time" is the concession you were after, the one that agrees that there will be other times in which you won't be refused "just because I, the boss, say so." You've made your point, and when that next time comes around you will be in a better position to use it. Your employer went as far into Leveler Mode as he or she was willing or able to go; now you switch to Computer Mode and close off the interaction.

> *Employee:* Well, undoubtedly there are more important ways to spend a Monday morning than talking about vacation schedules. Thank you for your time.

The final sentence is not Placating, it's part of a ritual sequence like "How are you? I'm fine." You have now moved from a discussion of your personal vacation and this specific morning to a discussion of hypothetical mornings and hypothetical vacations. You have established the fact that you're not afraid to question your employer's decisions and that you're willing to back up your questioning with logical arguments. You have also established that you don't intend to make mountains out of molehills. Many factors might enter into your decision about this; I won't try to consider every one. But barring some important additional factor, you have gone far enough and accomplished what you set out to accomplish if you have followed the script suggested above.

When You Are in the Classroom

Another situation in which dominance relations and status are often highly imbalanced is education, especially at the college level. All levels involve the built-in set of power relationships coming from the fact that teachers give grades and make rules, while students receive grades and follow rules. But when students are adults, that is only the beginning.

In a single class a teacher may have a dozen students who are young adults with little experience beyond their high-school education. Then there may be veterans who are returning to school, often after lengthy military service. There are businesspeople who are in class to advance their skills or accumulate continuing education credits. There may be senior citizens coming back to school after a break of many years. In this mixture, which can become far more varied than you might expect, there are often students accustomed in their daily lives to being in positions of power themselves who must now assume the subordinate position in the classroom; this can be difficult for both the students and the instructor.

Matters are further complicated by the fact that so much teacher-student communication goes on in public, in a setting that requires the teacher to be cautious about losing face before the class, while the student must be equally leery of losing face before his or her peers and perhaps looking foolish. This situation has inherent tensions, but if a little care is taken in advance you can usually work your way around them.

INTERACTION SEVEN
(A student has come to class without an assigned research paper, because of a crisis at home. When the instructor asks for the papers, the student has nothing to turn in.)

> *Student:* I'm sorry. My paper isn't ready.
>
> *Instructor:* You've known it was due for almost three weeks—
> that's *more* than sufficient time for anyone who takes
> class obligations seriously.
>
> *Student:* There's no need for you to be abusive about it, Dr.
> Lee. You haven't even asked me *why* I'm not through
> with the paper!
>
> *Instructor:* No, and I don't *intend* to ask you, either. Don't
> bother asking me if you can turn it in late.

Assume that Student's body language included a wooden expression and rigid shoulders, plus a direct stare into Instructor's eyes. Assume that Instructor has flushed deeply after Student's first utterance and has stood clutching the stack of papers turned in by others tightly against his or her body ever since. What are the Satir Modes being used?

Notice that the student did not say "I haven't finished my paper" or "I don't have my paper ready yet" or anything of that kind. (You will always want to remember that anything people say represents a choice—they have said that thing rather than some other possible utterance. It's therefore often as important to consider what *hasn't* been said as what has.) Instead, we have "My paper isn't ready," which is a denial of responsibility. The initial "I'm sorry" was a ritual utterance, and nothing in the body language used with it has given it any overlay of sincerity to make it believable. The fact that it's followed by a full pause—a period rather than a comma—tells us that it was a flat statement. The direct eye contact is not helping; it forces the instructor to respond, and in combination with the rest of the body language used it appears to be a statement of equal status and a challenge.

The instructor's flush in response to this opening tells us—and *should have told the student*—that the opener was interpreted by the instructor as defiance and a direct aggressive stance. The student isn't really sorry, and the opener is a mild, slightly disguised, Blaming sequence. Instructor Blames back; Student raises the ante with even more intense Blaming, accusing Instructor openly of hostility. And Instructor ties it off right there by going to full Leveler Mode and whacking the obstreperous pupil right between the eyes.

This is all wrong. For one thing, any student who has failed to meet some class requirement and has a good reason for that failure should present it to the instructor *in private*, not before the entire class. An insecure teacher—and the one above appears to be insecure—may be very reasonable in private, when there is no feeling of being "on stage." That is the student's first mistake, and it sets up a losing context before he or she utters a word.

But perhaps the student is a businessman at middle or upper management level, used to being in authority at his office, used to announcing decisions and changing plans and having his word accepted without question. If that is so, he may not even have considered the possibility that there would be any challenge to *his* authority. He may be a physician, in which case he is accustomed not just to respect, but to deference that in many patients and their families comes near to reverence—it may not have entered his head that this attitude would disappear when he wasn't wearing his stethoscope around his neck.

Nevertheless, once the student saw the instructor's reaction, he should have realized that he had made a tactical error and pulled back before damage was done. An example follows.

INTERACTION SEVEN, REVISED
Student: I'm sorry. My paper isn't ready.

Instructor: You've known it was due for almost three weeks—that is more than sufficient time for anyone who takes class obligations seriously.

> *Student:* You're quite right. I'll make an appointment to see you during your office hours and discuss it, if you have no objection.
>
> *Instructor:* No objection at all; I'll see you then.

The sequence of modes here goes like this: Blamer, Blamer, Leveler, Leveler. It's important to understand that the student has not done any Placating. A Placating third utterance would look like this.

> *Student:* I know you're right, and I'm really *sorry!* I really do try to always do my work on time, especially in classes I like as much as *this* one. And you know I'd never be late with my work if I didn't have a good reason, and I want to tell you about it if it's all right with you. Okay? I mean, if it wouldn't be a lot of trouble or against the rules or anything.

That will make much of the class sick to their stomachs, and the instructor as well. In the previous version, on the other hand, the student has simply stated the facts: the instructor is correct that three weeks should be time enough; there is a time and place to discuss the problem, and it isn't in class, it's during office hours. This doesn't represent knuckling under to the instructor, just skillful communication. Notice that the Leveling student did not say "Can I make an appointment to discuss it with you during your office hours?" which would have given the instructor another chance to talk about what people who take their obligations seriously should and should not do. The student has passed along the information that he or she knows there's a proper way to handle this and intends to handle it according to that proper procedure, and the instructor has acknowledged the information. Nobody has lost face.

When the student faces the fact that in the classroom, whatever his or her role outside it, the instructor has the dominant role, that is rational behavior and constitutes proceeding on the basis of what is true in the real world. You can be certain that most instructors have had to deal with a half dozen students who refused to acknowledge this reality and made determined attempts to convince both instructor and class that no such status difference existed. After the first encounter of that strange kind, an instructor has available a set of techniques for instant put-down and will tend to use them at the slightest sign that here comes another of those "You may have a Ph.D., but that doesn't mean one damn thing to *me*" types. If your goal is to use your student career as a political statement, you may want to adopt this very stance—but be quite sure that you do it in the full knowledge that there will be penalties.

This has very little to do with elitism in most cases, by the way. It's rarely that the instructor is concerned with power tripping; instructors don't *have* to be concerned about that. The problem is almost entirely one of *time*. Because classes in this country are so rigidly time structured, the instructor can't afford to entertain quibbles about what happens when and for what reasons. And that is, of course, a subject for another book.[3]

The instructor in the revised version of Interaction Seven could have made a number of mistakes. Responding to the Leveler utterance with another Blaming one would have been a mistake, causing the instructor to be perceived by the rest of the class as unreasonable and bullying. Placating is impossible—that gives the whole class the message that the teacher is more concerned with being liked than with anything else; such a teacher will never be able to get the respect of the class. Distracting is as useful to a teacher as a gag and straitjacket. The only possible second choice is a Computer utterance like this:

> *Instructor:* It's unlikely that any instructor would object to seeing a student during office hours, Mr. *X*/Ms. *X*.

Whether an instructor chooses a Computer option in a situation like this, rather than Leveling, depends primarily on the

---

[3]If the allocation of time as a mechanism of power interests you, it has a whole science of its own. Look under the heading *chronemics* for material to read.

dominance relationships that must be considered. If the student seems to the instructor to be someone who might well make a practice of trying to dominate in the classroom, Computer Mode will be chosen as a polite warning to the student *not* to try that. If there's no reason to anticipate a problem in the future and the instructor is not overly concerned with maintaining a wide status difference in the class, Leveler Mode is more likely. (Very young and inexperienced instructors may follow the rule about using Computer Mode when you don't know what to do; students should give them time to become more comfortable with their craft.) The important thing for students to remember is that whenever they set up an interaction before an audience, whether of students or faculty, they are taking a risk—they should be certain that they have good reasons for doing so. Not wanting to take the time to go to scheduled office hours does not constitute a good reason.

PUTTING THE SATIR MODES IN CONTEXT

When the Satir Modes are discussed in classes or training sessions, people often say something like this to me: "My boss (husband, sister, friend) talked to me this morning for nearly an hour, and never used any of those patterns you're describing. Does that mean I should say they were using Leveling Mode?" That is, if you can't fit language behavior into one of the other four modes, is it automatically Leveling?

The problem here is one of vocabulary. Any discussion of language behavior runs into this particular glitch rapidly, because of the looseness with which we use words such as *conversation, discussion,* and *confrontation* in daily life. Some scientists (for instance, Sacks, et al., 1974) have set up the cover term *speech-exchange systems* and have then divided those systems into *conversation, interview, debate, meeting, cere-*

mony, interrogation, and so on. I have been using the term *interaction* as a cover term because I perhaps define language somewhat more broadly than these scholars might wish, and that makes *speech* not quite right for my work. But I would go on to make the same divisions within the large class of "interactions." And in many interactions the Satir Modes aren't really relevant.

For instance, when someone is preaching a sermon or presenting a lecture, you might be able to classify his or her speech as primarily in a given mode—but such information is of little use to you. A professor who relies heavily on Computer Mode for all in-class language may turn out to use Blamer Mode almost exclusively during private discussions. Any time speakers are "performing," even in the informal sense—as when a visiting relative spends an uninterrupted fifteen or twenty minutes telling family members about the trials and tribulations of the trip to your house—they will shift their speech behavior into a performing style for as long as it takes to carry out that function. Identification of the Satir Mode being used is not helpful in such a situation.

For the most part, you will want to identify someone's Satir Mode in conversation and in any language interaction that involves a reasonably equal exchange of turns to speak, such as an interview, a small-group meeting, a business or personal encounter with your doctor, lawyer, accountant, or social worker, and so on—any situation in which, as in simple conversation, the turn to speak moves from one person to another according to the rules in Chapter Two.

If your physician always speaks to you in the office and examining room in Blamer Mode, that is important to you and is something you must think about and decide how to deal with. But suppose you hear a doctor give a public speech on the evils of overeating to an audience of several hundred people in an auditorium. Suppose you notice that she uses Blamer Mode almost exclusively. The situations in which that would matter to you are very few—the only really plausible one is if you are the person responsible for selecting and scheduling speakers. And you would be the only one in the auditorium for whom that was important.

Some people, even in one-to-one language interactions, try to keep the turn for a very long time.[4] If they are extremely interesting to listen to, you may be willing to allow that. If they have a great deal of power over you—for example, if you are sick and your doctor is explaining the illness to you, or if you are applying for a loan and the loan officer is explaining the financial arrangements to you—you may have to allow it whether you like it or not. Otherwise, someone who insists on monopolizing the turn in conversations is looked upon as a bore and a nuisance and will be avoided as much as possible. If you exclude those very interesting and very powerful people, you are safe in saying that a conversational turn will ordinarily not last longer than about three sentences of moderate length, after which someone else will have the opportunity to talk. And it is in that type of interaction that you want to put your knowledge of Satir Modes to use. (Presumably most of your language interactions will *be* of that type.)

We will come back to the Satir Modes all through this book, whenever it is appropriate. You will have them well sorted out in your mind at this point and should have no trouble using them. My favorite device for keeping them straight is to imagine that one person representing each Satir Mode is in an elevator that

[4]Some people set up mechanisms for holding on to the turn that involve body language rather than an unending barrage of words. There is the technique of pausing in mid-sentence to take a puff of a cigarette—done with obvious and deliberately exaggerated slowness—while the listener must wait for the sentence to be taken up again and finished. Scratching the head; removing the eyeglasses, cleaning them, and then putting them back on; anything of that kind—when it is obvious that it is done only to delay the progress of the conversation—is offensive and constitutes verbal abuse. It says: "I'm talking, and you have to wait until I'm through, and if I choose to tend to my personal needs in the middle of my sentences while you sit there with nothing to do but watch me, that's my right and my privilege; and if you don't like it, you can lump it. See how powerful and important I am?" If you are guilty of this technique, I strongly suggest that you make an effort to give it up. It may feel good when you do it, but people will detest you for it.

has suddenly stopped between floors. The language would then go like this:

> *Blamer:* Which one of you idiots pushed the STOP button?
> *Placater:* Oh, dear, I hope it wasn't me! I didn't *mean* to!
> *Computer:* There is undoubtedly a perfectly reasonable explanation for this.
> *Distracter:* If this is my fault, I'm sorry, you know? One always anticipates this sort of incident in older buildings during peak electric utilization hours. Why does this kind of thing *always* happen to *me?*
> *Leveler:* I'm scared.

SUPPLEMENTARY QUOTATION

With few exceptions, linguistic acts are performed by a speaker to apprise an addressee of real-world facts. But it is equally true that the majority of sentences uttered give clues, in one way or another, as to *how*, precisely, that utterance is to mediate between the speaker's mentality and the real world outside. That is, not only does language provide an outlet for information about the world outside the speaker's mind, but it also enables a speaker to encode internal information. This is not, in the strictest sense, information, though it is of course communication; but since it carries no immediately useful denotative content, practitioners of rhetoric are occasionally heard to advise speakers to eschew these internal-state signals, to restrict their communications to purely external information, and thus to save time and the listener's patience. What is realized too seldom is that this scorned information is at least as valid as the 'useful' kind; one should be aware that one is communicating on both channels, and one should be aware of the message one is sending via the internal signals, as much as the external [Lakoff, 1976, pp. 309–310].

71

SUGGESTED READINGS

ELGIN, S. H. *The Gentle Art of Verbal Self-Defense*. Englewood Cliffs, N.J.: Prentice-Hall, Inc., 1980, pp. 7–13. (More material on the Satir Modes.)

GRINDER, J., and R. BANDLER. *The Structure of Magic: II*. Palo Alto, Calif.: Science and Behavior Books, Inc., 1976, pp. 47–53. (A discussion of the use of the Satir Modes in therapy.)

LAKOFF, R. "Linguistic Theory and the Real World." *Language Learning* 25, No. 2, 1976, pp. 309–38. (As the use of the words *apprise* and *eschew* in the quotation above will make obvious, this is a scholarly article. But it is not very technical and is extremely useful as a resource for verbal self-defense. Highly recommended.)

SATIR, V. *Conjoint Family Therapy*. Palo Alto, Calif.: Science and Behavior Books, Inc., 1964.

———, *Peoplemaking*. Palo Alto, Calif.: Science and Behavior Books, Inc., 1972.

(These two books by Satir present the five Satir language patterns in detail, within the context of therapy. Both verbal and nonverbal communication are discussed.)

4
Using
the Sensory Modes

Our senses are the mechanisms by which we process the information from our environment for interpretation by our brains. In elementary school we learn that we have *five* senses: sight, hearing, touch, smell, and taste. Books for specialists may add a few more to that list; researchers may propose additions such as a "magnetic" or "homing" sense. Some of the large categories may be divided into smaller subcategories for special purposes. For all we know, we may have many more senses than the traditional five.

But there is one way in which the sensory information available to us is restricted, and it represents a phenomenon that isn't affected much by scientific discovery or discussion. I'm referring to the resources we have in the English language for *expressing* what our senses allow us to perceive.

For the visual sense, for the eye, there is a large vocabulary ready for our use. The ear's aural sense is not quite so abundantly provided for, but still has large amounts of material for expression. And that is just about where English stops. For touch, the tactile sense, the vocabulary is severely limited. As for the senses of smell and taste (olfactory and gustatory are their awkward technical names)—the vocabulary is literally impoverished. If a dozen more senses are part of our equipment for processing information about the world, that's very nice to know—but we have no way to talk about them.

RECOGNIZING DOMINANT SENSORY MODES

The reason this is important in verbal self-defense is because people have preferences about their sensory modes. Just as people can usually switch from one Satir Mode to another at will but have one mode that they prefer, especially under stress, so do people have a sensory mode that they rely on more strongly than the others. The word *preference* is perhaps not strong enough, because the processing and interpreting of information from the senses are so crucially important to satisfactory functioning in the real world. It is probably correct to speak of one sensory mode as being *dominant,* rather than simply preferred, for most people; I will use that term. And because of this dominance, moving from one sensory mode to another becomes difficult once you go beyond the eye and ear modes. The inadequacy is not in the sensory system itself—it is in the interaction between that system and the English language.

It is true that certain words, phrases, and patterns are more typical of one Satir Mode than of another. But in a very real sense the entire vocabulary of English is available to Blamers, Computers, Placaters, Distracters, and Levelers. All can make use of the same linguistic resources, using body language if necessary to provide information about the Satir Mode that isn't present in the specific words used. This is not true in the sensory modes, and later in this chapter we will turn our attention in detail to some of the real-world consequences of that fact.

There is another difference between the two types of modes. Remember that except for Leveling you ordinarily try not to match the Satir Mode being used by the other person involved in the interaction. For the sensory modes, just the opposite is true—and matching modes is the proper strategy. This can be as simple as answering "How does that look to you?" with "I *see* what you mean and I like it" instead of "It *sounds* great to me," or it can be very complex and subtle.

Matching sensory modes is one of the easiest ways to put into effect the crucial principle of effective communication often expressed by such phrases as "being on the same wavelength" as the other speaker or "being in tune" with someone. When the language resources are available, it doesn't require a lot of skill and practice, just attention. And unlike many other matching techniques in communication, it isn't likely to make other people think you are making fun of them.

The most readily available cue to a person's dominant sensory mode, or to the sensory mode of any particular utterance, is in the *predicates* used. Predicates in English will almost always be either verbs, or some form of *be* plus a chunk describing the subject, identifying the subject, or locating the subject in space or time. (This is true often enough to make the exceptions of little interest in ordinary conversation.) In Table One, you have an example of each type of predicate, to make this clear.

TABLE ONE

Subject	Predicate	
John	shouted.	(Verb)
Maria	was tall and thin.	(Description)
	was a surgeon.	(Identification)
	was in Tulsa.	(Location in space)
The party	was at eight.	(Location in time)

Each of the paragraphs below uses one of the sensory modes almost exclusively, and the key words in the predicates are in italics for your convenience.

75

Sight, Visual: "I *see* what you're trying to say, and it's perfectly *clear* to me. But it *looks* like we'd be better off if we put the money in an IRA instead of trying to get it *out of sight* in a gimmicky tax shelter. The tax people can *see right through* those avocado grove setups these days; they're not *blind* the way they used to be. You *see* what I mean?"

Hearing, Auditory: "Sure, I *hear* you, and I'm *listening.* And you may be right. But it *sounds* to me like the government is *making a lot of noise* about pension accounts just to trick people into giving up control of their money without having to *listen to a lot of static* about it. I'm willing to *listen,* but I'm not sure I'm going to believe much of what I *hear.*"

Touch, Tactile[1]: "Well, I think I *get* the idea. Maybe the best way to *get a good grip* on this problem would be just to *grab it and run with it.* I mean, if you *feel* the same way about leasing another fleet of cars as I do, we're probably wasting time here. I don't *have the feeling* that there's any real opposition from the rest of the group—if there is, I sure can't *put my finger on it.*"

Smell, Olfactory: "Does this whole situation *smell* as bad to you as it does to me? Frankly, I think it *stinks,* and I don't have any intention of being involved in a *rotten* deal that will only make everybody in town start *sniffing around* trying to locate the source of the mess."

Taste, Gustatory: "We're so close to figuring this out that I can *taste* it, but I can tell you right now, I don't like it. It *makes*

---

[1]A part of the sense of touch that is not always discussed is the *positional* aspect—that sense that lets us know without looking whether we are standing up straight, whether we are having to lean back because of the steep angle of a hill, how our toes are placed inside our shoes, and so on. (The technical name for this is about as handy as *gustatory* and *olfactory*—it's *proprioception,* or worse, depending on your source.)

There's a small vocabulary associated with this positional function, from which the following examples can be constructed: "It seemed a little shaky to me"; "The whole thing made me dizzy"; "I couldn't seem to get it straight"; "I was bending over backward to please her"; "It was like walking through molasses to try to do business with that crew."

me sick to think that anybody on this committee would be fooling around with the computer data on a *sweet* project like this—it gives me a *nasty taste in my mouth* even to consider such a thing!"

You'll see right away that it would be easy to make the paragraphs that focus on sight and hearing a lot longer. And touch could be extended a bit. But there's not much vocabulary material to choose from for smell and taste. That may be because human beings don't use those two senses as extensively as they do the other three. It may have something to do with the fact that smell and taste overlap physiologically, so that it's often hard to decide which mode you're dealing with. (When people lose the sense of smell, they lose most or all of their sense of taste along with it—that's why food is so boring when you have a bad cold.) It may be caused by a combination of these factors.

But we can be certain that the primary problem is the lack of vocabulary for *talking* about taste and smell. This is such an inescapable constraint that you are quite safe in limiting your concern with sensory modes to the first three: eye, ear, and touch. If there are individuals who are truly smell or taste dominant, they have no way to get that information across to other human beings.

MATCHING SENSORY MODES

The technique of sensory mode matching for the first three senses is so simple at superficial levels of conversation (so easy to see and hear and get a feel for) that people tend to make light of it. In their book *The Structure of Magic: II*, Richard Bandler and John Grinder discuss this, using the term *representational system* approximately where I would use *sensory mode*. They say that in their training seminars

the common reaction which we perceive to identifying highly valued representational systems by identifying predicates is one of disbelief.... Our students first go through a stage of not believing this; secondly they begin to listen to people in this new way and become amazed at what they can learn about themselves and those around them; thirdly, they learn the value of this knowledge [p. 11].

I agree with Bandler and Grinder on this and would recommend that you spend some time really listening for sensory mode predicates and other linguistic markers before you decide that they are too trivial to be worth your time. Most people have a distorted idea of what conversation in the real world is like— that's why it takes a professional writer to write dialogue that is believable and why most "dialogues" in foreign language courses are so awful. You may think that your own conversation is not peppered with *see* and *hear* and *feel* as my sample paragraphs are—but pay close attention before you make up your mind. And if you still think it's too easy, perhaps you should be grateful for that. Many of the skills required for successful communication are *not* easy; don't look a gift horse in the mouth!

Now let's look at a few hypothetical interactions in which we focus on the use of sensory modes and see what happens. (You will have noticed, I'm sure, that I tend strongly to the seeing mode.)

With an Equal

INTERACTION EIGHT

Husband: Look, I don't want to talk about how much I smoke? Can't you see that?

Wife: Yes, but I'm tired of hearing it. And I'm tired of hearing you pretend you're deaf every time I try to discuss it.

Husband: It's none of your business. If that's not clear to you yet, you're just plain not paying attention. If you'd spend as much time with your mouth shut as you do with your eyes shut, we'd both be better off.

> *Wife:* I can't believe what I'm hearing! Can't we just talk about it, without you starting right away with the insults?
>
> *Husband:* No, we can't. I don't see what right you have to—
>
> *Wife:* What *right!* What *right?* Now you listen to me for a minute! Smoking makes you cough, and it costs a lot of money, and it's going to give you a heart attack or lung cancer or worse, and *that* is what gives me the "right" to talk about it!
>
> *Husband:* You believe everything you see on TV, don't you? Everything you see in those dumb magazines! Show you a little hype, you don't even bother to think, do you?
>
> *Wife:* The way *you* talk, a person—
>
> *Husband:* Hey, you should see yourself right this minute! You should just see yourself. You look like *you* were going to have the heart attack, and I haven't seen *you* smoking. Boy, if you think the way you're carrying on is any pleasure to watch, you'd better go take a good look in the mirror! I don't see anything there worth giving up cigarettes for, let me tell *you!*
>
> *Wife:* How could you say a thing like that to me? How could you *possibly* say such a thing?
>
> *Husband:* It was easy!

This is a fine example of two people getting nowhere at all, and if it's typical of their language interactions their marriage is not likely to be much fun for either of them. WIFE is talking almost exclusively in hearing mode; HUSBAND is using seeing mode. Notice that they both started out Leveling—HUSBAND says he doesn't want to talk about it and WIFE says she does. But by the second time HUSBAND talks he has switched to Blaming. And from then on the entire exchange is Blaming up to the final line. "It was easy" is Leveling, if it's true. If, as is more likely, it wasn't all that easy for HUSBAND to say what he did, "It was easy" is just a ritual insult in this context, a way of trying to hurt.

There's a better way to do this.

INTERACTION EIGHT, REVISED
Husband: Look, I don't want to talk about how much I smoke. Can't you see that?

    Wife: Yes, I can see it. I can see it clearly, and I'm sorry it bothers you so much—but I still really do want to talk about it.

Husband: It's none of your business.

    Wife: Now that I *don't* see. Let's look at that a little more closely.

It may very well be that this interaction would degenerate into the same kind of who-can-be-nastier match that it became when the two people involved were using different sensory modes. Many other factors have to be taken into account, and just matching sensory modes is not going to make them all disappear. It's not a magical wonder drug for all communication ills. But it *is* a strategy worth trying and requires very little effort from the speaker much of the time.

In the revised interaction above, the two speakers are still Leveling. "It's none of your business" isn't pleasant to hear, but it appears to be the husband's statement of the simple truth as he perceives it, whether he is right or wrong. If they can continue Leveling they have a better chance to make some progress in communicating. And if they can continue matching sensory modes they have a better chance to continue Leveling.

The reason for this is as simple as the technique. To talk to each other in Leveling Mode, they have to feel safe doing that. They have to have a reasonable degree of trust in each other, so that being honest doesn't appear too risky. One of the things that makes you trust another person is your feeling, to use a current cliché that is exactly right for this situation, that he or she is *sharing your perceptions*.

Every human being has a way of using language that is different from that of every other human being; this is called an *idiolect,* meaning "dialect of a single individual." When one person makes an attempt, however slight, to communicate in the idiolect of another, the other person will have the feeling that they are "speaking the same language." You are more comfortable, more at ease, safer, when you and the person you are talking with speak the same language. Leveling therefore becomes easier. You are less likely to retreat to Computing or Placating, charge into Blaming, or flee into Distracting.

People that I work with on this often begin by saying "Well, why should *I* change sensory modes? Let *him* (or *her*) do the changing!" I understand that. But I wish you would stop and give that some thought. Let's assume that you genuinely do want to improve your communication with others. The basic principle should be this: In any interaction, the person who can *most easily* change modes should be the one to do so.

This ability varies widely from one individual to another. If the person you are talking to is so eye dominant that shifting to another sensory mode literally makes talking difficult for him or her, and you can move with very little effort from your own preferred mode to eye mode, what possible benefit is there in your refusing to make that change? At least in situations of stress when a confrontation or actual fight seems imminent, is there any reason for you to refuse to make an adjustment in your speech that is relatively simple for you but would require a major effort from the other person? Remember—your goal is to transmit information, not to impose your power on the other. And if you can ease that information transfer by a technique that is simple for you, not to do so is *self*-defeating. Deciding that others should be forced to use a sensory mode that is awkward and difficult for them is arrogant and cruel, unless you happen to have special training and skills that enable you to make such decisions and unless you have been asked to take on that task. It is one thing to recommend that someone try to shift among the modes just to experiment with them and see how it sounds or feels; it is quite another to force that, much like the old practice of forcing left-handed children to switch to right-handedness.

Don't be alarmed by the way that everyone you talk to after reading this chapter seems to be trapped in one sensory mode (or one Satir Mode, for that matter.) Don't jump to the conclusion that *you* are, either. If someone convinced you that it was important to pay attention to how many times everyone you talked with used a word beginning with the letter *n*, you would feel for a while as if people were "letter *n* addicts." That's a side effect of the new close attention you are paying to something you haven't paid attention to in the past, and it will go away. Medical students tend to believe they have every dread disease they study and to notice symptoms of that disease in everyone around them; your sudden perception of the communications environment as being made up entirely of mode fixations is the same kind of phenomenon. You will probably be very self-conscious and artificial in your own use of sensory predicates for a while also, until the newness wears off. Don't worry about it.

When You Are Outranked

Now, what about the use of sensory modes at work? The husband and wife in Interaction Eight are presumably of roughly equal rank and power at home, if only because they know each other so well that they know all the best ways to hurt each other. What if you are a salesperson and you are trying to deal with a customer, who is by convention "always right"?

INTERACTION NINE

Customer: I'd like to see something in a size eleven, please ... something in a good wool. Blue, or a dark green. And decent quality would be nice for a change.

    Sales: This sweater has been selling really well, and I have it in three different shades of blue.

Customer: Not in dark green. Naturally not.

    Sales: Frankly, I don't feel that dark green is your best color. But this medium blue—

Customer: Now *look*, I don't see how you could possibly know what was or wasn't my best color! If I want dark green, you're supposed to sell me dark green, not act like some kind of color consultant!

Sales: I'm sorry—I didn't mean to act like I was telling you what to do. I'll try to find you something in a dark green, like you said.

Customer: I did *not* say that I was only interested in dark green, for heaven's sakes! Do you always look at everything a person says absolutely literally like that?

Sales: But you said—

Customer: Never mind. I'll look somewhere else. There's bound to be a clerk in this store who knows the meaning of the word *courtesy*.

No sale, right? And a very good example of why this is not trivial. Look at the very first line of the interaction in which the customer says "I'd like to see something."[2] Your first reaction may well be that the choice of *see* doesn't arise from any kind of preference for visual mode. You may feel that it has to do with the vocabulary available. After all, you can't say "I'd like to hear something in a size eleven." "I'd like to touch something in a size eleven" would be an odd way to talk. You're quite right that the common predicates for this situation are *see* and *look* and *show*. All are visual, eye predicates.

But remember, it's useful to pay attention to what *isn't* chosen. A speaker who prefers noneye modes doesn't have a predicate available for use in this situation. Such a speaker will then *not* choose the visual predicates, but will substitute an entirely different sort of utterance, like one of these:

- "What I need is something in a size eleven."
- "What do you have in a size eleven?"
- "Do you have any sweaters in a size eleven?"

[2]Here I am, you'll notice, trying to persuade or inform you, or both, and constantly using visual predicates. If you prefer another sense, this won't help—and is one reason why scientific and scholarly work is written in Computer Mode, which allows an avoidance of all sensory modes.

If the customer has used an eye predicate not by preference but because it has been learned as a sort of ritual opener for this kind of situation, it will quickly become clear from other things that are said. If you find that the speaker's preference is really for a nonvisual mode, you can quickly change, with no harm done. If, on the other hand, the customer is eye dominant, you will have taken the first step toward putting him or her at ease and establishing a perception of you as someone who understands the customer's needs and wants to help. This is particularly important when the customer has already given you a cue that there will be resistance, by saying that quality would be "nice for a change." Anything you can do to reduce that hostility without sacrificing dignity is a plus.

This needn't be complicated. Your interaction would start out like this.

INTERACTION NINE, REVISED
Customer: I'd like to see something in a size eleven ...

    Sales: May I show you one of our sweaters that has been selling very well? I have it in three shades of blue, if you'd like to look at it.

Customers who receive this sort of service, linguistically speaking, will appreciate knowing that you see things their way.

When Money Is Involved
One part of reality that can always be counted on to contribute tension to language interactions is money. The necessity to talk about money, particularly if real money and not abstract economic principles is involved, brings built-in short fuses with it. If you are trying to borrow money from someone else, you're going to be anxious and uncomfortable. If someone asks you to loan him or her money, the necessity to make a decision, and perhaps to refuse, makes you uncomfortable. If you and another person disagree about money—perhaps the amount of a salary, or

whether a bill has or hasn't been paid—the interaction has a high probability of turning into a confrontation.

But precisely because money is so important in this society, we need to use our most finely honed language skills in financial communication. (Don't ever think, please, that money is not important to people who have lots of it. If it weren't, they would not be rich people very long.)

Consider a situation in which you want to get a simple $1,000 loan at your neighborhood bank. Let's assume that you are a respectable ordinary citizen; let's also assume that you have a good credit record and a reasonable income, but no substantial collateral. What do you say to the bank's loan officer, and how will you be answered? There'll be some sort of opening ritual in the "Nice bank you've got here" style; and then what happens?

INTERACTION TEN

> *Bank:* Hmmm. According to this application form you filled out, you'd like to obtain a $1,000 loan. That correct, Mr. X?
>
> *You:* That's right. All the information you need is there on the form, I believe.
>
> *Bank:* Mmhmm. Well, in going over what you've written down here, I felt a little uncertain about your real intentions, Mr. X. I wonder if you could give me a little additional information.

Let's stop for a moment and consider this exchange. You want to match the bank officer's sensory mode so that you will be perceived as trustworthy, someone to Level with. The officer has used four full sentences, and has had two conversational turns. Notice all the things that have *not* been said.

- "I see that you want to..."
- "I've looked over this application..."
- "One thing that isn't really clear to me..."
- "If I'm hearing you correctly..."

- "From reading your application, it sounds to me as if ..."
- "This sounds good ..."

Unless the officer is deliberately trying to avoid all sensory mode clues, you certainly should suspect that touch is the preference here. And there is the fact that a number of concrete predicates (*fill out, make, go over, give*) *have* been used. And there is the unambiguous touch predicate in "I felt a little uncertain." At this point, you'd be well advised to try a touch predicate yourself.

> *You:* Do you feel that you need more information about *me*, or about the purpose of the loan? I may not have a very good grasp of your requirements.

And now you listen. If she answers with "I can see that, just by looking at the way you filled out this form,"you've made a mistake. If she says "What I need from you is some firm indication of the use you plan to make of this money, and I can't put my finger on it from the information written here," you've made the right decision. Your next move is to shift to visual predicates in the first case or continue with touch predicates in the second.

> *Bank:* I can see that, just by looking at the way you filled out this form.
>
> *You:* I apparently didn't make myself clear. If you'll show me the problem areas, I'll see if I can do better.

The loan officer has made her own preference obvious here, finally, and you have immediately adjusted your own language behavior to fit that preference. This has not required you to knuckle under or sacrifice your dignity in any way. It's as if you had begun speaking to the loan officer in French and then—on discovering that she would rather speak to you in German—you had courteously switched to German. You may not be able to do that with entire languages or dialects; you may find it awkward when the requirement is for one of the rarer sensory modes. But when you can do it without undue strain, it's an excellent idea. And when all that is required of you is moving between eye and ear modes, you'll probably find that very little effort is required. The use of touch vocabulary may require you to do a little work with a dictionary and make a list or two, unless it happens to be your own preference.

If you examine the written language of money transactions you will discover that there does seem to be an attempt to avoid sensory predicates. The April 1982 issue of *Money Magazine,* in the space of 184 pages, had 30 advertisements in which someone tried to convince the readers to turn over their money for investment purposes. These ads were from IRAs, mutual funds, insurance companies, firms specializing in precious metals, and so on. In all that expanse of "Please let us invest your money for you" pitches, many of them a full page or more of written copy, only *one* used any sensory predicates. The following sequence occurred in a full-page ad for the Oppenheimer Special Fund: "Look at track records. Look around at all the various investment possibilities. See how they've done in these last turbulent years, which have been a test of investment ability. And be sure to take a close look at Oppenheimer Special Fund . . . ." And at the very end of the presentation we find the sentence, "See if anybody has topped that." The copy stands out by its unique use of all these sensory—visual—words.

I don't know if somewhere in the financial ad-writing community there exists a manual with a rule reading roughly, "When you want people to let you invest their money, use no sensory predicates in your advertising." Considering the rotten instruction people get in even the simplest communications techniques, there probably is no such rule. (If you're looking for a thesis topic, you might want to find out.)

What is more likely, and is reflected in the brochures that these firms send to people on their mailing lists, is that because they want to manage your money they are trying to write in Computer Mode. Written Computer Mode accomplishes a

87

number of things, among them establishing a formality that may seem appropriate in something so weighty as money management or investment counseling. It also achieves neutrality—that is, the language is carefully structured to *make no choice*. In that way, although the advertiser doesn't gain the advantage of having you perceive the firm as definitely "your kind of people," the equally definite turnoff that would come from an open clash of linguistic styles is avoided; the matter is left open. Later, when there are some data accumulated from personal contact, the neutrality can be abandoned.[3]

UNDERSTANDING PROBLEMS OF SENSORY MODE DOMINANCE

I promised at the beginning of this chapter to come back to a discussion of some of the ways that a strong preference, a dominance, in one sensory mode could affect people in the real world. Let's talk about what happens when someone has touch as the dominant sensory mode, and let it serve as an example for even more exotic situations.

In America today there is an overwhelming emphasis on ear and eye modes. All educational and mass media mechanisms are limited to those two modes, so that those whose preference is eye or ear (and especially eye) have an advantage truly impossible to overcome. Let's look at some of the major reasons for this and their effects.

First, except for the small number of people who use sign language—and therefore depend on sight and touch—all language processing in our culture is done through the sensory mechanisms of eye and ear.[4] We must see to read, we must see to

---

[3]If you wonder why the Oppenheimer people have deviated from this neutral path, there is a possibility worth considering. A lot of data indicates that people who are eye dominant also tend to be highly successful people who *have* money to invest. Oppenheimer may have a good idea going there.

[4]There are two obvious exceptions to this statement. One is the individual deaf and blind from birth, who is dependent on tactile alphabets for "speech" and on Braille

sign, and we must at least hear—and preferably see as well—to use speech. Despite what research tells us about the crucial character of body language, we receive no instruction in the subject, and it remains as mysterious to our conscious awareness as the far fringes of quantum physics.

Sensory Modes and the Brain

I doubt that you will have escaped the flood of recent stories and articles about left brain–right brain discoveries. Much of what the public has been told about this research is distorted, overgeneralized, premature, or misleading, as often happens with scholarly research that catches the media's fancy. You should take all such reports with a large grain of salt.

Having given that warning, I can tell you that there appears to be a connection of sorts between what we know about the left brain–right brain matter and sensory mode preferences. I'll do my best to pass it on to you without distortion.

Your brain is divided into two halves, called *hemispheres*, with a membrane between them that transmits data from one side to the other. In right-handed people and in a very large percentage of left-handed people as well, the left hemisphere is dominant for the processing of language and mathematics; the right half is dominant for processing spatial and nonlanguage information. When you hear your own language spoken it is processed by the left hemisphere; when a language you do not know at all is spoken at you, your right hemisphere tries to deal with the stream of sound.

This is *not* because—as you may have heard or read—the left brain is specialized for language and math. Rather, the left brain is specialized for processing information that comes to you in patterned, linear, segmented chunks, one item after another, as words and letters and numbers do. Because language and

for reading. The other is the blind person who may not be deaf, but who uses Braille for reading. The state of current research on these two situations is so chaotic and contradictory that I have no choice but to exclude them, with my apologies.

math are presented to us that way, the left hemisphere deals with them. The left brain attends to parts and sequences of parts; the right brain is more concerned with *wholes* and with information that is not neatly organized in "logical" patterns. The reason you do not process a foreign language with your left brain is because you don't have the necessary knowledge to identify separate patterned units of sound, separate words, and so on, in the stream of language coming at you. You hear the sound as undifferentiated and indivisible *noise*—that's right-brain work.

Because this is the manner our culture has chosen to transmit information, we can say roughly that the left brain favors the eye and ear sensory modes, while the right brain favors the touch mode. Very little, if any, information is presented in our society by mechanisms of touch. Thus, the effect of our concentration on training the left brain and letting the right brain flounder about without help also means that we educate and foster people whose dominant sensory modes are eye and ear, neglecting those who are touch dominant. As a culture, we are abysmally ignorant of shapes and textures, of sculpture, architecture, and handicrafts such as weaving. We look on the ballet, in which touch plays so great a role for the transmission of information, as a luxurious pastime, a frill for the rich.

How much of all this is biological, and how much is the cultural result of biological fact, we have no way of knowing. Perhaps if our alphabet were taught by presenting twenty-six different textures to our fingers, and if books were presented in those patterns of texture, written language would be presented by the right brain. There is no way to know, and no funding to find out.

Sensory Modes and Vocabulary

But whatever the theoretical facts, the situation is reflected clearly in one area: the English language vocabulary itself. Words are readily available and abundant to express the perceptions of the eye, less so but still overwhelmingly adequate for the perceptions of the ear (especially when the devices of music are counted in); but when you come to touch you find severe limitations. And it *stops* at touch. Vocabulary for the other senses is almost nonexistent.

Think, for example, of the basic task of describing a nonfigurative, "abstract" sculpture to someone who has not seen it. Most of us begin by saying that it "looks like" something—a horse, a fish, a bridge. If we are told not to do that, we may talk about such visually observable characteristics as size and color. And when that gives our listener no useful idea of what the work is like, we find ourselves saying "It goes like *this*" and then making gestures in the air to reproduce the shape. As for describing a fragrance or a taste so that someone else could identify it, if there are ways, they are not available to the nonspecialist. How would you describe the smell or taste of coffee? "It smells/tastes like coffee," right? Not very helpful.

Either we can perceive nothing about a sculpture except visual information, or—if we do perceive tactile information— we have no vocabulary for expressing that perception. There is every reason to believe that a person whose dominant sensory mode is touch perceives quite different information in a sculpture, but we cannot verify that reasonable belief—because there is no language to allow that person to tell us about it.

Touch Dominance

Consider what all this means for the person whose dominant sensory mode is touch. Let's call this person X, for convenience. What is X up against in the real world?

- X's first strategy in processing information from the environment is to focus on tactile data.
- X's strongest impulse in talking and writing to others is to use predicates and other vocabulary of touch.

- Because eyes and ears are little use for touch, X has a powerful inclination to use hands and other body language for communication.
- The faculty on which X depends most strongly has been allowed to develop with no direction, no education, no training, no provisions for direction in adult life. Tactilely, X is "illiterate."
- The English language offers X almost no useful vocabulary. There are specialized terms from various disciplines and professions (geology, for instance), but they are no help—most people X wants and needs to talk to will not know any of those terms. X will be frustrated at every turn because *there are no words* for the things he or she wants to say or write.

It would be very strange indeed if this situation did not cause X to have problems in relationships with other people. And the consequences are particularly severe because almost no attention has been given to this problem by our society.

It is common for those with dominant touch mode to have great difficulty talking when they are under severe stress. *Everyone* has problems talking under stress—for the person who is touch dominant, these problems are enormously worse. Such a person, frustrated past bearing by the lack of suitable words and desperately wanting to communicate, may behave in a way that leads to great misunderstanding.

Because of the way vocabulary is stored in the brain, certain kinds of vocabulary items come more easily to the tongue than others. These include: curses and obscenities; ritual items such as "Hi," "Thanks," "Help," and "Excuse me"; certain frozen chunks (often memorized in early childhood) such as proverbs, infantile jokes, and little jingles. All these are in a rough way "automatic." They have little meaning attached to them in the usual sense of the term. People who have lost much of their language capacity because of disease or trauma often retain just these vocabulary items.

What may happen, then, is that a touch-dominant person involved in a stressful language interaction will begin using these sets of automatic words and phrases, often very inappropriately for the situation. Such a person, particularly if he or she has acquired considerable facility at easy speech when not under stress, is all too likely to be perceived by others present as abusive, crude, offensive, or worse. And the feedback from that reaction in others naturally increases the stress level for the tactile person, which intensifies the problem.

The child whose preferred sensory mode is hearing is not quite so well off as the child who prefers sight. But there is ample reinforcement for such a child. If looking at a printed page is not the best way to learn, there are lectures, discussions, tapes, and radio programs to listen to. But the tactile child, the touch-dominant child, is left out. Neither looking at the letter *a* nor hearing the sounds it spells in English is sufficient to enable that child to distinguish all the multitudes of different real-world *a*'s in their varying typefaces and handwriting from the equal multitude of *c*'s and *o*'s and other *a*-like letters. The letters *m,n,w,u,r* all run together, as do *t,b,d,h* and *y,g,j,p,q*.

By the time such children enter the adult world, they are convinced that they are stupid, that they are slow, that they cannot learn, that they have "learning disabilities," and that they will not be able to function in society as other people do. They have heard those labels and judgments all their lives, and they have come to believe them. Finding that others perceive them as boorish and offensive in their communication then comes as no great surprise to them.[5]

I have gone into this at such length because it is responsible for so much misery, particularly during the present surge of enthusiasm for "assertiveness." Communication with other human beings is a powerful drive, like a need for food; that is one reason why solitary confinement is so effective as a way to punish human beings.

---

[5]This may lie behind some of the disturbing fuzziness in the use of labels like *dyslexia, autism, learning disability*. The experts who use these terms are as disturbed by their lack of precision as anyone else.

93

When you find yourself involved in a language interaction with someone whose verbal behavior, body language, or both seems to you abusive, gross, and completely inappropriate, I would like you at least to consider the possibility that that person has a strong preference for tactile mode. Perhaps it is someone locked into tactile mode when under stress. Certainly it is possible that you are facing someone who is drunk, drugged, mentally ill, or just plain *mean*—but it is also possible that you face nothing more alarming than someone for whom touch is as crucially important as sight and hearing are to you.

If you are a woman, this has a special significance. True, you may be dealing with the sort of "sexual harassment" that occupies not only the media but the law courts these days. On the other hand, the man who touches you without invitation and inappropriately *might* be doing that out of a desperate need to communicate and a severe limitation in available language. Babies grab you and scream at you because they can't talk—you don't interpret that as sexual harassment.

If you take the time to consider what is happening with an open mind, you *can* tell the difference between an articulate male who uses touch to harass you and a touch-dominant male who would use words if he only could. It seems to me that the two situations do not merit the same response.

If you are a man, you might give some serious thought to the straitjacket in which a tactile-dominant woman has been placed by American culture. Men, until very recently, have had a large set of touching behaviors permitted to them in interactions with both sexes. Women have never been allowed to touch men without that being interpreted as sexual invitation or a frank sexual act. And today they cannot touch other women without that risk either. It is no wonder that some women wring their hands and fidget.

Suppose you do find yourself interacting in a stressful context with someone you are certain is touch dominant; what can you do? First and foremost, you can temporarily set aside the idea of logical explanations—the more you talk with your eye and ear vocabulary, the more you increase the other person's frustration. Second, you can try to ignore the words the other person is using; never *mind* if they are curses or seeming gibberish—and pay scrupulous attention instead to his or her body language. When you do speak, use touch predicates if you can; at least avoid eye and ear predicates. If you are comfortable touching others, use touch as a means of communication. (Don't take on the task of touching a person who is completely out of control and is throwing wild punches or swinging a ball bat—use your common sense.)

As in any emergency, if you have no idea what to do, go to Computer Mode and stay there; and avoid sensory vocabulary altogether. Remember that panic feeds panic. Don't use Blaming language at a touch-dominant person under stress, however much his or her language may seem to deserve that; it won't help. Don't be logical; that's a waste of time. Don't, for heaven's sake, be *Assertive*—you will be completely misunderstood. Don't Placate—a person locked in tactile mode and already distressed has probably spent years being told that he or she is "childish," "irrational," "hysterical," and "behaving like a baby or an absolute idiot." Placating will only be interpreted as yet another way of humoring the foolish child—it will not help.

Keep your body language calm and nonthreatening. Listen carefully to the tone of voice and its melody; watch the body language of the other person as well as your own. When you must talk, say:

- "Is there anything that I can do?"
- "Do you want to tell me how you feel?"
- "Does this situation feel wrong to you?"
- "Would you feel more comfortable if ..."
- "I can't put my finger on what's wrong here, but if you feel like telling me about it, I'll do my best to understand."

Do not say anything that rubs salt in the wounds, like these examples:

- "I can see that..."
- "You look confused/miserable/upset..."
  "It's clear to me that..."
- "You sound as if you..."
- "Now, *look*..."
- "Listen here..."

If this all seems obvious, I'm pleased. The very last thing I want to do here is be obscure.

What if you have recognized your own behavior in all this and have suddenly realized that *you* are a touch-dominant person? For one thing, you can be glad. Be glad, because all the people who have been calling you stupid and slow and childish have been wrong. You don't have to believe them anymore.

For another, you might consider just explaining. Memorize this speech so that it becomes as available to you as curses are:

> I really have a hard time talking when I'm upset. I'm sorry, but I'd rather *not* talk right now.

This may not accomplish what you want it to. Chances are excellent that the person you're interacting with is going to insist that you talk, "for your own good." Chances are you'll get something like this response:

> Oh, come on! There's nothing wrong with the way you talk! You'll feel a lot better if you get it all off your chest instead of just clamming up and keeping everything bottled up inside you.

Notice, by the way, that this standard speech for getting people to talk who don't want to talk uses touch predicates and avoids eye or ear vocabulary! It may be a coincidence. Or it may show a kind of unconscious awareness of the proper way to behave.

Whatever happens, you will at least have stated the facts of the situation and put the other person or people present on notice. And you do *not* have to talk when you are certain that silence is best—please remember that.

If you have children, it would be excellent for you to supplement the tidal wave of eye and ear information they are subjected to at school and at home with some *touch* information. See that they have scraps of different kinds of cloth to play with, and encourage them to use pieces of different-textured substances to make collages and craft items. Encourage them to notice the textures and shapes of rocks, metals, and natural objects in the environment. If hands-on crafts using wood, yarn, clay, and metal interest them, encourage that. Many of the materials that would train the tactile sense are not only abundant but very cheap—dirt, soap, sand, string, paper, and rags are not high-priced items. Much of what you throw away as "junk" could be put to good use as a source of tactile information.

Sculpture is hard to find in America and even harder to afford. Pictures of sculpture only switch the information back to the visual mode. But if you can show sculpture to your children in galleries and museums or if you can provide inexpensive copies of sculptures and carvings, that's a good investment in normal communication. So is an investment of time and money in ballet and other forms of dance.

Your goal is not to make your children touch dominant; it is to make it easier for them to use the limited resources of the English language to shift to touch mode when that is needed. Your goal is to provide some education for the neglected tactile part of their sensory systems and perhaps for their neglected right brains.

This section is intended only to make you aware of some of the linguistic and social consequences of what might have looked to you (sounded to you, felt to you) like trivial information. It is not intended to teach you to "diagnose" problems with sensory modes, or—worse yet—to "treat" them. You have no more business treating such problems than you have doing brain surgery; you could do great harm, even with the best intentions in the world.

I also do not want to overstate the situation regarding specialization of the human brain. There is tremendous redundancy in the brain—that is, although certain areas customarily deal with certain functions, everything appears to be duplicated in the brain in many ways. The brain is probably far more like a hologram than it is like a filing cabinet. We are seeing people take the path of least resistance, not the one and only possible unique path.

My primary concern is to increase your own awareness and perhaps to prevent some misunderstandings. For more detailed information on these matters, you should go to the technical literature.

SUPPLEMENTARY QUOTATIONS

But beware. Any serious attempt at including unfamiliar phenomena in a certain verbal realm may change reality as perceived in that realm [Leonard, 1974, p. 46].

Only certain aspects of the universe and only certain kinds of human behavior have been identified and named in human history. (Only those phenomena of which a people are conscious are coded in speech, and only those things that are so coded play a conscious role in human communication.) For example, modern concepts of astronomic systems were not represented in language until about 1800. And only very recently has information about kinesics, dominance, and territoriality become linguistically coded and therefore generally knowable. Previously, this social regulatory system operated outside human awareness [Scheflen and Scheflen, 1972, p. 153].

Our educational system and modern society generally (with its very heavy emphasis on communication and on early training in the three *R*'s) discriminates against one whole half of the brain. I refer, of course, to the non-verbal, non-mathematical minor hemisphere, which, we find, has its own perceptual, mechanical, and spatial mode of apprehension and reasoning. In our present school system, the attention given to the minor hemisphere of the brain is minimal compared with the training lavished on the left, or major, hemisphere [Sperry, 1975, p. 33].

SUGGESTED READINGS

BENDERLY, B. L. "Dancing without Music," *Science 80,* December 1980, pp. 54–59. (Excellent nontechnical article on the history and structure of American Sign Language. Highly recommended.)

CAIN, W. S. "Educating Your Nose." *Psychology Today,* July 1981, pp. 48–56. (A rare item—an article on the sense of smell, with some information on taste as well. Reports experiments showing that people's skill at identifying smells increases when their vocabulary for the sense is increased.)

EDWARDS, B. *Drawing on the Right Side of the Brain.* Los Angeles: J. P. Tarcher, Inc., 1979. (Can't recommend this book too strongly—not only does it help wake up the right side of your brain as promised, but it provides a clear explanation of how this happens. Contains much useful information about languages you may not be aware that you know.)

FERGUSON, M. "Karl Pribram's Changing Reality." *Human Behavior,* May 1978, pp. 28–33. (A careful discussion for lay readers of a number of models for the human brain, ending with the idea of the brain as a hologram—with all information stored in every location for maximum redundancy.)

GRINDER, J., and R. BANDLER. *The Structure of Magic: II.* Palo Alto, Calif.: Science and Behavior Books, Inc., 1976, pp. 3–11. (A discussion of the use of the sensory modes in therapy.)

LEONARD, G. "Language and Reality." *Harper's,* November 1974, pp. 46–52. (See quotation above.)

SCHEFLEN, A. E., and A. SCHEFLEN. *Body Language and the Social Order: Communication as Behavioral Control*. Englewood Cliffs, N.J.: Prentice-Hall, Inc., 1972. (See quotation above.)

SPERRY, R. W. "Left-Brain, Right-Brain." *Saturday Review,* August 9, 1975, pp. 30–33. (See quotation above.)

The vocabulary of the emotions (hypothetically a right-brain domain) is very limited, but there is a controversial specialty called *sentics,* "the science of the communication of emotions." You might find it interesting, whether you found it outrageous or not; here are three references.

FINCHER, J. "The Joy (Grief, Love, Hate, Anger, Sex and Reverence) of Music." *Human Behavior,* April 1977, pp. 25–30.

JONAS, G. "Manfred Clynes and the Science of Sentics." *Saturday Review,* May 13, 1972, pp. 42–51.

_____. Review of *Sentics: The Touch of Emotions* by Manfred Clynes. (New York: Doubleday, 1977). *Psychology Today,* February 1977, pp. 98–99.

5

Identifying
Verbal Attacks

A person who shakes a fist in your face and shouts "You lunatic, I'll break your stupid neck!" is presenting you with a verbal attack and is well on the way to a physical one. No special skills are needed to recognize either. People using insults of class, race, and sex, no matter what the volume of their speech and no matter what their modes, are also mounting verbal attacks. Again, this requires no sophisticated detection strategies. When somebody calls you a honky, a hillbilly, or a broad, you know immediately what you're dealing with.[1]

However, the verbal attacks you will encounter in this Neanderthal form, nasty though they may be, are not the genuinely dangerous ones. In most situations it is the person putting out that sort of verbal abuse who loses such encounters and looks the fool, not you. Americans are not impressed by the

---

[1] I am assuming from this point on that those behaving in this way because they are touch dominant and panicked will be identified as such; they are not included in this discussion.

verbal bully beyond the age of nine or ten. Furthermore, attacks of this type are wide open—there can be no question in your mind but that they are happening, which means that you know you must defend yourself, if only by walking off and leaving the abuser ranting at the empty air.

I don't want to give the impression that such attacks don't cause pain or do harm. Of course they hurt! But I don't believe you need a book to tell you how to deal with them; I think you know. If the abuser is someone you don't have to associate with, someone you've encountered by accident, you just refuse to participate in such primitive behavior, and contempt is the only defense you need. Only the situation will tell you if that contempt should be accompanied by compassion. If the abuser is someone you are with a lot of the time—your spouse, your parent, your boss, your partner, your child—you have a much different problem. There is something drastically wrong with the entire relationship, in that case, and the verbal abuse is just a symptom of the larger problem.

If it's a relationship you can walk away from, that's a solution; if it's one you want to continue (or feel you must continue), you are in trouble. What you learn from this book will help, but you probably need the expert services of your minister, your doctor, a trained counselor, a support group formed specifically for the situation you face—something more than I am able to provide in these pages. In no way do I want to minimize your problem, but this book can only be one of an assortment of tools you will need to work out a solution.

My concern here, then, is with a different sort of verbal attack. Both in the occasional encounter and in long-term relationships, what I want to focus on is the verbal attack that is not so grossly obvious and may even appear on the surface not to be an attack at all.

The difference is like the difference between the danger you face from someone breaking into your home and abusing you physically and the danger that the elegant business building where you work assaults your body daily with toxic chemicals or other environmental contaminants you may not realize are there. The open physical assault may put you in the hospital for a few weeks and require psychological support for some time afterward, but the damage is usually brief in duration and accessible to treatment. And there do exist agencies to which you can turn for help, such as the police or social services.

In the other situation you may not discover that you have a fatal or disabling disease, or that your children have such a disease, until years after you've moved on from that particular building into an entirely different work environment. Unless you are very lucky indeed, there will be no equivalent of the police for you to call and nothing at all will happen to the corporation that did you serious harm. Damage of that kind goes on and on, year after year, often invisibly, while you pay all the costs.

The verbal attacks I will be discussing in this chapter and the next are like that. They are verbal pollution. They are exceedingly dangerous because so often you don't know they are happening to you and you therefore make no move to defend yourself. All too often you blame *yourself* for the havoc they cause in your life. This sort of thing I can help you with. A basic part of the art of verbal self-defense, the most basic part, is the recognition of such attacks and mastery of techniques for responding to them.

THE PRESUPPOSITION

These attacks rely primarily on one technique, that of *hiding the attack itself inside a presupposition*. We'll start with that term *presupposition* and define it carefully for this book, because it's used in many different ways and it has numerous definitions depending on the context in which you come across it.

For this book, *presupposition* is defined as follows: anything that a native speaker of a language knows is part of the meaning of a sequence of that language, even if it is not overtly present in the sequence. For example, consider this sentence:

"Even John could get an A in this class." If you are a native or near-native speaker of English, you know that the sentence includes as part of its meaning two more sentences:

1. John is not much of a student.
2. This class is really easy.

Someone who says "Even John could get an A in this class" hasn't called John names or shouted at him or cursed him; but John has been insulted all the same, and everyone present knows it. This insult to John has been hidden in the presuppositions of the sentence (represented by 1 and 2) exactly as a seemingly inoffensive and peaceful person might have a switchblade knife hidden away in a jacket pocket. The insult is a *concealed weapon*.

You could spend some time investigating the sentence "Even John could get an A in this class," as you would investigate a physical object. And you'd find out that the sentence *pattern* was crucial, and that two elements are responsible for the harm that it does. Look at these two sentences:

3. John could get an A in this class.
4. Even John came to the meeting.

Notice that Sentence 3 all by itself doesn't insult John. You'd have to hear it spoken, or read it in context, to find out if it did. It could be a compliment to John, as in "John could get an A in this class; I don't know anybody else smart enough, but *John* is." The fact that taking the word *even* away from the sentence cancels the automatic insult then makes us suspect that the word *even* is the source of the trouble—but Sentence 4 shows us that's not so. "Even John came to the meeting" is again not an insult unless there's other material that makes it so. Suppose we know that John never goes to meetings and is opposed to meetings as a way of solving problems. Suppose that nevertheless, because he is concerned about the feelings of the others who will be attending and wants to show his concern, he has joined them at least this once. You would then say "Even John came to the meeting," but you would not have insulted John.

For this pattern to constitute an attack it has to include *both* the word *even* and at least one of the set of English words called *modals*. The modals include *can, could, shall, should, may, might, will, would, must,* with *can* sometimes surfacing as *be able to, should* as *ought to,* and *must* as *have to*. The modals are inoffensive little words in isolation, but dangerous in combination with *even*.

The presuppositions set up by *even* plus a modal are so powerful that they can overrule the rest of the content of the sequence with ease. That's why the sentences below are all so strange to speakers of English:

5. Even Einstein could solve that equation.
6. Even an Eagle Scout can build a fire.
7. Even an expert chef should be able to cook an egg.
8. Even the finest musicians in the country would know how to play a simple little tune like that.

And that is why the next set of sentences is so sure to hurt and anger nurses, teachers, elderly people, and truck drivers.

9. Even a nurse can recognize severe pain.
10. Even a teacher would know how to spell that word.
11. Even an elderly person could understand that concept.
12. Even a truck driver might be able to do that.

Notice how little information there is in example 12—there's nothing there to tell you what *do that* refers to at all; nevertheless, it's an insult to all truck drivers.

105

THE IMPORTANCE OF
STRESS

If you read these examples aloud, you'll notice that it's almost impossible to pronounce them without one of the two patterns of stress shown below.

13a. Even *Ein*stein could...
13b. *Even Ein*stein could...
14a. Even an *el*derly person could...
14b. *Even an el*derly person could...

If English is your language, you know all this. You may not have realized it, but you do. You've known it since you were little. ("*Even Bil*ly's mother lets the kids play in the garage, for cryin' out loud!")[2] But nobody ever taught you anything about it, and you won't find it written down in any English grammar book or dictionary. You can look up *even* or the modals till you're blue, and nothing you read will provide you with the information that they are crucial to a common English insult pattern.

You can, of course, find this pattern described in articles by linguists, just by looking for titles including the word *even*. But unless you've studied linguistics the articles aren't likely to be of much use to you, because they are written in technical jargon. They are absolutely useless to anyone trying to learn English. (And notice how very different "you can even find this pattern" and "even you can find this pattern" are! It must be done just so, or it doesn't work.)

I once gave a lecture for a group of about one hundred teachers of English as a Second Language. They were excellent teachers, with many years of experience, and they spoke English

---

[2]One of the things that bothers me most about the many otherwise excellent books I read on communication is their total disregard for marking stresses. You would think, from reading such books, that stress had no effect at all on meaning. I think this must be because their authors take it for granted that anyone reading their examples will put the stresses just where they did—and this is *not* safe.

fluently. Not one was a native speaker of English (or a language closely related to English), however. And when I gave them the example sentence "Even John could get an A in this class" *not a single one* knew that the example was an insult to John. How would they know, after all?

You can't look it up anywhere, and you aren't taught about it in English class—it's just something "everybody knows." And that is exactly the point with presuppositions. They are what everybody knows, whether they can explain their knowledge or not. When someone hits you with a presupposed verbal attack, even though you may be so unable to explain your reasons for feeling hurt that you think it's ridiculous of you to be bothered at all, you *do understand* that something in the words caused you to feel pain. The problem is that you often have no idea why, and that you have been trained in such situations to assume that the fault must be yours. It's not that the nice man or nice woman has verbally abused you, your trained reactions tell you. It's that you are childish or emotional or oversensitive or hysterical or, heaven help us all, "sick." This is not one little bit funny.

You cannot possibly anticipate every sort of concealed verbal attack that will come at you. If I had the skill and the space to list every such attack known as of this moment, that wouldn't do it; somebody would invent a new one before the book went to press. But you *can* learn the concept of the presupposition; you can learn to listen closely for what is presupposed by the things you say and hear, as well as those you read and write; and you can learn to be familiar with a set of very common attack patterns that come up again and again in almost everyone's daily life.

In the first book I wrote on verbal self-defense, I concentrated on eight attack patterns. Years of careful observation and record keeping had convinced me that eight attack patterns made up such a whopping chunk of the verbal pollution that learning to deal only with those would guarantee a substantial improvement in communications skills. They were not the only attacks I heard, but they were far and away the most frequent. I am going to repeat them here, along with their presupposed verbal abuse, before going on to some new examples.

In all of them the stress placed on certain parts of the utterances is crucial, because—and this *matters*—without the extra stresses indicated they may be the neutral utterances of someone who is Leveling, rather than being attacks. Because stress is so important, I will indicate where it falls (roughly, which is all that our writing system allows) by putting the stressed portions in italics; if more than one pattern is common, I will try to show them all. Stress is a complicated matter physiologically and acoustically, but our concern here is with how it is perceived by the listener, and that is not so difficult. It is perceived as higher pitch combined with louder volume.

THE BASIC EIGHT
VERBAL ATTACKS

Now let's go through the eight elementary attacks. I'll comment on them as we go along.

SECTION A ATTACKS:
If you *really* loved me, you wouldn't smoke."
"If you really *loved* me, you wouldn't smoke."
>   *Presupposed:*
>   You don't really love me.

SECTION B ATTACK:
"If you *really* loved me, you wouldn't *want* to smoke."
"If you really *loved* me, you wouldn't *want* to smoke."
>   *Presupposed:*
>   You don't really love me.
>   You are able to control your personal desires if you want to do so.

Let's compare these two for just a moment. In both, the real attack is in the presupposed material; in both, the last thing to come along is what we will call the *bait*. The bait is what your attacker expects you to respond to—and *when you do* you have accepted the presupposed material by default, in letting it go by without protest.

The two attacks are very similar—both use smoking as the bait and "You don't love me" as a hidden attack. But a Section A is much less skilled than a Section B. Notice, no matter what you do you cannot get out of the bind that a Section B attack places you in. Not if you accept those presuppositions. You might prove the attacker wrong, demonstrating the reality of your love by giving up smoking, if the attack is a Section A. But Section B attacks can't be handled that way. If you go on smoking, you'll feel guilty; if you give up smoking, you'll *still* feel guilty— because you will still want to smoke, thus proving that you don't love this person. Accepting those presuppositions in Section B attacks is like playing in heavy traffic—you can't win.

SECTION C ATTACK:

"Don't you even *care* about your wife?"

"Don't you even *care about your wife?*"
>   *Presupposed:*
>   You don't care about your wife.
>   You should care—any decent person would.
>   Therefore, you should feel guilty and ashamed.

SECTION D ATTACK:

"Even a *wo*man should be able to change a tire."

"*Even a wo*man should be able to change a tire."
>   *Presupposed:*
>   "There is something very wrong with being a woman."

You've met this one before, in the discussion of example sentences. This is an all-purpose attack, because in a pinch all anyone has to say is "Even *you* ..." and fill in the rest of the pattern. The presupposition is then that there is something inherently wrong with you, no matter what your identifying characteristics.

SECTION E ATTACK:

"Everyone under*stands* why you can't get along with other people, my dear."

Presupposed:

You can't get along with other people.

If there weren't something wrong with you, you *could* get along with other people.

Everybody knows what that something wrong is, so don't think you can hide it away.

This one is particularly vicious, because every last one of us has something we consider "wrong" with us, something we don't want others to know about. It may be an imaginary wrong, but it feels very real to us, and Section E goes straight to it.

And this is a good place to illustrate how little faith you can place on the surface form of utterances in deciding whether they are attacks or not. The skilled attacker doesn't shout curses and threats and brutal blunt insults—that's strictly for amateurs and small children. The skilled attacker may bury the verbal abuse under a regular smorgasbord of tenderness and affection, for example:

15. "Sweetheart, there's just no *reas*on for you to torment yourself the way you do. Everybody under*stands* why you can't get along with other people, love ... and b*e*lieve me, nobody holds it against you! Try to remember that; try to remember that everybody, *e*verybody, is genuinely concerned."

If sequence 15 had started out with, "*List*en, stupid, there's just" and gone on like that, you'd have had no trouble spotting it as an attack. But when the abuse is carefully packaged as in the example, the surface signals are flashing loud and clear: *This is tender loving care you are hearing; be grateful for it and know how lucky you are.* Much of the time this means that if you feel hurt after hearing something like this you have a second layer of hurt to deal with—the one that goes "I'm ashamed of myself for being hurt when X is doing everything humanly possible to be

110

good to me—I must be completely crazy." This is precisely the way you are supposed to feel; and that is why I consider attacks like this far more dangerous than the "Listen, stupid" variety. This kind of attack can go on for your whole life without your ever spotting it for what it is, and that means a life of bewildered misery and bewildering guilt. I'll take "Listen, stupid" right out front where I know what's coming at me, *any* time.

If you customarily divide people up in terms of their language behavior toward you by relying on the surface signals, you are a perfect verbal victim. You will perceive the person who genuinely cares about you but is a poor communicator and says clumsy things, including the occasional "Listen, stupid," as an enemy. The person who has enough verbal skill to stick to attacks like those in the examples will be perceived as on your side and deserving of your affection or respect. That's a very dangerous situation indeed.

SECTION F ATTACK:

"A person who *really* wanted to be promoted would get to *work* on time/work on *time*."

Or

"A person who really *wanted* ...
Presupposed:
You don't want to be promoted.
You never get to work on time.

This is in Computer Mode, of course, since it never once says that you are the "person" in question; but its presuppositions are unmistakably directed at you.

SECTION G ATTACK:

"*Why* do you always criticize me in public?"
Presupposed:
You always criticize me in public.
You couldn't possibly have any good reason for doing so; therefore, it is wrong of you.

This is straight Blamer Mode. But it can be easily disguised with sweeteners, like this: "Darling, you know I love you with all my heart ... but there's just one thing I cannot understand no matter how hard I try. *Why*, sweetheart, do you always criticize me in public?"

SECTION H ATTACK:

"*Some* fathers would re*sent* it if they had to listen to smart remarks all day long."

Presupposed:

You make smart remarks all day long.

Any ordinary father would resent that—it's wrong of you.

I'm not an ordinary father, I'm very special and exceptional.

Considering how lucky you are to have a father like me, you should feel very guilty about making smart remarks.

You should feel extremely grateful to me for being so special and wonderful.

Yes, indeed, that simple sentence up there does pack all that presupposed material in it. And where a three-paragraph lecture that spelled them all out on the surface might fail to do much harm, because the person being spoken to would just turn it all off, the Section H attack is a way of getting in there and landing one blow for each presupposition—and getting right back out before there's time for anything but pain.

The Section H attack, like the Section F, is in Computer Mode. Neither one openly identifies the person being spoken or written to as the person described in the bait—they never say *you*. When someone says to you, "A person who *really* cared about getting good grades wouldn't turn in their work late," that someone has not identified you as guilty of either late work or lack of concern about grades. So far as the surface, overt, form of the utterance is concerned, the subject of discussion is some hypothetical person. This makes it harder for you to complain that you are being abused. The same thing is true for "*Some* fathers would" whatever; the speaker or writer has not said *I*.

The attacker is talking about a hypothetical father, not himself, according to the surface form. And when he goes on to say what sort of behavior that hypothetical father would object to, he doesn't openly accuse you of it. Native speakers of English know that he is talking about himself and about you, but neither fact appears on the surface. Both attacks are favorites of people who want to appear objective and superior; that adds an automatic claim to higher rank to the rest of the damage they do. Don't let them confuse you.

You may be wondering why the Section G ("*Why* do you always...") attack is included here. It's not subtle and it's not clever—the most you can say for the technique is that it uses a question instead of a flat statement.

I include it because, like the other seven attacks, it is so common in your language environment. It tends to come at you from people who can use it to hurt you badly, despite its crudity, because they are close to you and know exactly what *will* hurt you. The chair of a committee you serve on isn't likely to attack you with "Why do you always eat too much?" even if you *do*. That's not appropriate. However, if you are in fact not overweight at all, but you perceive yourself as overweight and worry about your image of yourself as an overweight person, that is probably well known to your intimate circle. When people who are truly close to you want to hurt you, they don't have to be subtle. They know just where to put the knife and exactly how many turns to give it. Because most of us have at least two or three people in a position to know what things we are deeply sensitive about, this attack pattern has to be included in the basic set. Every one of us has to learn to deal with it, usually on a long-term basis; that makes it important far beyond the level of technical skill that it demonstrates.

In Table Two you will find the bare-bones pattern for each of these eight attacks.[3] To fill in the pattern, look back at the

[3]If you find this brief discussion of the eight basic attacks not quite enough, you might want to look at the first book in this series, pp. 15–191.

examples; the symbols *X, Y, Z,* and *W* mean "anything at all can fill this slot." They are called *variables*.

TABLE TWO

A. If you *really (X)*, you would/wouldn't *(Y)*.
B. If you *really (X)*, you would/wouldn't *want* to *(Y)*.
C. Don't you even *care* about *(X)?*
D. Even *(X)* should *(Y)*. (or other modal)
E. Everyone under*stands* why you *(X)*.
F. A person who *(X) (Y)*.
G. *Why* do you always/don't you ever *(X)?*
H. *Some (X's)* would *(Y)* if/when *(Z) (W)*.

The pattern for Section H attacks is sufficiently complicated, with those four variables, to need one more explanation. I'll underline the sections that match up with the variables.

16. "*Some* <u>parents</u> would <u>really find it hard to understand</u> if <u>one</u>
        X   Y
<u>of their children</u> <u>was out of work for the third time in one year.</u>"
        Z   W

(Be careful in reading this to remember that the underscores are meant to identify the material representing *X, Y, Z,* and *W;* the stress is marked by italics.)

And now let's summarize a bit. The *words* in the eight basic attacks listed above are not in themselves evidence that you are under verbal attack. When they appear in these patterns, they are cues that should make you alert—you should react to these groups of words by listening with particular care. But they may not be attacks at all. The evidence that they are attacks is in the way they are spoken or written—in the melody that accompanies them, which is called the *intonation* of the utterance.

Look at this pair of sentences:

114

17. John called Mary a Republican, and then she insulted him.
18. John called Mary a Republican, and then *she* insulted *him*.

The only difference between those two sentences is the intonation—the words themselves are exactly the same. But only in the second sentence is "You are a Republican, Mary" a presupposed insult. And that information is carried not in the words but in the extra stresses on *she* and *him*. Stress in English carries a heavy freight of meaning; you must learn to listen to stresses and hear them accurately, not only in the speech of others but in your own as well.

The use of these patterns is a cue; it says, "Listen with care." But only when they are used with the stresses indicated by the italics should they be considered verbal attacks without other evidence of hostility. Without those stresses, you are probably hearing a *Leveler*. Perhaps a tactless and unpleasant Leveler, but a Leveler all the same. And you are not under attack in that case, you are just engaged in a discussion.[4]

WRITTEN ATTACKS

We have a strong tendency to feel that the rules of English punctuation are about as important as the rules of table setting, and to react to the suggestion that we've put a comma in the wrong place as we would to the claim that we ought to have our

[4]Another possibility to keep in mind when you hear these patterns is that the person speaking doesn't know about the presuppositions. I would hesitate to assume an attack if the speaker were obviously a native speaker of some language other than English. That person could have picked up the pattern from hearing it used, but may not have understood *any* of the presupposed meaning attached. A foreign speaker may use one of these patterns with complete innocence and should be given the benefit of the doubt until you have something more to go on. You would also want to be wary of interpreting these patterns as attacks from someone having a speech handicap, or when some other special circumstance existed. By all means use your common sense in situations like that, and wait for more information. It's much harder to learn the correct intonation of a language than its pronunciation or grammar rules.

salad fork somewhere else in the lineup of utensils. Many people are almost proud of their lack of skill with punctuation, perhaps because they feel that it is elitist and nit-picking to be concerned about it.

The reason for this is the strange way that punctuation is taught in our schools. Teachers either do not know, or forget to mention to students, that punctuation is the only way we have to indicate intonation in written language—and that is its only real purpose. It's not a very accurate system, and it's a rotten substitute for actually hearing the words pronounced and seeing the body language that goes with them—but it's *all we have*. Incorrect punctuation means incorrect intonation, which often means some other meaning than the one you intended for your words. And *that,* not pompous verbal table manners, is why punctuation matters.

It is false to say that "uneducated people" don't know where to put their punctuation marks. If you listen to the oral language of an "uneducated person," however you want to define "uneducated," you will *hear* all the punctuation marks in their proper places. The problem is that instead of being taught that the comma between 3 and 1982 in *February 3, 1982* is the way we write down the pause between the two numbers, we are taught a rule that simply says, "Put a comma between the day of the month and the year." With no reason given and no connection made between the symbol and the sound, the rule is quickly forgotten. If teachers would tell students what commas really are, they would not have to teach all those rules, because there is really only one rule.

Why am I making such a fuss about this? Because unfortunately the chaotic state of punctuation usage in America today makes it impossible for you to judge written language accurately for intonation patterns that signal a verbal attack. This can lead to much confusion. When you react angrily to a statement in a letter from your sister and she then tells you aloud that that wasn't what she meant *at all,* the chances are very good that at least part of the problem is either her misuse of punctuation or your misreading of it. (That is, it doesn't help much for her to put the punctuation marks in the proper places if you've been taught some fictitious "rule" of punctuation that causes you to interpret them differently than she meant them.)

The only mechanism we have in English punctuation for indicating the kind of heavy stress that is indispensable to understanding meaning is the underscore. In this chapter I've been using italics for that purpose, as a way of making it even more clear; but I had to explain to you in advance what I was doing. There is no provision in our system of punctuation for the fact that frequently the stress is only on a part of the word, as in "Even a *wo*man should be able to. . . ." The rules of punctuation oblige you to write that as "Even a *woman* should be able to . . ." as though the heavy stress covered both syllables. You know this is false, but you have no choice in the matter.

Because of this unreliability and plain inadequacy of the punctuation system, when you spot one of the attack patterns above in something written for you to read, you can do no more than be aware that it *might* be an attack. You can't be certain until you have more information.

If your situation allows it, have the writer read the dubious utterance aloud to you, with a sentence before and after it to make natural intonation more likely. For example, if your boss sends you a memorandum that contains the words of one of the attack patterns, the best possible way to check intentions is to take the memo to the boss and say, "I wonder if you'd read these three sentences out loud for me? I'm not sure I understand them." If your relationship with the boss allows you to do that, you have a way of checking the question. Which leads me to a warning—

Be very careful when you hear someone read aloud the words of another person. If a person is talking to you on the telephone, which means you can't see any body language, be even more careful. You cannot have even a rough probability of being certain that when X reads what Y has written, the intonation will be what Y intended. Y may have used punctuation incorrectly, and X may only be reading back what's there, errors and all. Y may have punctuated correctly, but X may not be skilled at reading aloud. Y may have punctuated properly, but X may have a different feeling about the words and *read in* punctuation that *isn't* there—pausing in places where Y intended no pause, stressing material that Y did not intend to stress.

FOUR NEW
VERBAL ATTACKS

Now let's move on to some new patterns that aren't quite as common as these eight, at least in my experience and that of my students and clients.

The first pattern has had quite a lot of attention from linguists, who call it a *Hedge*. Hedges have two functions in English. One is the "I'm a willing victim, please abuse me" signal—it is commonly heard from students who begin their questions in class with "I know this is a stupid question and probably everybody else already knows the answer, but. ..." Eliminate that sequence, and all sequences like it, from your language behavior. Everyone already knows that you may be wrong, since anyone may be wrong; starting your questions with "I may be wrong, but..." is not impressive. However, the Hedge also turns up as a verbal attack pattern, like this.

SECTION I ATTACK:
"You *know* I'd never tell you what to do, my friend, but it would not be a good idea for you to send that letter."
Presupposed:
I *would* tell you what to do, and I *am* telling you what to do.
I have the right to tell you what to do.
I'm a very nice person and very polite, and I expect you to notice that and behave accordingly.
Don't send that letter.

The third (and perhaps the second) presuppositions may seem to you to take us beyond the limits of our definition. That is because we are unaccustomed to thinking of the real-world context in which words and gestures are used as being part of their meaning.

We understand "Good morning, how are you?" as a set of words, and we expect that set to go along with a pleasant, or at least a neutral, expression. But we tend to forget that "Good morning, how are you?" has two possible meanings. If it's only a greeting, the person using it doesn't want to know how you are, and the proper answer is "Fine, thank you." If the utterance comes from the nurse who has just come on the morning shift and is entering your hospital room to see whether you've made it through the night, it *is* a question—not a greeting. And you are expected to answer with information about your health and your present physical condition.[5] *Only the context* makes it possible for you to decide which one of those meanings is intended, and the context is therefore a very important part of language. The term used for this interaction between the real world and the words and body language we use in it is *pragmatics*.

When someone says to you, "Don't send that letter" or "It would be a good idea for you not to send that letter," he or she is giving you a direct command or a piece of direct advice about your behavior. Behind every command is this presupposition: I have the right to tell you what to do. A speaker who doesn't want to have to deal with the consequences of that presupposition resorts to the Hedge. This allows the speaker to get across to you the illogical message: I have the right to tell you what to do, but I'm not going to say that I have the right to tell you what to do, I'm going to make an end run here instead. This has, as part of its pragmatics, the chunk about how very nice and polite this is

[5]Health workers, including physicians, would be well advised never to greet a patient with the words "How are you?" at all. The social pressure to treat that as a greeting and say "Fine, thank you" is so strong that many patients can't comfortably do anything else. Such a patient then resents the fact that the health professional "didn't even bother to ask how I was." A greeting followed by "Tell me how you feel" would avoid this problem.

of the speaker. And it warns the listener to be polite back. That is, it's a warning not to answer, "You can't tell me what to do!" After all, the speaker has just *said* that.

Hedges can be complicated and time consuming to construct, and some people don't want to be bothered with all those words. They then substitute "Never mind," as in the following example:

19. "If you send that letter, you're going to be sorry, because—oh, never mind."

Never mind is an abbreviated Hedge, and a way of allowing speakers to say exactly what they want to say and know they should not say—and then take it back. There are very few more annoying verbal habits, and if you do this often I'd suggest you try to stop it.

As with any of the patterns, pay close attention to the stresses. "I *know* I shouldn't say this, but ..." is probably an attack. "I know I shouldn't say this, but ..." without the strong stress on *know*, is very probably used by Levelers stating the simple fact that they know they should not say something but intend to say it anyway. The Leveler is not trying to avoid responsibility for what is said—you're just being warned that the Leveler is well aware that he or she shouldn't say whatever it is. When the utterance is Leveling, there is probably a good reason for it. When it's a Hedge, the only reason is to let speakers cheat on taking responsibility for their words, in which case something nasty must be hidden in them that you need to pay attention to. The difference is considerable.

You will remember that the phony Leveler is probably the most dangerous communicator of all. The next attack pattern is one of the favorites of the phony Leveler.

SECTION J ATTACK:
You're not the *only* patient I have to worry about, you know."

Presupposed:
I have other patients besides you to worry about.
You are behaving as if I had no other patients except you—
stop it.

Attack pattern **J** almost without exception is used to say something that is not only known to the listener or reader but overpoweringly obvious to the whole world. Consider the following:

20. "You're not the *only* person capable of understanding economics, you know."
21. "You're not the *only* person with problems, after all."
22. "You're not the *only* dentist in town, you know."

Listen carefully for the strong stress on *only*. Without it, the doctor in Section J meant to say, "I wonder if you have forgotten that I have other patients that need my time and attention as much as you do—I wish you'd try to remember that." When the doctor thinks that's what she said, and you think that she was attacking you because you didn't notice the absence of the stress cue, you have a serious misunderstanding that will lead to more of the same.

Even worse is the doctor, or other dominant person, who *did* use the strong stress and was abusing you, but has somehow managed to convince himself or herself that the utterance was absolutely innocent and that "nobody in their right mind" could take offense at it. If you are ordinarily in a dominant role, listen to yourself and see if you are guilty of this—you may be surprised at how the proportion of people who "overreact" to things you say grows smaller when you are more careful.

In my seminars and workshops people usually raise at this point the issue of deliberate versus unintentional abuse. A frequent suggestion is that the person who uses a pattern such as "You're not the *only*" is not aware that the strong stress makes the utterance a verbal attack and therefore doesn't "really mean it that way."

This is a handy excuse for the person using any attack pattern. People who say, "Listen, stupid..." or "See here, stupid ..." or "Get this, stupid ..." can't pretend not to know they're being abusive. But might the situation be different with the hidden attacks?

No. Not if the person is a native speaker of English. I defy any one in 1,000 such speakers to tell me that he or she never had to listen to "You're not the *only* person in this house that needs to use the bathroom, you know" while growing up.

It is certainly possible for speakers to have used attack patterns all their lives long and become so accustomed to using them that they have lost all conscious awareness of the pain they cause. This is much like the situation with dominant people who have used touch as a power mechanism for so many years that they've become deadened to what they are doing. It is *not* possible for such people to be unable to understand the presuppositions of their own language.

The more important, busy, and powerful people are, the more likely it is that someone will be on hand to defend their abusive language behavior and offer a little ditty like this on their behalf.

23. "That's just his way—he doesn't really mean it."
24. "She doesn't really mean that like it sounds—she's just so busy."
25. "He just has an awful lot of important things on his mind right now—don't take what he says personally."

Some people feel that they are so important in this world that others should have to clean up the dirt they make; they leave their dirty socks right where they take them off, in the serene conviction that someone less important will come along and pick them up. Others have the same attitude about their verbal messes, and may go so far as to hire someone who presents everyone about to be ushered into their presence with a long introductory excuse like this:

26. "Now, everybody thinks at first that he's gruff and bad-tempered and not really interested in them—but believe me, it's not true. It's just that he's really too busy and has too many life-and-death matters on his mind to worry about whether he hurts people's feelings or not. Just don't pay any attention to the way he talks. You couldn't have a better doctor/lawyer/professor/agent/company president, and that's what really matters."

(The version of this that referred to a woman would not be different enough to require comment.)

The paragraph in 26 is a gigantic *Meta-Hedge*. It says this: "You have no right to feel verbally abused, no matter how rude and abusive I am, because you are so unimportant in comparison to me and my enormous problems. But we will pretend that you do have such a right by discussing it as if you did—and please notice how polite that is of me and behave accordingly. It would be extremely rude of you to object to my verbal abuse after all the trouble I'm going to on your behalf here." Obviously, the hired hand can't come right out and use *those* words, and therefore 26 is used to get the same information across. This is the technique of choice—and it ordinarily works.

In the same way that you hear people at parties bragging about who has the longest abdominal incision, you will hear them bragging about which one has the rudest doctor. ("You think *that's* bad—let me tell you what *my* doctor said to *me!*") The technique has worked so well that people now seem to assume that only incompetent doctors are polite, which is an interesting measure of the verbal skill that doctors are alleged *not* to have.

You can get out of having to share in the car pool by claiming that you can't drive; you can get out of having to wash dishes by claiming that you always break things; and if you are sufficiently high in status in American society you can get out of having to participate in the system of mutual verbal courtesy by claiming that you don't know how to use language courteously. Even if you are not in one of the high-status professions, if you provide a service that people can't get along without—as do auto mechanics and plumbers—you may adopt this excuse and use it with success. This is one of the reasons that people need to study verbal self-defense, and in the next chapter I'll tell you how to handle this abuse.

Right now, we'll move on to Attack Pattern K, which looks like this.

SECTION K ATTACK:

"You only *do* that to get at*t*ention/cause *trouble*/em*barr*ass people, you know."

(The phrase "*do* that" may be replaced by a word or words that specify the particular item of behavior being criticized.)

Presupposed:

There could be no other reason for your behavior except the completely unacceptable one I'm presenting.

What you're doing is therefore rotten and awful, and you should be ashamed of yourself.

This attack is a tricky one, because it contains a double accusation that's tangled up in itself. Suppose you want to claim that getting attention is *not* the "only" reason you have for doing whatever you're said to do. Then is it *one* of the reasons? And while you are making this muddled point, you are unfortunately accepting the presupposition that what you are doing is wrong —if it weren't, why would you be defending yourself?

If you decide instead to begin by claiming that what you do is not wrong and is nothing to be ashamed of, you are accepting the presupposition that you have no reason for doing it except your desire to get attention (or cause trouble, or embarrass people, or something equally distasteful)—and who can be proud of *that*?

No matter which of the twin heads of this attack you decide to wrestle with, you are letting the other flourish. And it may come at you in even more devastating form with yet another presupposition added to it, like this:

27. "You *only want to do* that because you're trying to get at*ten*tion, you know."

This, like the Section B attack, throws in a presupposition that you're perfectly capable of controlling all your personal desires if you'd only do so. Because that is never true, it traps you in the bind of feeling guilty because you don't stop wanting to do whatever it is, even if you actually stop doing it. When the item filling the "do that" part of the utterance is something you can't help doing (and perhaps hate yourself for doing), having to listen to this attack pattern causes misery.

Nesting one verbal attack inside another is vicious, and common, and it greatly complicates the problem of verbal self-defense. Consider this mess:

28. "*Some* professors would say that even a *fresh*man should be able to manage a simple little task like a neatly typed term paper."

Or—to the professor rather than to the student—

29. "Everybody under*stands* that *some* professors would say even a *fresh*man should be able to manage a simple little task like a neatly typed term paper."

The stress patterns in nested attacks like these are very confusing. Only small children and people who are willing to be perceived as childish put multiple strong stresses in a single sentence. The usual practice is one, or at most two, such stresses per sentence, and not in every sentence either. Anyone with sufficient status (or making a claim to sufficient status) to use attacks with multiple stresses is by definition not someone willing to be considered childish. The person must therefore find a way to put in the crucial emphasis that carries the abusive presuppositions *without* slipping into the juvenile style. This is done by putting very heavy stress on one or two chunks of the utterance and a less obvious stress on the others, and it takes skilled control of the modulations of the voice to bring it off.

When it's done successfully, the listener will find it hard to tell which of the attacks is most important to the attacker. This is not something to worry about. It matters to specialists, such as the trial lawyer in open court or the expert sent to try to talk a terrorist into releasing hostages. But if someone is throwing an assortment of attacks at you in ordinary circumstances, trying to rank them in order of their importance or unpleasantness is a waste of your time. Notice them, be aware of them, but deal with any one that happens to occur to you first.

The last attack pattern I want to introduce here is this.

SECTION L ATTACK:

"Even if you *do* lose your job/fail the course/forget the answer/get a low score/get a headache again/forget your speech, *I* won't think any less of you!"

You will notice here another problem with using written symbols to convey real language. In this example the only way I can indicate strong stress on the word *I* is to underline it. Be sure that you hear both stresses indicated before you identify this sequence of words as an attack—neither of the examples below qualifies.

30. "Even if you *do* lose your job, I won't think any less of you."
No heavy stress on "*I*"—not an attack.

31. "Even if you do lose your job, *I* won't think any less of you."
No heavy stress on *do*—not an attack.

126

Except in negative sentences and in questions, the English word *do* is always an emphatic marker, and it always carries extra stress whether it is indicated by punctuation or not. English speakers once said things such as "I do sing this afternoon" with the word *do* having no more significance or stress than it does in "Do you like broccoli?" But today, *do* in anything but negatives and questions is automatically emphatic.[6] This means that when *do* appears in a verbal attack it will have an exaggerated stress that is impossible to miss, and this lets you know it is meant as part of an attack.

THE DOUBLE BIND

You will be familiar with the concept of the *double bind*—the situation that appears to allow only two choices, both of which are wrong. The old joke in which someone who has been given a blue sweater and a green sweater doesn't dare put on either one, because the giver will immediately demand to know what's wrong with the *other* one, is a situational double bind. The quandry you're in when one of your guests is a professional pianist—if you don't ask her to play you look as if you don't appreciate her talent, but if you do ask her you look as if that's the reason you invited her to your party—is a double bind. And beyond the double bind lies the multiple bind, in which even more choices, all of them wrong, are offered.

When you offer a number of choices, you are presupposing that the other person is free to make his or her own decision; but in reality you have that individual tightly bound by the fact that none of the choices can possibly be right. And the act of using a double bind, coming from someone in a dominant position, says, "I order you to choose one of these alternatives, all of which are the wrong alternatives for you to choose."

[6]English has a different verb *do* meaning "accomplish, carry out," as in "Do the dishes." You'd need both to ask a question, as shown by "Do you do the dishes?" Don't confuse the two.

The highly skilled verbal abuser will often set up one of the attack patterns from this chapter in such a way that it contains a double bind, for example:

32. "If you *really* loved me, you'd *never* be angry with me."

This binds the listener into knots—it's impossible for any human being to "never be angry," and that immediately leaves no way to prove that the attacker is "really loved." Worse yet, the natural reaction to a statement like (32) *is* anger. All it takes to turn a Section A or Section B attack into a double bind is something in the "If you *really* . . ." section that the speaker knows the listener will want to prove false, and something impossible as bait. Section B double binds look like these:

33. "If you *really* loved me, you wouldn't *want* to work."
34. "If you really *loved* me, you wouldn't *need* to smoke."

Because nobody can control what he or she wants or needs and the attacker chooses something the victim is *known* to want or need, this pattern always creates a double bind.

Another way to structure attacks as double binds is to use words such as *realize, know, be aware,* which presuppose the truth of whatever follows them. Then the impossible choice is tucked into the bait as usual. Consider a situation in which a husband doesn't want his wife to work, but knows that she wants to very badly; they have one or more children still at home. *Ordering* her not to work would be amateurish; if he has any verbal skills he won't do that. What he might do instead is this:

35. "A woman who was *aware* that the major cause of juvenile delinquency is the working mother wouldn't *want* to work."

Tricky, isn't it? That "the major cause of juvenile delinquency is the working mother," true or not, is presupposed by the "was *aware*" that comes before it. Because the woman has heard the statement, she can't claim *not* to be "aware"; even if she wasn't aware of it before, she has just been *made* aware. The husband has presupposed that once she is aware of the presupposed statement she won't *want* to work—but of course that is impossible.

If she says that she isn't aware of the bit about juvenile delinquency, she is wrong, now that he's brought it up. If she says that now that she's aware of it she doesn't want to work, she is lying. If she says that he is wrong, she is claiming that "a woman who knows that the major cause of juvenile delinquency is the working mother" would want to work anyway. If she says that he is right, she is claiming that she can do the impossible and deliberately not-want to work. And so on, through any number of choices. All of them will be wrong, because of the manner in which the attack has been constructed. She is multiply bound.

This sort of thing is not confined to men, or to the home. Here are two other examples:

36. "A son who was a*ware* that his parents would be broken hearted if he didn't go to college wouldn't *want* to become a mechanic!"
37. "An employee who *real*ized that high salaries are the primary cause of unemployment wouldn't *want* to get a raise."

Always consider any utterance that is a double or multiple bind to be a verbal attack, whether it fits any pattern in this chapter or not, no matter what its other characteristics may be. There is no such thing as a fair or neutral double bind.[7]

All right—there you have an even dozen, a very dirty dozen, of the verbal attack patterns you need to be able to recognize. The formal structure for Sections I through L is shown in Table Three.

[7]It's common for therapists to construct double binds and use them in clinical situations; you will find this much discussed in the professional literature. The value of the technique depends on the skill of the therapist; in good hands it can be useful.

TABLE THREE

I. You *know* I'd never (X), but (Y).
J. You're not the *only (X)*, you know.
K. You only (X) to (Y), you know.
L. Even if you *do (X)*, I won't (Y).

The focus in this chapter has been confined strictly to how verbal attacks can be recognized, how to tell the difference between such attacks and the Leveler utterances that often contain exactly the same words, and how to find the meanings hidden away in presuppositions inside attacks. In the next chapter we will move on to the techniques for responding to verbal attacks after you have recognized them.

SUPPLEMENTARY QUOTATION

It's pouring down words, all day, every day. You are surrounded by, inundated with language from morning till night, every day of your life. And what does this mean to you? It means that language is your business, as it is everybody's business, unless you are one of those rare individuals who is going to be able to isolate himself or herself totally from society. It means that the day when the analysis and understanding of all language other than simple conversation could be left for the scholar and the expert is long past. It means that you must, in self-defense, become an expert on language yourself. [Elgin, 1975, p. xiii].

SUGGESTED READINGS

ELGIN, S. H. *Pouring down Words*. Englewood Cliffs, N.J.: Prentice-Hall, Inc., 1975. (A textbook on dealing with various modes of language, including the language of politics, journalism, advertising, with special attention to the characteristics by which we recognize various language forms.)

_____. *The Gentle Art of Verbal Self-Defense*. Englewood Cliffs, N.J.: Prentice-Hall, Inc., 1980, pp. 15–191. (Takes up each of the first eight verbal attacks discussed in this chapter, in detail, giving a separate chapter to each one.)

6

Responding to Verbal Attacks

Remember that the key to the twelve verbal attacks discussed in Chapter Five is that *they hide the actual content of the attack inside a presupposition*. Remember that the usual surface cue that lets you know this is happening is not specific words in themselves, but unusual stress—heard as higher pitch and louder volume—on a word or words *fit into* those patterns. Obviously Chapter Five did not cover all possible verbal attacks of this type. However, the twelve that were discussed are so common that mastering their forms should make it relatively easy for you to spot not only variations but completely new examples.

Now we need to turn our attention to the techniques for responding to verbal attacks once you have recognized them and identified their abusive content. The first principle of self-defense in this situation is:

ALWAYS RESPOND DIRECTLY
TO THE PRESUPPOSITIONS.

That is, you have identified the presuppositions and their content; now you respond to *that* material directly.

THE BAIT

Verbal attacks that are not just open insults of the "Listen, stupid ..." variety ordinarily have two parts for you to be concerned with: the *presupposition* and the *bait*. The attacker expects you to respond to the bait because that is what usually happens in his or her experience. And the bait will be made only as irresistible as seems necessary. If you have been through many of these episodes with a particular opponent and you have always responded instantly to the bait—no matter how trivial—your attacker won't go to much trouble to construct a bait you can't resist. This is a real advantage for the verbal bully. Once you as victim have been trained to take any old bait that's handy, both your opponent and anyone else who happens to be listening will be able to point out the incredible triviality of the things you get upset over. If you let yourself acquire a language habit like that, you are going to be miserable.

Let's begin with the simplest example, the Section A attack.

1. "If you *really* loved me, you wouldn't stay *out* so late."
                               BAIT

Anything at all can go in that bait slot. It is in fact irrelevant what goes in there, because your opponent is only interested in the claim that you don't really love him or her. Here are some examples from other life areas:

2. "If you *really* wanted your promotion, you wouldn't always leave half your work for other people to do."
3. "If you *really* wanted me to get well, you'd bring my pills when the doctor *said* I was supposed to have them."
4. "If you *really* wanted me to get good grades, you'd buy me a calculator like all the other kids have."

The better the attacker knows the person attacked, the more likely he or she is to be familiar with the sorts of accusations that will really hurt when used as bait. If the victim is a stranger, there are all-purpose formulas like this example:

5. "If you *really* cared anything about other people, you wouldn't *act* the way you do."

Because the accusation that is the bait is usually so irritating—and often unjust or plain wrong to the point of absurdity—the person listening has an almost automatic tendency to respond to that bait. And that is exactly the wrong thing to do. Your opponent is aware that the bait is absurd in most cases, and the fact that you fall for it only decreases his or her already limited respect for you. If you want to put an end to this kind of pollution in your language environment, you must learn to ignore the bait and go straight for the presupposed attacks.

THE PRESUPPOSED ATTACK

INTERACTION ELEVEN
Patient: If you *really* wanted me to get well, you wouldn't neglect me like you do.

Nurse: I don't neglect you, Mr. Jones! I bring you your pills, I check your vital signs, I take you for walks—how can you say that I neglect you?

Patient: Oh, sure, sure, you do *those* things! That's your *job*, that's what they *pay* you to do! But I'm not a human being to you—you don't care anything about me—I'm just a number. Just a sta*tis*tic, that's all I am to you!

Nurse: Mr. Jones, that's unfair and I resent it. I take *very* good care of you. And you don't make it any easier by getting yourself all upset like this, you know.

Patient: Getting myself all upset? *You're* the one that's getting me all upset!

Nurse: I'll come back later, Mr. Jones, when you've had a chance to calm down. Excuse me. (Exit, tight lipped and rigid.)

This isn't likely to improve the patient's physical or emotional health, and it went wrong the instant NURSE responded to PATIENT's opening sentence. PATIENT doesn't really feel that the nurse neglects him. He is just as likely to attack the way the nurse talks, something he overheard someone say the nurse *thinks,* or anything else about the nurse's real or imagined behavior. What's bothering Mr. Jones is that he has begun to feel that nobody cares whether he gets well or not.

This may be nothing more than his lack of experience with hospital routines. It may be the result of any number of misunderstandings. But what Mr. Jones wants to hear is that his health *matters* to somebody. If he were comfortable with Leveler Mode, he could just ask "Do you care whether I get well, or not?" But many adult Americans have a hard time Leveling, even under ideal conditions. Mr. Jones is sick, perhaps in pain, and in a hospital—that's about as far as you can get from ideal conditions without doing something criminal. Because he can't Level and desperately wants to know, he hides his suspicious question inside a presupposition and throws a bait on the end to cover up what he's doing. And NURSE, unfortunately, takes the bait.

Once NURSE has admitted that PATIENT's suspicions are correct by ignoring his plea for reassurance and has responded to the bait with an outraged retort, there's no saving this interaction. It ends with PATIENT just as worried as he was to begin with, and now humiliated and hurt as well. NURSE is not a great deal better off, although the position of dominance health-care professionals have in this situation allows them to "win" the encounter.

INTERACTION ELEVEN, REVISED

Patient: If you *really* wanted me to get well, you wouldn't ne*glect* me like you do.

Nurse: Mr. Jones, I do want you to get well. That really does matter to me.

Patient: Oh. Well, sure. I guess it does. I guess I'm just being silly.

Nurse: I don't think so, I think you were just worried, and that's natural. Being in a hospital is no fun. Now, do you feel like taking a walk down the hall?

Please notice that if we are concerned here with medical economics rather than compassion, this technique is a more efficient and cost-effective use of the nurse's time than the useless argument was. It is *not* true that effective communication can only happen if you have all day to stand around talking.

"ASSERTIVENESS"

In the original version of Interaction Eleven, the nurse's second response begins with a line that can be identified as an intended "assertive" speech. The patient has accused the nurse of neglecting him, of caring nothing for him, of treating him like a statistic, and so on. NURSE's perception of the situation is that this is untrue and unjust; however, only a few years ago the most probable response would have been something like "I'm sorry if something has happened to make you feel that way, Mr. Jones." Nowadays such a response, especially from a woman or a subordinate, is labelled "submissive" behavior. (The range runs from "submissive" through "assertive" to "aggressive," with instructions to avoid both extremes and strive for the middle.) I mention this because, although I have much respect for the intentions of the assertiveness training experts, I see a great deal of confused and potentially dangerous language behavior growing out of assertiveness training and self-help books. Sometimes it is dangerous for the person speaking assertively, sometimes for the listener or listeners, and frequently for everyone involved. This may not be the fault of the assertiveness expert at all; for instance, the person taking the training may not have paid close attention, may have misunderstood, or may be taking a rule intended for one situation and extending it to others that the trainer never anticipated. Nevertheless, this is a source of much confusion, and we will be discussing it from time to time throughout this book.

The nurse in Interaction Eleven is being assertive because he or she has learned that patients must not be allowed to abuse the nurse, that the nurse has rights which the patients are obligated to respect, and that unless nurses stand up for themselves they have only themselves to blame if they are taken advantage of. The nurse has been taught that the fact that patients are paying for nursing services does not entitle them to bully or otherwise abuse the provider of those services and that nurses must *assert* themselves for the patients' sakes as well as for their own. All of which is true.

However—in this instance the argument is the result of the nurse having made a mistake in the first place. The technique of answering a verbal attack by responding to the presuppositions and ignoring the bait does not require any enormous investment of time or energy. It is much easier to do than keeping track of medications and giving injections. The nurse, not the patient, is the professional here; the patient is in the nurse's care and is entitled to expect competence. It is as much the nurse's responsibility to use language competently as it is to use a hypodermic competently. Under these circumstances, the "assertive" response is inappropriate and unprofessional. Predictably, it not only doesn't help matters, it makes them worse.

BAITS AND RESPONSES

In the examples below, the portion of the utterance that is the bait and should be ignored is marked off at each end by double slashes, like this //.

6. "If you *really* wanted to lose weight, //you wouldn't *eat* all that candy."//
7. "If you *really* cared about your health, //you'd *want* to exercise."//
8. "Even an as*sist*ant professor should be able to keep from //giving tests so hard they drive the students into a different major."//
9. "Everyone under*stands* why //you spend most of your time saying rotten things about your sergeant."//
10. "A person who really *want*ed to stay on a budget //wouldn't even con*sid*er buying an expensive wardrobe like yours."//
11. "*Some* patients would think their dentists didn't even *care* about them if //they never listened to a single word the patients said."//
12. "You *know* I would never interfere in the way you raise your children, dear, but //if you keep on feeding the girls junk food all the time, you're going to ruin their health as well as their characters."//
13. "You only //pre*tend* that you can't eat anything but soup and toast//to make people feel sorry for you,//you know."[1]
14. "Even if you *do* //keep making such foolish decisions that your business goes into bankruptcy,//I won't hold it against you."

For every verbal attack of this type the same strategy should be followed—ignore the bait, no matter how infuriating it may be,

[1]The claim that you are trying to make people feel sorry for you—and worse, that that's your only motive for your actions—is also bait. The two chunks of bait are so entangled here that it isn't really possible to separate them.

and respond directly to the presupposition. An example of a possible response for each of the attacks in 6-14 follows.

6A. "I really do want to lose weight—no kidding."
7A. "Of course I care about my health! I care very much."

Or

"The idea that people are able to control their personal desires is an interesting one."

Here there were two presupposed accusations to choose from. The first response is addressed to the claim that you don't care about your health and is in Leveler Mode; the second responds to the presupposed statement that you are able to deliberately not-want or want things and is in Computer Mode. We could switch the modes, and would then get a pair of possible responses like these.

7B. "It's always difficult to know where a sensible concern for personal health ends and hypochondria begins."

Or

"When did you begin to think I was able to control my personal desires?"[2]

8A. "The opinion that assistant professors are in some way inherently inferior to their senior colleagues is a common one—I'm very surprised to hear it from someone like yourself."

9A. "I'm sure they do; and I want you to know that I appreciate their concern."

10A. "I couldn't agree with you more. Staying on a budget is an admirable goal."

11A. "Really? I'd be interested to hear *your* opinion about that sort of problem."

[2]Any question that begins with *when* contains a presupposition that can be useful. Here you have presupposed that at some time the attacker *did* begin to think you could control your wishes.

12A. "I do know—and I want you to realize how much I appreciate the way you resist the temptation to interfere. Not everyone is capable of that."

13A. "How nice of you to feel sorry for me!"

Or

"How observant of you to notice that I can't eat anything but soup and toast!"

14A. "It's unfortunate that not everyone can have your good sense and sound judgment."

In every one of these responses you have played by the rules. You have allowed the topic chosen by your attacker to succeed and have responded to it. You have simply developed a topic that was presupposed, instead of a topic that was serving as bait. This may surprise your opponent, but it violates no rules of conversation and is a demonstration of your linguistic skill.

RELUCTANCE TO USE THESE TECHNIQUES

Some of my students and clients tell me that they don't believe responses like these will work. I suggest they try them out and see what happens, because we know for certain that responses to the *bait* will never work. They discover that these responses work very well indeed and that people don't consider them nearly so much fun to pick on anymore. And that is always very satisfying both to them and to me.

But there is another sort of resistance that isn't so easily dealt with. Some people tell me that they do believe the suggested responses will work, if only because they've heard other students and clients report that they do. They tell me they have every intention of using those responses. *But,* they just can't seem to get started. Why? Because "when somebody says something like that I can't just stand there and let them get away with it!" That is, they cannot resist the bait. They tell me that each time they recognize one of the twelve attacks they take the bait and the inevitable row that follows it. And even as they are walking into the punch, they tell me, they're thinking, "Now *this* time it's so awful I can't stand to let it go by, but *next* time I'll use a verbal self-defense response instead!" Unfortunately, every chunk of bait is as tempting as the one before, and "next time" never arrives. What, they want to know, can they do about that?

I only wish I knew. I do know that logic alone won't help, because there is no logical reason that can be offered for countering a verbal attack with a response that is certain only to (a) turn the interaction into a fight, (b) leave all individuals involved—except the deliberate verbal sadist—feeling rotten, and (c) encourage the attacker to use the same technique again because it always works.

I am not going to say what I'm afraid these people expect me to say: "If you *really* wanted those verbal attacks to stop, you'd be able to follow my in*struc*tions!" I know better. I listen with great care to keep the distasteful dozen out of my own speech. I can only keep encouraging people to try for sufficient self-discipline, *just one time,* to ignore the bait and follow verbal self-defense strategy. In my experience, if they can resist just once they can continue to resist, because the surprise it causes their attacker and the increased respect it wins for them are such welcome changes from what they are used to.

I'd like to separate the two causes of this problem because I suspect they are inherently contradictory and because in many people's minds they've become so entangled that they are a real barrier to communication. First, there is the idea already mentioned—the feeling that to let the accusations thrown out as bait go by without protest is to let the attacker get away with something. The victim is afraid that he or she will *lose face* if the accusations in the bait are allowed to stand—much like two children who are shouting "You did!" "I did not!" "You did, too!" in an endless cycle from which neither knows how to escape.

141

Then there is the difficulty—also relating to loss of face—that comes from perceiving the verbal self-defense responses as submissive, cowardly, toadying, Placating, and so on.

The two problems ordinarily coexist in the student or client, and it's impossible to tell which is the major barrier without long investigation on a one-to-one basis. (Even then, as with private clients, I often find that the two factors vary in importance from one context to another.) It's best, therefore, to discuss each one as if everyone were equally bothered by both.

Let's begin with that idea that the attacker will be getting away with murder if you don't counter the accusation used as bait.

INTERACTION TWELVE

Professor: If you *really* cared anything about passing this course, you'd pay attention in class instead of sitting there working on your *other* courses while I'm talking.

Student: Working on my other courses? I don't *do* that, Dr. Martin! You may have students that do—but I'm not one of them!

Professor: Oh, come on. I've been teaching for almost twenty years. Don't you think that by now I'm able to tell when somebody's putting me on? Or do you think I'm too stupid to figure that out?

We can stop right here in mid-disaster to see just what STUDENT has accomplished by this. Let's assume STUDENT is innocent; if not, there's a different problem that we don't want to muddy our waters with now. Let's assume STUDENT really has been taking notes on PROFESSOR's lectures, not doing work from other courses while the lecture was going on as PROFESSOR has claimed. The student's response—the classic "I did not!"—has escalated the initial accusation into a real attack in force. PROFESSOR is now saying, "You're a liar and I have twenty years of teaching experience plus a Ph.D. backing me up in that judgment—what have *you* got?" Not only that, the student has just accused the professor of being wrong; in this context that constitutes issuing a challenge to one of superior rank and power. Predictably, PROFESSOR has thrown in a little something extra, and now STUDENT can choose from among a variety of "Yes you did/No I didn't" dead ends.

Should the student ignore the question of whether he or she thinks the professor is stupid and concentrate doggedly on maintaining innocence of the original charge? Like this: "Dr. Martin, I said I don't do work for other classes during your lectures, and I mean that. I don't know how you got the idea that that's what I'm doing when I'm taking notes on what *you* are saying—but you're wrong." That's very satisfying to STUDENT, I suppose, but it continues the open challenge to the prof's judgment, and it lets stand unchallenged the prof's charge that STUDENT is saying he or she is stupid.

Should the student let drop for the moment the question of whether other work is being done during the prof's lectures and turn to the matter of who is stupid here? Like this?

> *Student:* Of course I don't think you're stupid! I didn't say anything of the kind, Dr. Martin, and I resent you putting words in my mouth.
>
> *Professor:* Oh, *do you re*ally?
>
> *Student:* Yes, I do. It's not fair, and I don't think I have to put up with it.
>
> *Professor:* Indeed you don't! In fact, you don't have to put up with *any* aspect of my behavior that you find unsatisfactory. I suggest you transfer to another section, with a professor who can meet your high standards—and the quicker the better. Now if you'll excuse me, I have an appointment with a student who doesn't feel that her skills include evaluating the qualifications and character of her professor.

We now have an interesting muddle to consider. The student's strategy is quite clear: Stand up for your rights, insist on being respected, and don't let the prof get away with anything. The result of this set of moves is supposed to be a clarification of the relationship between STUDENT and PROFESSOR, with a new respect for STUDENT dawning in the instructor and remaining as a basis for further communication. You will notice that that is *not* what has happened.

Whether STUDENT will have to transfer to another section of the course—usually very inconvenient and no help to a student already struggling to keep up—will depend on the school. Almost anywhere students have mechanisms available to bring pressure on the professor and force him or her to withdraw the order to change sections. These mechanisms are valuable to students and should be used when they are needed; they include grievance committees, the dean of students, the ombudsman, and so on. They take time away from one's studies—in some instances, they lead to numerous meetings and negotiations up to and including a formal hearing. They create ill will in all directions, because other profs will take note (and make a note) that the student is a troublemaker. The prof who is forced to give in is not ever going to forget that—and the student may need that prof farther down the road for another course, for a letter of recommendation, as a member on a thesis committee, or for a multitude of other things.

Let me make myself very clear at this point. I don't want you to have any trouble seeing, hearing, or grasping what I mean. There are times when it is necessary to follow this route, whatever the risks. Some thoroughly rotten professors (or bosses, or doctors, or military officers, or any other power figures) abuse their privileges. For the sake of everyone obliged to deal with these stinkers, as well as the individual, some people have to gird up their loins and say, "Enough!" Otherwise, it will go on forever. And if nobody has the guts to challenge the person, or if everyone is either too lazy or too selfish to follow through on the long, weary procedure of making the challenge stick, they *deserve* to have it go on forever.

But it is absolutely crucial to be sure that that really is the situation, and that the confrontation is for that purpose and worth the price.

Students ask me *why* professors act like that. That is, why on earth, given the fact that they have their students outranked and outgunned in every direction, do professors stoop to verbal abuse? And that is precisely where the clue is to be found. *No* professor (or boss, or doctor, or military officer, or any other power figure) who is confident of his or her power does this. You can rely on that. The professor who behaves like the one just described doesn't believe he or she is powerful, respected, in control of his or her classes or career; and such people are terrified that somebody will discover all these unpleasant things. You should realize that given the amount of power a prof has to throw around, the one who is reduced to picking on *students* to prove status is a pitiful case. You may safely assume that either the rest of the faculty and the administration make this person's life a torment or at least that the professor perceives the situation that way.

This should change your *own* perceptions of your opponent. This is not a powerful and dominant individual using clout to abuse a subordinate; this is a pathetic person. There's no reason for the student to feel anything but compassion for such a professor. Therefore, if he or she "gets away with it," so what? It may be the only opportunity you have to do a good deed that week—let it pass. Rather than saying that you are toadying and submissive if you let the accusation stand, try to remember that *you* lose face if you stoop to taking the bait in such a case. The interaction should therefore be revised; let's do it.

INTERACTION TWELVE, REVISED

Professor: If you *really* cared anything about passing this course, you'd pay attention in class instead of sitting there working on your *oth*er courses while I'm talking.

> *Student:* Dr. Martin, I do care about passing. It matters very much to me.
>
> *Professor:* Well, it doesn't *look* that way. Aren't you working on your other classes while I'm talking—tell the truth, now—aren't you?
>
> *Student:* No. That would be a waste of my time as well as yours. I'm taking notes on your lectures, and I'm paying attention just as closely as I can.
>
> *Professor:* I must have you mixed up with some other student, then. I'm sorry.
>
> *Student:* I'm sure it's hard to keep students straight when there are so many—I can see that. Now, I wonder if you'd explain this section of the homework to me? I know I'm doing something wrong, but it's not clear to me where the trouble is.
>
> *Professor:* Let's take a look at it. Let me see—

Notice what has happened in this revision. The student has understood that the professor suspects nobody really cares about passing his or her class—and has used a verbal self-defense (VSD) response to offer immediate reassurance. The presupposition was "You don't care if you pass my course or not" and the response was directly to that presupposition, an immediate "I *do* care." (And once the student hears the heavily stressed *look* in the professor's speech, a switch is made to sight predicates where possible. This is certain to increase the student's trustworthiness in the judgment of the professor.) The result of the interaction is exactly the one the student wanted; the prof has given up the foolish accusation, has demonstrated a new regard for the student, and has in fact apologized. The two are now on a friendly footing that should serve as a foundation for effective communication in the future.

Neither student nor professor has had to behave in an undignified or dishonorable manner; neither has lost face. The professor can afford to offer the apology, because he or she has the higher status and is able to think of a plausible reason for the mistake. The student has won this round in every sense of the word, but has done so by demonstrating skill in the use of language. The interaction was nonviolent, completely free of abusive counterattacks, and entirely successful.

Negotiating Instead of Submitting

Here is one more example for your examination. This time the attack is a bit more subtle.

INTERACTION THIRTEEN

Doctor: *Some* doctors would be inclined to be annoyed when one of their patients insisted on repeating tests that are already *per*fectly clear.

Patient: Sorry, but I don't agree that the test results are clear. And I want them done over. As long as I'm paying the bill, I don't see what difference it makes to you, Doctor.

Doctor: You don't, eh?

Patient: No. I don't.

Doctor: Well, let me see if I can clarify this for you, all right? In the first place, you are *not* qualified to judge whether your test results are clear. *I* have a medical degree—*you* do not. In the second place, you are *not* the only patient whose care I am responsible for. And when you insist on a wasteful investment of time and effort from my lab technicians, not to mention an equally wasteful repetition of *my* tasks in going over needlessly repeated tests, it is my *patients* that you are taking advantage of. I'm willing to let you get away with taking a certain amount of advantage of me personally; that appears to be important to you. But I absolutely will *not* have you interfering with the care I can give to other patients with very real illnesses.

This is a mess. PATIENT is perhaps wondering how the simple request for a repeated test or two turned into this series of accusations. In five conversational turns PATIENT has been

147

transformed into a callous and selfish person who cares nothing about the health of the doctor's other patients and wants all the doctor's attention and facilities for himself or herself. Furthermore, the patient has been turned into an egotistical ninny who presumes to claim medical expertise on the basis of no qualifications whatsoever. This doctor is extremely skillful with language, and the patient is boxed in tightly. No matter what PATIENT says now, it will probably only make matters worse. I have given much thought to this, and I cannot think of *any* response from PATIENT that would improve the situation. (Note also that this is an example of an interaction in which matching sensory predicates—sight words, for both persons involved—did not provide a magic solution.)

This is a good place, I believe, to comment on the language skills of physicians. It is commonplace to claim that doctors are poor communicators, that they aren't trained to communicate, and that patients should be grateful for their medical skills and not insist on linguistic skills as well. An examination of the medical curriculum will provide reinforcement for the position.

Doctors (and nurses) may have one or two courses in "human communications" or "the interview." Their content will be a mishmash of platitudes and garbled extracts, as free of theoretical foundation as the Flat Earth Society publications. Such courses can be summarized as follows: (1) Listen carefully. (2) Be pleasant, but don't fraternize. (3) Use your communication time in an efficient and cost-effective manner. (4) Avoid technical terms when you can and explain them when you can't—if you have time. (5) Watch out for the manipulative patient or client. (6) Don't make promises. (7) Don't discuss your fees. (8) Don't discuss other medical professionals. (9) Be sympathetic, but don't become involved. (10) Never let a patient or client put you down—your image as a confident physician in control of the situation is essential if the patient is to get well and maintain health.

Most of these statements are in the "thou shalt not" mode, and what little positive instruction is provided is of dubious usefulness. "Listen carefully." For *what?*

Just as there is a difference between the overt (open) information in an utterance and the covert (hidden) information, there is a difference between overt and covert content in a curriculum. Almost every class an individual takes in the American educational system has as part of its hidden curriculum the training given in perceiving *time* in the American way. It is very much the American way to expect patients in therapy to arrange their crises into fifty-minute chunks on scheduled days, just as students are expected to learn verb endings in fifty-minute chunks on scheduled days. It is similarly American to expect patients to learn that an illness at three o'clock in the morning is ill-bred and inconsiderate. A part of the medical curriculum is devoted to helping doctors learn how to teach this sort of thing to patients—it is part of "patient management." And although there is no course so labeled, all American physicians receive superb training in one language skill: That of using language as a means of achieving dominance and maintaining power.

The problem in medical communications is not that doctors aren't skilled communicators. It's that they are highly skilled, but only in one narrow communication role. So finely honed is this skill that it often becomes a language trap for the doctor as well as the patient. Doctors become unable to communicate in any other way but the one they are taught as part of their profession. And when they try to use that same language style with nurses, salespeople, and family members, it leads to much confusion, with painful results for everyone. Furthermore, when the patient reacts to this language behavior by perceiving the doctor as a sort of priest, while the doctor perceives the patient as a sort of product, the possibilities for misunderstanding get entirely out of hand.

What if we revise Interaction Thirteen, using some of the techniques we've been discussing?

INTERACTION THIRTEEN, REVISED

Doctor: *Some* doctors would be inclined to be annoyed when one of their patients insisted on repeating lab tests that are already *perfectly* clear.

Patient: I'm sure they would—and I don't blame them one bit.

Doctor: You don't, eh?

Patient: Not at all. With health-care costs so high, it's the doctor's obligation to make good use of time and facilities. No question about it.

Doctor: Well, if we are in agreement on that as a basic principle, perhaps we can come to some kind of consensus about those tests you wanted me to repeat.

Patient: Oh, I'm sure we can. Which test was it that you didn't want done again?

I would hope that the patient has planned ahead in this situation, has anticipated that there will be an objection from the doctor, and has included at least one test that he or she does not feel it absolutely necessary to repeat. This is called *negotiation* and is completely ethical behavior.

If the doctor surprises the patient by giving in to the entire request, the patient can then remark that the question raised about unnecessary repetition has made him or her see the whole thing more clearly and perhaps it *is* excessive to ask for another run on Test X. The doctor is then free either to say that all the tests should be done—presumably for good reason—or to agree that the dubious one should be dropped.

Whenever you must negotiate with someone whose dominance (perceived status plus real-world power to punish or reward) outranks yours, you should routinely request just a bit more than you actually feel obliged to get; this leaves you with something you can give up gracefully. Little boys learn this by the time they are five; little girls are not so likely to and may have a serious problem with seeing the strategy as dishonest. This is unfortunate, and is much like insisting on playing baseball without using a bat because you feel that the bat might be a symbol of aggression. You can be reasonably sure that in a situation such as just described, only two possibilities exist:

- Everyone else present is playing the negotiation game by the rules and has included in the demands something he or she is prepared in advance to surrender for the sake of letting the other side maintain face.
- Some people present don't know about the rule and are there with their actual demands, right up front.

In neither case will the fact that *you* have chosen to play by the rules do any harm. In the first case the other side will also give up things they didn't intend to insist on; in the second case, only you will. In both cases this will result in agreement.

If you are going in as chief negotiator for a labor contract between General Motors and its union, of course, this is not sufficient. If that's what you're doing, however, you are an expert negotiator and you already know how to proceed. For everyday negotiations between patient and doctor, student and professor, client and lawyer, car owner and mechanic, loan officer and loan applicant, the information is sufficient and accurate.

ANALYSIS OF THREE
VERBAL ATTACK PATTERNS

Now I want to take a closer look at three of the twelve attacks we've been working with—the three shown in the examples below, repeated in their formula patterns for your convenience.

15a.   Don't you even *care* about (X)?
15b.   *Why* do you always/don't you ever (X)?
15c.   You're not the *only* (X), you know.

These patterns require separate attention because a suitable response to them is not so obvious, and because many people tell me that they are the three that are most difficult to respond to without counterattacking. They are apparently, for many of my students and clients, the hardest to "let somebody get away with."

Section C Attack

"Don't you even *care* about (X)?" is a way of saying "Any decent human being would care about X and you don't—therefore you are not a decent human being and should feel guilty and ashamed." It is a way of saying all that without having to use Blamer Mode. The pattern is a disguised Blaming attack and represents a slightly more sophisticated way of Blaming than the head-on open accusation. Here are some typical examples.

16. "Don't you even *care* about the problem of world hunger?"
17. "Don't you even *care* about the way your smoking endangers the health of everyone around you?"
18. "Don't you even *care* if your attitude about my smoking—not to mention your constant harping on the threat it's supposed to be for other people—makes it impossible for us to communicate?"
19. "Don't you even *care* about your grades?/credit rating?/colleagues?/squad?/promotion?" and so on ...

This pattern is framed so that whatever is included in (X) can fall on a scale from the most minutely personal item to the most grandiose of abstractions. Here are the two extremes carried to their ultimate degrees:

20. "Don't you even *care* about the color of your shoes?"
21. "Don't you even *care* about universal justice?"

You'll notice, if you say these aloud, that your tendency is to hold the heavy stress all the way from the word *care* to the end of the sentence. The extent to which this is done will vary from person to person, but there will always be even more stress on *care* than on any other part of the sequence, and that is what identifies the pattern as an attack.

The two extremes shown in examples 20 and 21 are not worth wasting your time over, especially if they come from people you don't have to deal with constantly. Answer the trivia examples like 20 by simply saying, "No." You are responding directly to the presupposition and are pointing out that the claim that such matters as shoe color require passionate convictions from all human beings impresses you as silly. Let your opponent take on the burden of arguing for the claim, if it really matters to him or her. But don't waste your time or energy in something like

22. "*Shoe* color! Why on earth should I care about *shoe* color, for crying out loud?"

When you do that, you are behaving as if the absurd presupposition is entitled to serious consideration. You are *giving* it serious consideration and inviting its defense. That's playing right into your opponent's hands. It's exactly what you are expected to do—don't do it. Say "No," and leave it at that.

The total abstraction should be met with something just as absurd as *it* is. Nobody is going to admit that he or she doesn't care anything about universal justice, or world hunger, or the rights of humankind, even if that is the solemn truth. The terms are free-floating and undefined and could mean almost anything. Unless you have very good reasons not to do so, I suggest that you use this sort of response move.

INTERACTION FOURTEEN
X: Don't you even *care* about human suffering?
You: Indeed I do—especially since the publication of the Allegheny Barthenwhacker et al. studies on the subject!
X: The what studies?

153

You: (Solemnly, with full eye contact if possible) Anyone who *really* cares about human suffering has *surely* read the Allegheny Barthenwhacker et al. studies!

X: Oh. Of course.

It doesn't make any difference what you call your invented "studies." The Fritzelbagen Studies. The Chelsea–Skunk Hollow–Addlepation Project Report. It makes no difference at all, because your intention is to inform your attacker politely that you are aware the original question was nonsense. If attackers then want to try saying "You made that up!" without looking like complete ninnies, you can wish them luck.

Are there any very good reasons not to do this? Yes. If the person using the attack is a small and innocent child or someone obviously confused, in pain, or disturbed—that is, anyone you can tell is not in fact *aware* of the absurdity of the question— treat the attack as if it were Leveler Mode and respond to it as carefully, completely, and seriously as you can. That's a special situation, and when it comes along it's the person using the pattern who needs defending, not you. If you can make it plain in your response that such questions need to be made more specific if they are to get useful answers, so much the better. But anyone using this pattern without realizing its foolishness deserves your help; it is not honorable to defend yourself in that situation. You do not defend yourself physically against the infant hitting you with a teddy bear—you make an honest effort to help the infant understand why such behavior is not appropriate.

When this attack falls in the middle range (not trivia and not an abstraction) it becomes more difficult to manage. You will then want to reply directly to the presupposition that you don't care, using either a neutral question or an utterance in full computer mode, like this.

INTERACTION FIFTEEN

Boss: Don't you even *care* about the way your constant lateness upsets everyone in this office?

You: When did you begin to feel that I don't care about the other people in the office?

Or

You: The question of the actual effect of lateness on employee performance and morale is an extremely interesting one and can be explored from a variety of different points of view, among which the perceptions of an individual at management level no doubt will be directly relevant.

Notice the way BOSS has framed the question, using the phrase "your constant lateness." In English, the possessive presupposes the existence of the thing possessed. That means that when I say "You are constantly late," I must go on and support my claim. But if I say "Your constant lateness puzzles me," it is *presupposed* that you are late all the time, and the only claim I have to support is the one about my being puzzled. Navajo allows native speakers to use a sentence such as "My new hat doesn't exist"; in English, that is impossible as an example of ordinary language and could only be a sentence from poetry, a joke, or perhaps an example in a linguistics class.

Furthermore, by turning the sequence "be late" into the noun phrase "lateness," BOSS has added one more layer of presupposition. English has a regular process that converts verbs and adjectives into nouns; it is called *nominalization*. And anything nominalized is also presupposed. "You are late" is a flat accusation; "your lateness puzzles me" presupposes "you are late" in two ways, using the possessive "your" and the nominalized "lateness." This hides the accusation securely away in a pattern roughly like "Gravity puzzles me." And it blandly assumes that "You are late all the time" is so obvious and so self-evident that it requires no proof.

Finally, BOSS has topped off this presupposition sundae by putting "constant" before the nominalization. To say "You are constantly late" would weakly presuppose "You are late" and require proof for the "constantly." By putting the whole thing into a possessive— "your constant lateness"—Boss is able to

155

dump the entire accusation into a pile of things that are *obviously* true. All that must be proved is that this self-evident constant lateness of yours *upsets* people. That's a great deal packaged into one small noun phrase.

If you respond by asking when BOSS first began to feel that you don't care, you aren't agreeing with any of those presuppositions. You are responding to them by acknowledging that they—the presuppositions—exist and asking when their existence began. The chances are very good that you will get a specific incident as a response if you do this, and specific charges are a lot less hard to handle than vague ones. For example, if we carry Interaction Fifteen a bit farther:

> *Boss:* Don't you even *care* about the way your constant lateness upsets everyone in this office?
>
> *You:* When did you begin to feel that I don't care about the other people in the office?
>
> *Boss:* Last Tuesday—the day you came in at eleven o'clock when you knew perfectly well that we were taking inventory and needed everybody here *early* if humanly possible, that's when.
>
> *You:* Last Tuesday ... that would be the day my bus broke down on the intercity bridge and they wouldn't let any of us get off because of the traffic hazard.
>
> *Boss:* Oh, I see—I didn't know that.

In this example you had a good excuse, and presumably you are *not* "constantly" late. If the accusation is not only presupposed but true in the real world, things won't be quite so easy. Having a good excuse in the specific case BOSS brings up won't clear the decks and will be useful in only one way: It will probably get BOSS started on a long list of examples of your lateness, to each of which you can offer an excuse, until both of you run out of interest in the whole discussion. It would be far better not to get into that unless you just happen to be looking for a fight. Instead, say this:

156

23. "You're absolutely right, there was no excuse for my being late last Tuesday. In fact, there's rarely any excuse for it. But it's not because I don't care; and I'll make a real effort to do better in future, now that you've called my attention to the problem."

This is not toadying, it's Leveling, and it's appropriate. (Unless, of course, you have no intention of trying to be on time, in which case it's not Leveling but lying and represents a problem this book can't deal with.)

If you use the full Computer Mode response pattern instead of the neutral question, you'll want to tailor it to the degree of truth in the accusation. If you aren't constantly late, you can afford to go to the extreme shown in the Computer response on page 155. What you are really saying is "I perceive that you want to play a game in which you accuse me of always being late, and I'm willing to play that game for a while if we switch from personal to general terms." If the accusation is accurate—if you *are* constantly late—you'll need to be more careful. Use only a brief sentence about the interesting nature of the question, and keep your body language in absolute Computer Mode also. Neutral. Calm. Without emotion either positive or negative. Otherwise, you are going to get back something like this:

24. "Are you *trying* to see how offensive you can be, or is that just your natural way of talking?"

It's hard to find the bait in "Don't you even *care* about (X)?" because there are so many places to put it. I'm inclined to think it's primarily in the presupposition that you're the sort of trash that *wouldn't* care about (X), and that's very unusual. It may be that that explains why people react so strongly to this particular attack pattern and find it so hard to deal with calmly. They are hearing "You no-good rotten creep, you!" way back in the layers of stuff hidden away, and the temptation to respond with an insult of the same kind is very strong.

Section G Attack

The pattern in the Section G attack is not dependent on subtleties and is much easier to handle. The bait is always right there in (X), where you can get at it easily. If it comes from a stranger, it probably won't bother you—how could a stranger know what you "always" or "never" do about anything? But when, as is usually the case, it comes from someone you know well, it can trick you into dreadfully foolish moves. Look at this interaction.

INTERACTION SIXTEEN

Spouse: Why do you never try to make me happy?

    You: Waddaya *mean?* What kind of talk is that? Didn't I just buy a stupid washing machine we didn't need and I didn't want, just to make you happy? Didn't I just tell one of the best friends I ever had to watch his language in my house, just to make you happy? Didn't I . . .

This is a fail-safe recipe for Instant Fight. If it appeals to you, you like fighting; I will assume that it doesn't. Let's do it a different way.

INTERACTION SIXTEEN, REVISED

Spouse: Why do you never try to make me happy?

    You: All right . . . how about if we go to your cousin Marion's for the weekend? If that would make you happy, I wouldn't mind at all.

    Spouse: Good grief, I don't want to spend the weekend right in the middle of the city!

    You: Okay. Then we won't do it.

Isn't that better? SPOUSE will have to make a deliberate effort to turn that into a fight.

The English question words (*why, where, when, what, who, how, whose, which*) presuppose a response that matches their role in the sentence. To a *why* question, you are expected to answer with a reason; to a *when* question, you are expected to answer with a time. A *where* question presupposes an answer that contains a place. And so on through the list. The Section G attack stresses the opening *why* as a way of demanding, "Give me a *reason* for doing what I am accusing you of doing." Don't ever fall for that. If it doesn't get you into an endless recitation as in the original version of Interaction Sixteen, it will get you into a mess like this one.

INTERACTION SEVENTEEN

Spouse: Why don't you ever try to make me happy?

You: Because I don't *know* what makes you happy.

Spouse: Oh, is *that* so? Listen, I think I make it absolutely clear that it would make me happy if you'd stop eating all that junk food.

You: Oh, no. You're *not* going to start that again!

Spouse: See? It's not that you don't know what makes me happy, it's that you don't even *care! Isn't* that so?

You: Whatever you say, dear. What the hell.

There's no way to turn this into useful communication. Your strategy should be the one demonstrated in revised Interaction Sixteen. The steps are set out for you below.

A. Respond directly to the presupposition that you always or never do what is being claimed by your opponent.

B. Ignore the request for a reason. (Or for a time, as in "*When* did you ever think about what *I* might want to do?" Or whatever other structure is anticipated by the question word.)

C. Use as your response something that proves the accusation false, right then and there. That is, if the claim is that you never try to make SPOUSE happy, offer *immediately* to do something that will have that effect. Offer something you know for certain SPOUSE will not want to do, and then agree with the refusal—which makes *two* attempts on your part to "make SPOUSE happy" in one short conversation. Or offer something that you know will please your opponent and that you are genuinely willing and able to do.

159

You will have to decide between these two alternatives on the basis of the real-world facts.

Here's an example of the second alternative, in which you make a real offer rather than one you know will be refused.

INTERACTION EIGHTEEN

Spouse: Why don't you ever try to make me happy?

You: Okay . . . let's go out for Chinese food tonight.

Spouse: Are you serious?

You: Certainly. Would you like to?

Spouse: I'd like to very much.

You: Good enough—let's do it.

The strategy shown in Interaction Eighteen is certainly a simple one, and it's often almost heartbreaking to see how small an effort you have to make to carry this off, considering the gravity of the charge. But I have one caution to offer.

If you find yourself in a *long-term* communication situation with someone who incessantly uses the Section G attack, giving in to it as in Interaction Eighteen is not a good strategy. It will only encourage your opponent to keep using the pattern. You should instead use the offer of something you know will be refused, doing that just as incessantly, as a way of demonstrating to the other person that you absolutely will not play this silly game. Eventually, he or she will give it up, provided it never works—that is, provided you never fall for the question structure and respond with a *reason*.

The technique of using a question word as a way of drawing someone into a particular response pattern is a favorite of trial lawyers and other professional interrogators. The question "Did you throw the drugs out the window of the car?" is a call for a yes or no, nothing tricky about it.[3] But the question "*Why* did you

---

[3]This is because it is a short form for the formal "I am asking you *whether* you threw the drugs out the window of the car or didn't throw the drugs out the window of the car." The response to *whether* (or the less formal *if*) is presupposed to be *yes* or *no*.

throw the drugs out the window of the car?" presupposes that you did throw them and that your doing so is a self-evident fact. All it asks for is your *reason* for doing what you are presupposed to have done.

Certainly the witness can still say, "I *didn't* throw the drugs out the window of the car." (Whereupon the lawyer will ask "Oh? where *did* you throw them?") Or the witness can say, "I didn't throw any drugs anywhere!" (And the lawyer can then ask, "Oh? What *did* you do with them?") Lawyers, who have the advantage of quite a lot of training in the use of language, know that they can count on one of two types of responses to this sort of thing. Either the witness will fall for the question word for at least a few seconds and then switch—after a brief, but suspicious, pause—to a denial; or the witness will see the question as a trick and be foolish enough to charge right into Blamer Mode with "Whaddaya *mean,* why did I. ..." Either response is useful to the lawyer. The first will make the judge and jury wonder why the witness hesitated before denying the accusation. The second will allow the lawyer to say, "I see that you'd really rather not answer that question, so ..." and leave you looking very bad indeed.

This is why trial lawyers today are rehearsing their witnesses in simulations of real courtroom scenes, with a videotape setup for the rehearsal so that witness and lawyer can watch it afterward and discuss it. Just "going over the testimony" is no longer considered sufficient.

The Section G attack, for all its seeming simplicity, can take vicious form. Consider this example:

25. "*Why* are you completely indifferent to the effect that your constant selfish extravagance has on your children?"

Notice all the traps in there! There's the initial question word *why,* with heavy stress, which presupposes the accusation and asks only for a reason. There's the possessive *your,* which presupposes the real-world existence of whatever comes after it. There's the nominalization of the adjective *extravagant* in the form *extravagance*, again presupposing its real-world truth. And because of all these layers of presupposition, the adjectives that come *before* the nominalization are automatically presupposed as well. That means that the attacker has presupposed all the following statements:

26a. "You are indifferent to the effect that your constant selfish extravagance has on your children."
26b. "You are extravagant."
26c. "Your extravagance is constant—you're *always* extravagant."
26d. "Your extravagance is selfish—you're *always* selfish."

That's an awful lot of content to have to counter. All the following responses are sure failures:

27a. "I am *not* extravagant!"
27b. "I am *not* selfish!"
27c. "I am *not* indifferent to the effect ..."
27d. "I'm only extravagant once or twice a year—whaddaya *mean* 'constant' extravagance?"

Oops, right? That last one is very easy to do, if you aren't paying attention to what you put your foot in. Notice that if you deny the accusation of indifference in that way you can only do it by *accepting* the accusation about selfish extravagance. And whenever the presupposed accusations are stacked up like this, you have that problem; respond to any one of them and you risk accepting the others by default. The key to achieving this attack is, of course, in a *possessed nominalization*.

Nominalization in English takes two regular forms: special noun endings added to the verb, or the all-purpose ending *ing*. Table Four shows you the verb or adjective on the left, with its possible nominalizations on the right.[4]

[4] I am often asked how we know which ending to use with which verb or adjective. So far as I know, it's a mystery.

TABLE FOUR

Verb or Adjective	Nominalization
you are careless	your carelessness
	your being careless
you neglect (X)	your neglect of (X)
	your neglecting (X)
you abandoned (X)	your abandonment of (X)
	your abandoning (X)
you confiscated (X)	your confiscation of (X)
	your confiscating (X)
you are hostile	your hostility
	your being hostile

Nominalizations are very powerful. The skilled attacker puts a horrendous accusation inside a nominalization, adds a possessive to increase the presupposition of truth, and then throws in some totally innocent predicate to serve as the surface claim, like this;

28. "Your disgraceful refusal to honor the terms of the contract is very interesting."

Interesting is about as close to a word with no content as you can get in English and still keep any meaning at all. When someone you don't want to hurt shows you something you think is awful and asks for your opinion, you say that it is "interesting." Almost anything at all, including accusations like those in (28), can be said to be interesting, without much of a burden of proof falling on the speaker.

The only safe ways to respond to a question like the one about your extravagance are these two:

29. "When did you begin to feel that I was indifferent in the well-being of my children?"
30. "Indifference to the well-being of one's children is a rather rare phenomenon in American society, even among single parents." (Or "even in Massachusetts." Or "even in times of stress." Or

163

anything at all of the same kind that is sufficiently general and is nonthreatening to the particular individual you're speaking to.)

Section J Attack

And we come at last to "You're not the *only* ..." something or other. I'm pleased to be able to tell you that the immediate response is usually easy. (Usually—not always.) You just agree, because there is no possibility of the presupposition being false in the real world, and you leave it up to your attacker to decide what to do next—like this:

> *Parent:* You're not the *only* person with problems, you know!
> *You:* You're absolutely right.

You do this with minimal body language attached, smiling in a neutrally pleasant way and looking mildly interested in what's coming next. PARENT will then have to think of something else to say. Because the chances of a situation in which you really are the one and the only whatever-it-is are extraordinarily slim, agreeing will in almost every case be a direct response to a presupposition that truly *is* self-evident. Someone who responds to your agreement with, "Aha! Then you *admit* it!" is either very confused or not a native speaker of English. This is uncommon enough to be something we can safely ignore.

DOUBLE BINDS

The previous chapter ended with a discussion of the ways in which verbal attacks can be set up to create double or multiple binds for the victim. Now the question is, how do you deal with this extra level of verbal violence?

The answer depends heavily on your relationship with your attacker. That is, do you want to try to change the situation, and are you free to do so? If the person using the double binds has real-world control over you, you may be afraid to do anything at all—which is, of course, the whole point of a double bind. It is intended to immobilize you. If that is your situation, you need expert help and this book cannot provide it.

Otherwise, you have several possible courses to follow. Assume that you're reasonably sure your attacker doesn't consciously mean to put you into a double bind, and your goal is just to make him or her aware of what is being done. In that case, the best move is to Level. You point out exactly what is happening, saying, "If I say (X) I will be wrong because (Y). If I say (W) I will be wrong because (Z). There's no way I can respond to what you said, because of the way you put your sentence together." You explain, step by step, until it is clear. And you make it equally clear that if the speaker wants any response from you, the utterance will have to be reworded. If you were right that the abuse was not consciously intended, this should help matters. (If the use of double binds has become an unconscious *habit*, of course, you'll have to spend a lot of time in these careful explanations—be prepared for that, and be sure it's worth it.)

If, on the other hand, you can be sure that the attack was intentional and that Leveling is only going to lead to more abuse, your goal is to demonstrate that you know what's going on and you aren't going to participate. One way of doing that is silence—say nothing until the attack is restructured. That's not usually easy to do, and it can drag on for days and weeks, but it is sometimes the proper move. Or you can throw a double bind right back, like this:

X: If you *really* loved me, you wouldn't *want* to work.
You: If you *really* loved me, you wouldn't *want* to keep me from working.

Or

You: If you *really* loved me, you wouldn't have *said* that.

What you are saying is absurd, yes, but so is what provoked you to say it. In fact, the more absurd and obvious it is, the clearer

165

your message will be. You are saying, "Using double binds on me won't work—you're wasting your time."

Finally, there is the shock treatment response, done this way:

> *X:* If you *really* cared anything about me, you wouldn't *want* to buy a new car.
> *You:* You're absolutely right.

This comes perilously close to a counterattack. You'll want to think carefully before you do it. It's an even more emphatic refusal to play the double bind game, and it has none of the possibilities for humor that are present in the foolish exaggeration of responding to double bind with double bind. When you do this you are pretending to agree with the presupposition that you don't care about the attacker. You are saying, "Right, I must not 'really care anything about you' after all."

That's going to hurt. If you proceed in that way, and if you really do care about your opponent, you'll want to do it so that it becomes obvious that you're saying, "You're right" *only* as a way of breaking him or her of the double bind habit. That means extra work for you in the relationship, and extra care and attention. It may be the best move, however, if your primary purpose is to avoid reinforcing the double bind by allowing it to work.

Remember, whatever you decide to do, that anybody who uses a double bind has stepped outside the boundaries of fairness completely and has sacrificed the right to courtesy from you. The only question you have to consider in such a situation is how much force is appropriate to your self-defense.

These two chapters about common patterns for verbal attacks don't cover the subject thoroughly. Entire books could be written on the problems posed by any one of them. But we need to move on to other things, and we will do so. In later chapters, whenever these attack patterns are relevant to the subject under discussion, we'll take them up again.

For now, master the twelve patterns presented, along with the responses that are suggested. Say them aloud, so that you become familiar with the stress patterns. Both the recognition of the twelve, and the responses, should be so automatic that you don't have to pay them any conscious attention—but this takes time. At first you'll miss some of them, or you'll fall for the bait and escalate the interaction. You're certain to mistake for attacks some utterances that aren't attacks at all. And you will feel self-conscious about using responses that are not part of your usual language behavior. All this will pass, if—as in any art of self-defense—you *practice*. You can count on the world to offer you plenty of opportunities to do so.

And when something comes along that seems to you to be an entirely new pattern, by all means write it down so that you will remember it.[5] Identify its special characteristics—whatever caused you to recognize it. Identify the presupposition(s) and the bait. And proceed as always: Respond directly *to* the presupposition(s) and let the bait go by.

SUPPLEMENTARY QUOTATIONS

One last point about indirectly aggressive communicators we wish we didn't have to make. Some indirectly aggressive types consider themselves to be appropriately assertive and, labeling themselves as such, have unfortunately misled others to believe that their brand of "truthful directness" is what assertiveness is all about. We can't tell you the number of indirectly aggressive people we've encountered who, having learned what they wanted to hear about assertiveness, have made themselves self-appointed

---

[5]I would be a very grateful writer if you also let *me* know about the new pattern, so that I could share it with others and credit you for your help. You can reach me at Route 4, Box 192-E, Huntsville AR 72740.

missionaries whose life goal is to carry the banner of the virtues of "assertiveness" to the unenlightened masses [MacNeilage and Adams, 1982, p. 13].

SUGGESTED READINGS

ELGIN, S. H. *The Gentle Art of Verbal Self-Defense*. Englewood Cliffs, N.J.: Prentice-Hall, Inc., 1980, pp. 15–191. (As previously mentioned, this section takes up each of the first eight attacks in a separate chapter. The "sample scripts" given as suggested responses to confrontations present a number of different possible ways to reply to an opening sequence in a confrontation and discuss the probable outcomes of each.)

ANDREWS, L. B. "Mind Control in the Courtroom." *Psychology Today*, March 1982, pp. 66–73. (Description of the language techniques used today by trial lawyers, especially in the preparation of witnesses and questioning of potential jurors.)

LANDEFELD, J. "Speaking Therapeutically." *Human Behavior*, September 1975, pp. 56–99. (A good nontechnical discussion of the communications strategies of psychologist Gerald Goodman, who is a specialist in "remedial talking." Particularly useful for its material on questions.)

MACNEILAGE, L. A., and K. A. ADAMS. *Assertiveness at Work: How to Increase Your Personal Power on the Job*. Englewood Cliffs, N.J.: Prentice-Hall, Inc., 1982. (Superb source of *accurate* information on assertiveness as a communications technique. Contains many scenarios with sample dialogues, all believable. Many useful self-help exercises and aids for analysis and development. Despite the orientation toward the workplace, this book is appropriate for almost all communication situations.)

SHUY, R. W. "The Medical Interview: Problems in Communication." *Primary Care* 3, No. 3 (September 1976), pp. 365–86. (Excellent discussion of the way patients perceive their doctors' language behavior during medical interactions.)

7
Matching Realities

One of the hardest things for people to accept about human communication is the uselessness of logic. You grow up hearing that things must be reasonable and logical, you learn that your culture places a high value on reason and logic, and you know that to be labeled "illogical and irrational" is likely to cause you to be perceived as not only different but literally *sick*. It then comes as something of a shock to go to the research literature and discover that logic has been proved to have almost nothing to do with the effectiveness of language. Language can be so far out on the limits of total nonlogic that it approaches madness—that will not keep it from functioning superbly as a means of persuasion.

That is why commercials and advertisements are so foul, for the most part. Advertisers know that a tasteful commercial causes people to remember the *commercial*, not the product. Only a firm that has massive built-in security (such as IBM or Xerox) can afford to ignore this ugly fact and use tasteful advertising. There's nothing logical about this. There are very logical people who really will make an absolute decision not to buy any product that is associated with a tasteless piece of advertising, and that is rational of them. But they are a tiny minority of the buying public. Most consumers are not directly affected by either the presence or absence of logic in advertising language.

CONSTRUCTED REALITIES

Psychologist George Miller (1980) has given us the most crucial principle for all communication strategies. Because he understands what he is talking about completely, he has provided that principle simply and concisely and in the ordinary language of daily life, as follows: "In order to understand what another person is saying, you must assume that it is true and try to imagine what it could be true of [p. 46]."

Notice that he does not say you must assume that it is true provided it is logical and reasonable and all the rest of those qualities we claim to admire so much—just assume it's true and proceed. He is absolutely right. If you assume that what you're hearing or reading is false, and if you maintain that assumption militantly, you are not going to understand the message. Being "reasonable" with a closed mind is impossible.

We understand fiction, fairy tales, and television dramas because we are willing to give up our real-world knowledge for a while. Certainly we know, at some level, that the man being shot by the television police officer is in no danger. But if we didn't briefly suspend that knowledge and assume that his death was real, we wouldn't be able to understand the story we were watching—we would see the man's wife weeping and wonder why she was doing that when the man is unharmed, and he isn't really her husband anyway. And we would be alarmed about a person watching with us who asked us, "Why is that woman crying?"

170

When you agree to believe in the worlds you see on film and read about in books, you are accepting *constructed realities*. Those realities are made up of sets of statements put together by other people. And you behave as if they were true, to be able to understand. This has nothing to do with logic.[1]

What does all this mean, now, for the person who wants to communicate effectively with someone else? It means that, whether you are trying to understand others or cause them to understand you, one basic rule holds without exception: You must find a way to enter the reality of the other person(s) involved in the language interaction.

You may believe that reality is made up of objects and living things, with some sort of extension for abstract concepts that is tied directly *to* objects and living things. Some scholars will agree with you, and the position is a respectable one with a long history. But there exists no way to *prove* that you are right or wrong.

You know that this page is "real" because you can see it. Correct? But that doesn't mean anything. When you look at a railroad track and you see the two tracks come together in a point at the edge of the horizon, you don't think that point is real. Linguists have done many experiments in which they taped a sentence such as "A dog was crossing the road with her three puppies" and then cut the sound of *p* in *puppies* out of the tape and spliced in a *g* sound from another tape. When you play such a tape, the sentence "really" says, "A dog was crossing the road with her three guppies"—but that's not what people hear. They hear *puppies*, and the fact that *guppies* is "really there" won't change their perception. In fact, so strong is this constraint for many people that even after the linguist tells them what has

---

[1] In my workshops and consultations there is often someone who points out that this *is* logical, because the person adopts the behavior in order to understand. For a perfectly good, logical, and rational reason, in other words. To make that clear, we need that useful prefix *meta-*. To do something illogical for a logical reason is *metalogic*, being logical about logic or illogic. To say something about language and use language to do that is to use *metalanguage*. Any time you use a system to refer to a system you are involved in a metasystem; it can't be avoided.

been done, they will still insist that they hear a *p* rather than a *g*. George Miller can help us again; he says, "That's the way the mind works. You have your conclusion to begin with, and you're very clever at searching for evidence that directly—or indirectly—by arguments you cleverly invent—leads to your conclusion [Miller, 1980, p. 49]."

Touch is no more reliable than sight or hearing as a way of knowing reality. You know this page is real because you can feel it with your fingers? All right. Cross your middle finger over your index finger and touch a single marble at the point where they cross. You will feel *two* marbles, and no amount of logical assurance based on the evidence of your eyes or such statements as "There was only one marble there when you picked it up and there can only be one marble there now" will keep you from feeling two marbles. Your senses, the only mechanism you have for judging reality, are simply unreliable.

And scientific instruments (which depend on your senses to observe their results) are not useful either. It makes no difference how many prestigious scientists with superb technological devices prove that this planet is traveling at a speed of many thousands of miles per hour through space. You, and I, will continue to perceive the earth beneath our feet as motionless unless it is violently deranged by some force like an earthquake.

You have to deal with this strange situation, whether it is logical or not. Without opinions about what is and isn't "real" you would be unable to function in any way in this world. You therefore have no choice but to make decisions that constitute a set of statements representing what reality is, for you—for example:

a. Water is a liquid.
b. I cannot fall off the earth.
c. Ronald Reagan won the 1980 presidential election.
d. Sugar tastes good.

e. Railroad tracks don't come together in a point in the distance even when they look as if they did.

REALITY CONSENSUS

When enough people agree on the same or almost the same set of such statements, you have a culture. A culture is made up of people who have a *reality consensus*, itself made up of statements like *a* through *e* which they all agree to believe. There may be specialized subsets of statements within that culture (such as the set subscribed to by the wine taster or the game hunter or the ballerina), but unless the specialist agrees to the set that makes up the reality consensus he or she cannot ever be part of that culture. The uneasiness called "culture shock" comes from having to interact with people when you aren't certain what statements make up their reality consensus and don't know how much it may differ from your own.

If people talk to you in a way that never conflicts with your personal set of statements about reality, you perceive them as "speaking your language." You are likely to trust them, even if you don't agree with them. That trust, however limited, is the small wedge that makes it potentially possible for them to persuade you that they are right in what they say to you.

The skill of entering other realities is the most important communication skill of all. That's what you are doing when you try to match another person's preferred sensory mode. And when you answer "If you *really* loved me, you wouldn't go back to college" with "Of course I really love you" you are entering a reality in which the statement "You don't really love me" is part of the set that must be dealt with. What you are trying to do is *match* the reality of the other person, for whatever period of time is needed to communicate—and the more statements from the reality consensus the two of you have in common, the easier this task will be.

THE USES OF METAPHORS

We have been discussing a number of ways to match realities in previous chapters. This chapter will focus on yet another mechanism for the purpose: the *metaphor*.

The formal pattern for the metaphor is not complicated. Have you ever worked a cryptogram puzzle? It's set up like this:

English Alphabet: a, b, c, d, e, f, g, h, . . . z

Cryptogram Alphabet: z, y, x, w, v, u, t, s, . . . a

The cryptogram sets up a metaphor that says, "This alphabet is like the ordinary English alphabet, except that it is reversed. And for every point in the English alphabet there is a corresponding point in the cryptogram alphabet. *A* corresponds to *Z. B* corresponds to *Y.*" And so on. By looking at the points where the two alphabets match each other, you can understand the message written down in the cryptogram. It doesn't matter whether the alphabets are set up so that one is the reverse of the other or in some other arrangement (for example, so that each letter of the cryptogram alphabet corresponds to a letter two spaces over in the English alphabet, or to every other letter in the English alphabet). The two alphabets show a perfect match, with every point in one system corresponding exactly to a point in the other.

Metaphors in the real world, outside the artificial and the formal, don't have that degree of perfection. When the poet tells us that his or her love is like a swan, we can be quite sure that no reference is being made to some part of the sweetheart's anatomy that is in perfect correspondence to the insect parasites that infest a swan's feathers. (And eyes like woodland pools would be repulsive if taken seriously, point for point.)

When you respond to a double bind by a careful explanation why each of the possible answers open to you is wrong, you are using logic; and logic is the only thing you have going for you in that situation. It is precisely because logic is so weak as a method of persuasion that this choice takes so much time, patience, and weary effort. People are not simply going to say, "Oh, dear, I didn't know I was doing that, and I'm sorry." (It's like pointing out to someone the illogic of racial prejudice and expecting that the prejudice will therefore disappear.)

Responding to a double bind *with* a double bind is usually faster, because it uses metaphor. It says, "Your situation in this interaction is like *my* situation in this interaction," and it gives the other person a chance to enter a reality in which he or she is the one in double bind.

The best book I know about metaphor, although some sections are rough going for the nonspecialist, is Douglas Hofstadter's *Goedel, Escher, Bach: An Eternal Golden Braid* (Basic Books, 1979). He mentions the possibility of a metaphor in which the vice-president of the United States is called "the spare tire on the automobile of government." And he goes on to say:

> If you were told, "See our government as an automobile" without any prior motivation, you might come up with any number of correspondences: steering wheel = president, etc. What are checks and balances? What are seat belts? Because the two things being mapped are so different, it is almost inevitable that the mapping will involve *functional* aspects. Therefore, you retrieve from your store of conceptual skeletons representing parts of automobiles only those having to do with function, rather than, say, shape [p. 670].

That is, in setting up the automobile as a metaphor for the United States government, you wouldn't try to find a match at every point as you would with alphabets. A spare tire, Hofstadter points out, is round in shape—that doesn't mean we expect the vice-president to be round in shape. Shape is one possible place for the matching of points within realities, but it won't work in the metaphor that matches the vice-president with a spare tire, and so it is ignored.

Metaphors that are used frequently in a culture save vast amounts of work in communication. People are used to them and know how to match the points. In the cryptogram example we can safely leave out much of the alphabet and count on people to be able to supply the missing letters. Similarly, we can mention only one or two matching points for a metaphor such as the Old West, the Old South, the (Football) Game of Life, and so on and count on Americans to be able to fill in the rest of the matching points without our help.

In January 1982 a plane went down in the Potomac River shortly after takeoff. Government helicopters came to try to rescue passengers from the icy water. In addition, a bystander named Lenny Skutnik jumped into the Potomac and pulled a woman to safety. Michael Kinsley [1982] sets up a metaphor using this tragedy, with the matching points shown in Table Five.

TABLE FIVE

Potomac Tragedy		Tragedy of Poverty
Potomac River	(matches)	United States of America
Accident victims in the water		Poor people in the United States
National Park Service helicopters		Government social agencies
Lenny Skutnik		Private charity

Lenny Skutnik serves here as a reality point matching the private citizens and corporations that Ronald Reagan predicted would donate money and resources to the poor of America. The National Park Service helicopters are matched with all the agencies such as Social Security and the Department of Health and Human Services, that spend tax monies to help the poor of America. Kinsley carefully discusses the fact that people saw Lenny Skutnik as a hero—as something rare, unusual, and special. And he winds up his attempt at persuasion by claiming that just as the accident victims would drown while "waiting for Lenny" to come along and rescue them, so would poor people go under while waiting for the rare and idiosyncratic examples of private charity.

176

You may not agree with Kinsley at all. But you have no problem understanding exactly what he means. The metaphor is many times more powerful as a way of communicating his argument than any number of pages of logical reasoning standing alone could have been.

Now, how do you counter a metaphor like this? Not by the rational argument that it replaces, you can be sure. The only effective defense against a powerful metaphor is another metaphor, for example:

TABLE SIX

A garden		United States of America
Plants in the garden	(matches)	Poor people in America
An ornamental fountain		Government social agencies
A garden hose		Private charity

This metaphor lets you argue that using government agencies to help the poor is like trying to water the plants in your garden using an ornamental fountain—the water goes in all directions, but it reaches only a few of the plants and does *that* haphazardly. With the garden hose of private charity, you would claim, you can put the essential water directly and specifically on each plant that needs it.

I happen to agree with Michael Kinsley on this matter. I am firmly convinced that the private citizen or corporation is as unlikely to rescue America's poor as the average bystander (including myself) is unlikely to leap into freezing water and swim after an accident victim. But that is not the point here. The point is that my own opinions do not make it impossible for me to set up a metaphor that argues *against* what I believe. I need only assume that the Reagan position is true and imagine what it might be true of—I can then enter that reality and construct my agricultural metaphor, being very careful not to go too far and risk being funny rather than effective.

It's because it is so easy to go too far with metaphor—"Shall I compare thee to a summer's day?" (with ticks and ants and tornadoes and all the potato salad spoiling?)—that you have the alternative choice of *exaggerating* the metaphor you are trying to work against, spoiling its effect the way the heat of the summer's day spoils the potato salad. Michael Kinsley is safe against that sort of countering action because his metaphor involves a horrifying tragedy in which real people died. You don't try to turn that into a matter for laughter. But suppose someone were to use the structure mentioned by Hofstadter, in which the American government is matched with an automobile and the vice-president is its spare tire. Suppose that the intent was to make you feel sympathetic toward the vice-president. You could counter that easily by carrying the metaphor into the ridiculous extreme in which the vice-president as spare tire was seen as round, inflated, and empty in the middle—this would make it difficult for the desired sympathy to develop.

The set of statements that make up the reality in which Kinsley's metaphor works includes at least the following:

a. The people drowning in the Potomac needed immediate and effective help.

b. Poor people in the United States today need immediate and effective help.

c. Government social agencies are set up to provide immediate and effective help; that is their function, not a matter of choice.

d. Private citizens and corporations are not set up to provide immediate and effective help. Whether they will help at all is a matter of choice in every case.

e. Most government agencies will do what they are set up to do; therefore, most poor people will be helped.

f. Most people and corporations will not choose or be able to extend charity; therefore, most poor people will not be helped.

g. For a government agency to help the poor is routine.

h. For a private citizen or corporation to help the poor is rare.

i. Government agencies are suitable mechanisms for helping the poor.

j. Private initiative is not a suitable mechanism for helping the poor.

178

I can only attack this metaphor by looking at the set of statements that lie behind it and looking for one that will let me create a corresponding counterreality. Many of the statements in the list can't be disputed—for example, everyone will agree with Statement *b*. We all know that a hungry child needs food at once, not after Congress returns from a recess. But we also know that government social agencies are cumbersome bureaucracies, and this lets me attack the constructed reality of the metaphor at Statement *e:* Most government agencies will do what they are set up to do; therefore, most poor people will be helped.

I have found a weak statement in the set. Now I need to think of something that channels a substance to living things in need in the same way that government social agencies are supposed to channel money to people in need; the set of objects that can be used to channel water to plants comes to mind. I need something from that set that is also ineffective. An ornamental fountain, which shoots water straight up into the air in pretty patterns, with only a few drops accidentally falling outside the pattern and onto plants, is an excellent example. All I then have to do is set up my matching points. Because everyone in the American culture is familiar with gardens, plants, fountains, water, and hoses, my metaphor allows me to enter their reality. Notice—I can be certain in advance that they have the following statements in their reality set:

a. A garden hose is for putting water directly on plants.
b. An ornamental fountain is for decoration.
c. A garden hose is not expected to be pretty.
d. An ornamental fountain is only expected to be pretty.
e. All plants need water to live.
f. No plants need an ornamental fountain to live.
   And so on.

I can use all the statements that I know my listeners or readers will already have in their reality consensus about growing plants;

I can count on all those statements to give me an entry into that reality. And once I am inside it, I can be reasonably certain that I will be understood.

It's not an accident that our standardized tests contain so many of those problems asking us things like "Cub is to bear as calf is to ?" and expecting us to fill in *cow* in the blank. Our satisfactory functioning in this world depends in many ways on our ability to understand metaphor and to discover quickly the essential matching points, such as the parent-offspring relationship that makes a cub and a calf a set. Little children have a hard time learning about metaphor, and they must deal with it constantly as they develop their language skills. Look at the following sentences.

1. "Would you run that past me one more time, please?"
2. "He shot down my argument before I even got started."
3. "I didn't have a chance to run through my lines before the play started."
4. "I can't put my finger on the source of your problem."
5. "The answer is probably staring me right in the face."

All such sentences rely heavily on the understanding of metaphor to "get their message across." The child who says of Sentence 2, "What does that mean ... did he have a gun?" is not yet comfortable with the store of metaphors that pervade the English vocabulary. The child is looking for a perfect match at all points, instead of focusing on the matching points that are important to the particular metaphor.

DISRUPTION OF
THE REALITY CONSENSUS

Sometimes a new fact or concept comes along in the real world and clashes violently with the reality consensus but cannot be avoided or hidden away. When that happens, the entire culture will go into a kind of squirming effort to force the new bit of reality into the existing framework. We have seen this human tendency at work in the recent discoveries about pain and painkillers. Once we had evidence that painkilling drugs work by locking into specific receiving sites in the brain—at actual anatomical sites, not figurative ones—we had a real problem with the equally inescapable evidence that pain can be eliminated without drugs. An immediate search for some way to fit all this into one reality resulted in the "discovery" that the brain, when properly stimulated—for example, by hypnosis—manufactures its own "painkilling drugs," which lock into anatomical receiving sites just as morphine does. It was then possible to be comfortable with the known facts about pain again.

Our reality statement about the manner in which pain is eliminated from human consciousness required a chemical component. Hypnosis, because it does not include introduction of chemicals into the body, was an embarrassment—it should not have worked and it was in conflict with our reality statement. We already had our conclusion, and we were not anxious to give it up; we therefore set out to find a way of cramming hypnosis *into* that conclusion. And sure enough, now that we knew where to look, we managed to "discover" the solution. The very facts about hypnosis then became sources of evidence for the conclusion that we started out with. This process is essential to human beings, because it protects the reality consensus that holds the culture together.

You may never find yourself obliged to make some troublesome new scientific breakthrough fit into the current picture of reality held by an entire culture. Most of us will never have to face that task. But the same process, on a smaller scale, faces us every time we are obliged to tell other people about a change they had not anticipated and aren't prepared for. You will always be able to do that better if you package the new information carefully into a metaphor and match it, point for point, with something that is already familiar to your listeners or readers.

Be careful, however. When a small child is suddenly faced with the completely unexpected and awful fact that the family dog must be killed by the veterinarian, the child's parent is likely to look for ways of presenting that information that don't involve the ugly word *kill*. If the first metaphor that comes to mind is expressed as "The doctor has to put Rover to sleep," because sleep is familiar to the child and death is not, the parent has an excellent chance of finding that the child is now afraid to go to sleep. You can't count on the child to match up the metaphor, death = sleep, at those points you were thinking of—the ones about rest and freedom from pain and a happy ending to a long hard day. The child is just as likely to go straight to the part of sleep that matters most to children—the waking *up* from it so that you can *do* things—and is then going to be immediately aware that this is a place where the two halves of the metaphor don't match. So far as the child can determine, Rover is not going to wake up from this new kind of "sleep" you are suggesting. Choose your metaphor from elements familiar to those you want to communicate with. But examine that familiar element and be certain that just because it *is* familiar you have not overlooked something about it that is frightening enough or distressing enough to make you fail in your goal of reassurance.

We have been concentrating up to this point on situations in which your main concern is finding a way to fit something into a reality that is just what you yourself believe in. And it's true that a lot of the time you have no reason to do anything more than that, so long as you are interacting with people of your own culture. But every once in a while you are going to need to consider the possibility that the reason things aren't going as you want them to go has something to do with a picture of reality that differs from yours, even in the most familiar situations.

Assume that you were supposed to get your paycheck in the mail on Monday, but it's now Tuesday and it hasn't arrived; you go to the payroll office to talk to a payroll clerk about your difficulty. This is no ivory tower theoretical matter. This is the painful real world, with all its bills to pay. How do you use your knowledge of matching realities and constructing metaphors in such a situation?

You know in advance that you and the payroll clerk share a large number of statements from the reality consensus, because you see at once that the two of you are from the same culture. You are certain that the clerk, like you, has bills to pay and food to buy. And you tell her about what has happened, which leads to this interaction.

INTERACTION NINETEEN
Clerk: Look, it's only Tuesday. If your check doesn't come by Friday, you come back and I'll take care of it.

You: But what am I supposed to live on till *Fri*day?

Clerk: I'm sorry—that's not really my problem.

You: There's gotta be *something* you can do in a case like this!

Clerk: No, there's nothing I can do. The *rule* is, if your check's late you have to wait till Friday.

You: But couldn't you just go see if—

Clerk: Look, *don't* give me a hard time, *okay?* I only work here. *I* don't make the rules.

Your immediate reaction is probably going to be anger. The clerk is insensitive, callous, and a number of other ugly things. Now what? You can be assertive, refuse to give up your turn in line, and insist on your rights. You can demand to see a supervisor. You can try being more obnoxious than the clerk. You can give up and go home.

Before you do any of those things, I'd like you to stop and follow George Miller's rule: *Assume that what the clerk is saying is true, and try to imagine what it could be true of.*

One of the things people have to do to get by in this world is accept small sets of auxiliary reality statements that are only "real" as part of a particular role. Our military forces live in a culture that accepts and agrees to the statement "It's wrong to

183

kill another human being." They can only function in combat by *temporarily* accepting the conflicting statement "You must kill as many human beings of a certain specified kind as possible" as part of the role we call "soldier." The soldier does not go home on furlough and set aside the statement that killing other human beings is wrong.

Each of us has to learn these extra sets of reality statements necessary to the roles we fill in life. We have the statement "You are not allowed to hit other people" in the reality consensus set; but as part of a role—as parent, perhaps, or as prizefighter—we have a very different statement. We have the shared statement "You are not allowed to destroy another person's property," but as part of the role "fire fighter" you know that you can take your hatchet and chop your way right through a certain specified kind of other person's doors and walls.

The language you use because it is tied to a particular role in life is called a *register.* The more registers you have control of, without becoming confused by their conflict with one another, the more successful you are going to be. The child who can switch with ease from the street register ("Hey, man, how's it goin'?") to the school register ("Good morning, Mr. Jones!") and the home register ("Hi, Mom, everything okay?") is succeeding in this world. The specialized academic register used on standardized examinations like the college entrance exams is efficient as a filter precisely because that register is not part of most people's experience.

Your payroll clerk has a register that is part of being a payroll clerk. It includes a certain vocabulary, a certain body language, and a certain set of statements about reality. When you want your check, the payroll clerk is in the position of dominance and has to be *convinced* to give it to you. You already know that logical argument is not likely to convince her. Your strategy has to involve entering her reality while she is being a payroll clerk.

Think. What set of statements about reality is the clerk agreeing to, temporarily, while on duty? What kind of metaphor has she constructed for her working world? If you look at Interaction Nineteen carefully, you'll see that she has given you lots of clues. And from those clues—notice all the talk of rules?—you can be pretty sure that her work register includes at least the following statements:

a. There are a lot of rules.

b. Rules can't be broken, and there are no exceptions.

c. Rules don't have to make any sense, either taken one at a time or taken together.

d. Somebody (or a bunch of somebodies) made the rules.

e. Considering what the rules are like, those responsible couldn't be basing them on logic; therefore, appealing to the rulemakers would be a waste of time.

f. I didn't make the rules; therefore, appealing to me is also a waste of time.

g. Because I didn't make the rules, I'm not responsible for them or their effect on other people.

h. Any change in one rule would mean changes in the whole system, which would be a mess; that's why there are no exceptions.

i. Nobody who isn't part of this could possibly understand it, especially because it doesn't make any sense; therefore, trying to explain is a waste of time.

All right—does this set of statements sound familiar? What does it remind you of? In what situation in the real world do people solemnly follow silly rules made by unknown outsiders, rules for which they are not responsible and which they cannot explain? Do we have a metaphor available for this kind of situation?

Indeed we do; the metaphor is some version of the Game of Life. When you play Monopoly, there's no logical reason why you do the things you do; you just follow the rules somebody made up. When you win all of somebody's money in Monopoly, he or she isn't really hurt. In fact, if losers become angry or upset, they clearly aren't rational people. The only thing it is legitimate to be upset about is a violation of those same silly rules. Your payroll clerk is using the Game of Life metaphor as a basis for her behavior at work.

Now you can't get anywhere with this clerk unless you enter her reality, which means that you have to play this game *with* her. Let's go on with Interaction Nineteen with that in mind.

INTERACTION NINETEEN, CONTINUED

You: I should *hope* I know better than to give you a hard time! What I *need* is somebody like you, who has a clear picture of all the rules and sense enough to stay with them 100 percent.

Clerk: Thank you—lots of people don't see it that way.

You: Well, I do, and I know I'm lucky you're here. I *could* have gotten some ding-a-ling.

Clerk: You sure could.

You: Now, let's see. The *rule* is, my check has to be delivered on the first Monday of every month. That's the rule. And I'd appreciate it very much if you'd find out who *broke* that rule so I can take this matter up with them.

Clerk: You've gotta be kidding.

You: I *never* kid about rules. You can get in big trouble that way. You start breaking rules, there's no tellling what you'll end up doing. And I intend to see that whoever broke *this* rule learns that rules are not a joking matter.

Notice what you're up to here. You've entered the clerk's reality and are playing her Game for all you're worth. You have skillfully chosen the weakest point in her set of statements, which is the one about rules having no exceptions. The clerk is now in a difficult position. She can't say that although the rule says checks arrive on the first Monday of the month the rule isn't really meant to be taken seriously. If she says that, she is admitting that rules have exceptions. And if she admits that *one* rule can be broken, well, there's no reason why she can't make an exception to the "wait till Friday" rule and have a new check issued to you right now.

If you had been logical and insisted that of course there was something she could do and that you weren't leaving until she did it, then she could have declared you out of the game and ignored you. But you're playing the game, too, and that means she has to go on with it. The fact that you've noticed her preference for visual mode and are matching it isn't hurting anything, either. Part of the metaphor is being a team player; she can't just decide she's having no fun and *quit*. Her next move should be this one:

> *Clerk:* Look, maybe there's been some kind of mistake. Hold on a minute while I go look.

Why couldn't you just have said, logically, "I bet my check is sitting on somebody's desk and never even got mailed. I'd appreciate it if you'd go look"? Because this is what happens if you do that.

> *Clerk:* That's impossible, sir.
> *You:* Impossible?
> *Clerk:* That's right. Our staff does not *make* that kind of mistake.
> *You:* But—
> *Clerk:* Next!

THE GAME OF LIFE AND
OTHER SYSTEMATIC METAPHORS

There is no way to know absolutely, in advance, what sort of metaphors you will be faced with in real-world encounters. They may come as a total surprise and be unique, exotic, and new. But when you are dealing with a bureaucracy of any kind, from the smallest local one to giants like the Veterans Administration, you always have one strategy that's worth considering. Nine times out of ten, the metaphor in use inside the bureaucracy will be the Game of Life, or some variation, such as the Football Game of Life.

The staffs of bureaucracies are faced with absurdity all day long, every day. They have to function surrounded by nonsense that no logical person could defend. If they run out of paper for their mimeograph machine they can't order more paper; they have to order a new mimeograph machine, with an accompanying budget for paper. If they have money left over at the end of the year they can't return it to the central treasury it came from; they have to spend it, even if they don't need anything— otherwise, their budget will be cut and they might not have enough money next year. They have to submit budgets and schedules three years in advance when they know perfectly well, and the people they submit them to know perfectly well, that there's no way they can possibly have any idea what their budget or schedule will be even six months from now, much less three years. Nothing makes any sense, but they can't just sit around and laugh. They must behave *as if* it did make sense.

The only way people can function in such a system and maintain either sanity or self-respect is to staunchly insist inside themselves that the whole thing is just a game, with no real-world effects. And the Game of Life metaphor will then provide a set of reality statements to go by while they are at work.

Therefore, even if you don't yet feel skilled at spotting other people's metaphors and the reality statements behind them, you are going to do well most of the time if you just try playing the game when you interact with people in bureaucracies.

And if it doesn't work? What if you try to join the team and the staffer you are facing won't play? If that happens, you have two possibilities to consider.

A. The staffer is brand new, doesn't know the system, and has no idea what the rules are. Therefore he or she can't play the game with you. In this case, insist on seeing a more experienced staffer, as politely and as nonthreateningly as possible.

B. You have met a living glitch. This person does *not* have the set of
    reality statements the rest of the group has and is not using the
    Game of Life as a metaphor. To this person, it isn't a game, it is a
    deadly serious business.

Assume the payroll clerk is a glitch—she probably subscribes to
this reality statement. "Because I mail out the checks, and I am
responsible for the checks, they are really *my* checks." A clerk
with this statement as part of her reality will do nothing at all to
help expedite your check. It hurts her to let any of those checks
go, and if she can hold on to yours, she will. She is not aware of
this and would be outraged if anybody suggested such a thing.
But she will cling to those checks as fiercely as if it were indeed
her own money being spent. This happens sometimes, particularly with highly ethical people who have trouble seeing
their work (or *any* work) as anything other than serious business.

Consider the librarian who rigidly limits everyone to only
one book if he can, never offers to help anyone find a book, slaps
on overdue fines for late books even if you were in the hospital,
and so on. A library is a kind of bureaucracy, but this librarian
doesn't seem to be involved in the game. What could be going
on?

There are at least two possible ways to view a library.

A. A library is a mechanism for getting as many books as possible
    read by as many people as possible (the metaphor of the library as
    Fountain of Knowledge).
B. A library is a mechanism for storing books so that you will always
    know where each one of them is at any moment (the metaphor of
    the library as Safe Repository of Knowledge).

A librarian who happens to subscribe to the second metaphor
doesn't really *want* anybody to check out books. He is responsible within that metaphor for seeing to it that every book is in its
designated place on the shelves at all times. (And with that much
responsibility, they may well become *his* books and *his* shelves.)

He may be completely unaware of this and may dutifully recite the set of statements that goes with the first metaphor, but his behavior will betray him.

Faced with one of these people, what can you do? You have only two choices. You see somebody else, or you give up. There is no way you can interact with such people and get your check, or check out your books, or whatever your project may be. You cannot reason with them, and if you enter their reality you will no longer feel that you *ought* to get your check or your book. Be glad you know that and can avoid wasting your time.

If you have no choice but to deal with one of these people, you are in a no-win situation. If you are going to have to interact with them for the rest of the foreseeable future, you may want to take on a long-term project in which you work to *change* their metaphors. But there is no quick fix available to you and you should not expect one. A bureaucrat who takes his or her work seriously inside a bureaucracy where everyone else is playing The Game always constitutes a serious problem either for the bureaucracy itself or those who must deal with it. Treat such people with the tender care you would show live rattlesnakes— don't startle them, don't bump them around, don't upset them, and avoid them whenever you can.

Because everyone you have to interact with in role situations (and there is almost nobody else to interact with, so far as I know) will be functioning within some metaphor based on a set of reality statements, it will be useful for you to learn to identify metaphors quickly. In the mainstream American culture a number of metaphors will turn up over and over again. It's worth becoming familiar with them to cut down the time you have to spend identifying them. The list below will get you started.

The Proud Ship Sailing. Captains go down with the ship. Women and children first. There's always land ahead. For every ship, there's a safe harbor. The wind fills our sails because we sail

for God and country. It's always darkest before the dawn. Proud
ships always have trusty crews. The captain's word is law. Proud
ships are always tidy and shining, no matter what.

The Glorious Battlefield. Soldiers are brave, strong, and
right. No soldier ever gives up so long as there's breath in his or
her body. It is a privilege and an honor to be hurt, even to die, in
battle. God is on the side of *our* soldiers. A soldier follows
orders, always and without exception. Duty is more important
than anything else, no matter what. We soldiers are closer than
brothers, closer than sisters, closer than lovers. All soldiers are
gentlemen and gentlewomen; they do nothing dishonorable and
their word is always good. We're all in this together.

The Happy Factory. It's *fun* to work! Good workers don't
care about money, they work for the sheer joy of it. The boss
cares about the firm, but his or her primary concern is the well-
being of the workers. The workplace is clean, safe, and cheery.
When workers grow old, the boss will take care of them; when
the boss grows old, the workers will weep at their loss—and if
they are lucky, the new boss will be a child of the old one. If any
worker is a bit slow or having problems, all the other workers
will do that much extra to protect him or her, and they will do it
gladly.

Daniel Boone's Place. Anybody worth a damn stands alone.
If you have to tackle a bear, you have to tackle a bear—no
complaining allowed, and no dawdling. There's plenty of everything for everybody, and if you're doing without it's your own
fault for being shiftless and cowardly. The cabin floor is always
clean. There are no weeds in the garden and no fleas on the dog.
Don't be beholden to anybody. If the Indians come—and they
will—it's all right to fight them, but you're not allowed to resent
that; it's a way of demonstrating your abilities. Work is grim, but

it has to be done; if you don't work, you don't eat. There will always be copperheads and mosquitoes, ticks and poison ivy—if you don't see them, be suspicious. You only sing on Sundays.

The Rose-Covered Cottage. For every man there is one perfect woman, and vice versa. There is no bathroom in the cottage, because the perfect couple don't have bodily functions. Nobody is ever angry, or even irritated, in the cottage. The cottage may be poor, but it is always clean and comfy-cozy. The perfect couple who live in the cottage don't need friends or family or anybody except each other—but a baby is allowed. Any baby in the cottage will be a perfect baby. Nobody ever grows old in the cottage, although the perfect man is allowed to become *mature*. The roses that cover the cottage are always in bloom, and there are no thorns in them. There are no bugs in the cottage.

You should also expect to find people who have chosen as their metaphor for some life role a particular *person* from American culture. Instead of "my home is the Rose-Covered Cottage" or "my work is the Glorious Battlefield," they are opting for "I am _____ " and filling in the blank with: Cinderella, John Wayne, Florence Nightingale, Sleeping Beauty, Joan of Arc, Mr. Spock, Romeo (or Juliet), Geronimo, and so on.

PROBLEMS WITH METAPHORS

Bookstore and library shelves are filled today with books about "role playing" and "game playing." These are useful books and can be read with profit. But they will not help you if you use them *only* as a kind of metagame in which the sport is identifying the games you and other people are playing. You must also consider what happens when the identified metaphors come in contact with each other. If you are being John Wayne and the person you are interacting with has the Happy Factory as metaphor, nothing is going to work very well until you find a niche for John Wayne *inside* the Happy Factory reality (or until one of you is willing or able to switch metaphors, at least temporarily). You have to act on your knowledge and put it to use.

Your strategy calls for you to follow these steps:

- Listen to the other person carefully and identify the metaphor being used.
- Consider the set of reality statements that makes up the metaphor you have identified.
- Now, behave *as if* you also considered that set of statements to be true, for so long as is necessary to achieve communication.

There's no questioon about the usefulness of this strategy. It is infuriating to those who believe that communication should come from simply being logical, rational, and consistent, but it works. However, be careful—what does it presuppose? It presupposes that people can move easily from one metaphor to another and back again. It presupposes that people can behave *as if* they believe something and then abandon that stance without difficulty, as they do when they switch channels or turn off the television set. This is an oversimplification, and some cautions must be set out right now. The results of clashing metaphors can mean centuries of trouble—consider the conflict between the mainstream American who views the earth as a kind of storehouse of goodies for distribution and the Native American who views it as a sacred temple to be guarded.[2]

First, there is the problem of participating in other people's metaphors that contain negative statements about *you*. One of the ways that the language of others can hurt you is when you allow your "*as if*" behavior to include such statements without taking sufficient care.

Suppose that the other's metaphor includes the following false statement about you: "You are cruel to other people and

[2]This sounds familiar because it is so much like the two views of a library discussed a few pages back, which means that you could use a meta-metaphor to compare the two and point out that one is a small-scale version of the other.

should be ashamed of yourself for that." When you enter the metaphor and behave *as if* that statement were true, you do that for only one reason: To be able to understand *why* the other person holds that as part of his/her reality. Once you've accomplished that goal, once you understand what lies behind the statement, *drop it*. This is very, very important, or I wouldn't be using all those italics to get your attention. You have to assume that the statement is true to understand it, just as you assume that the television bullets are real to understand the actions and reactions of the characters in the drama. But once you understand, you've gone far enough. You must not make the mistake of continuing to assume the truth of the negative statement after your assumption has served its purpose.

This is not easy. And I understand very well those who refuse to follow George Miller's rule because they refuse to take the *risk* of entering another's reality even temporarily—they have logical reasons for their behavior. But I do contend that although it isn't easy, it is possible. The fact that you are now *aware* of the process is usually enough to keep you out of trouble. That is, if you make a conscious decision to enter a metaphor for a brief time, with a specific goal, you will be aware of what you are doing and able to make an equally conscious decision to come back out. The risk is only sizable when you wander in and out of metaphors without realizing that that's what you are doing.

The second problem is more dangerous than the first, because you have far less control over it. This is the problem that comes up when other people choose to perceive you as playing a full-scale role in their metaphors. If the role is an attractive one, your behaving *as if* you filled it will feed the metaphor and provide you with many tempting rewards. Suppose you are a man whose wife has chosen the Rose-Covered Cottage as a metaphor. She has chosen you to function as the Perfect Husband within the metaphor. When you behave *as if* that were true, you reinforce her choice, and she may treat you as if you were in fact perfect. This can be extremely pleasant. You can get to like it very easily indeed.

It will cripple your wife, who really needs a human being for a husband and has a right to one. And it may confuse the rest of your life, because you'll have a tendency to let it leak into other life areas and to be annoyed when people other than your wife don't seem willing to recognize your perfection. But you may find it so pleasant that you're willing to put up with these disadvantages.

If you are a woman whose family perceives you as Wonder Woman—always strong, always able to cope, never unable to rise to the occasion no matter what the challenge, invulnerable to the stresses and strains and physical limitations that hamper ordinary women—you can literally destroy yourself playing the role. The constant admiration and respect that Wonder Woman gets are powerful temptations. In my part of the country it has different labels and a slightly different set of surface characteristics, but it is so culturally dug in that all females are presorted into one of three slots: the Southern Lady (that's Wonder Woman, without the bracelets); the Mountain Granny (that's Wonder Woman, grown old); and the Traipsin' Woman (that's everybody else, the *failed* Wonder Woman.)

Watch out for this. *Resist* it. Once you have discovered why the other person sees you in the role, stop behaving as if it were true. In the same way that you can set up a little loop in your head to repeat hurtful statements over and over until you suffer from them, you can set up one that says, "You are *not* perfect [or whatever label is needed in your situation]," over and over and over until it convinces you. Do that, for the sake of your own well-being.

The third danger is that you will become confused about your own reality. Assume that your metaphor of choice at work *is* I Am John Wayne, but your boss sees you as one of those glowing eager beavers inside the Happy Workplace, bent on industrious togetherness. You assume that she is right, that what she says is true, and you behave *as if* it were true. She reinforces your behavior and rewards you for it, because you are feeding *her* metaphor of choice. And one day you realize that you're not quite sure if you're the Happy Worker or John Wayne or somebody else entirely.

This is a clear signal that you're following Miller's rule to excess. You're not limiting your reality sharing to just the time necessary for communication. If this is a problem for you, set yourself an artificial limit and stick to it until you've learned not to overdo. Establish a rule that you'll enter nobody's metaphor for longer than ten minutes, or for longer than three conversational turns on each side, or any other brief arbitrary limit. You'll wreck some of your interactions that way, but it's less a hazard than the alternative. When you've learned to follow your artificial rule you can drop it and return to the more flexible one: Match realities for just as long as it takes, in each interaction, to achieve communication.

Finally, there is the problem of being *locked in,* trapped in a single metaphor for every situation. This is exactly like being locked into one Satir Mode or one sensory mode in all situations. It is anything but a trivial matter and deserves serious concern.

At the end of this chapter you'll find as one of the suggested readings an article called "Feminists and Other Useful Fanatics." It describes the function of fanatics in our society and shows that we need them. They are useful, essential as antidotes to cultural disorders of many kinds. But let us be frank—the fanatic, whether saintly or wicked, is a *damned nuisance*—not only to other people, but to his or her own self. The line between the useful fanatic and the destructive maniac is a narrow one, often clearly visible only with the hindsight of hundreds of years.

I know no solution to this problem. It is a matter for experts, including the expert within you that cannot be denied. But I can at least counsel you to be aware of the problem. If you find yourself militantly maintaining a single set of reality statements *in all situations without exception,* you might stop and ask yourself two questions:

- *Why* am I doing this?
- Do I really want to do this?

If you can't answer either question, you need help. By all means, find some.

Remember that any skill, if misused, can be dangerous. Karate is meant to be self-defense; misused, it becomes a terrifying skill for physical abuse. Rhetoric is meant to cut through forests of useless words and make communication more efficient; misused, it becomes a weapon for verbal manipulation. Reality matching is no different. It is a skill, a tool of living, with equal potential for good or for bad—what you make of it is your own choice.

It's possible that after reading this chapter you will make a conscious choice not to use it at all if you can avoid it—and that's fine. That's fine, because it *is* a conscious choice. You now know that it exists as a technique, and you have learned a lot of things about it. You are basing your own decision not to use it on knowledge, and you will still come out ahead in your language interactions. Because when other people use reality matching against *you*, you will know what is happening. That can only be a help to you.

SUPPLEMENTARY QUOTATIONS

Various interest groups claim that public opinion is behind them on a certain matter, appealing to the illusion that there is enormous interest in and support for a policy. They commission polls, quite valid in their sampling procedures, but which load questions about a particular issue—for example, "Do you favor creating a vast new bureaucracy costing billions of dollars in your tax money to administer socialized medicine?"—and selected results are presented in testimony before Congress and other forums as evidence of public opposition to socialized medicine [Nimmo and Combs, 1980, p. 120].

Every semantic environment is controlled by metaphors, frequently hidden from the view of those who have created them, but through which people interpret the meaning and value of what is happening. Where people have a roughly similar construction of a situation ... the environment will function with a minimum of disruption. Serious difficulties arise, however, when people's metaphors clash, and especially whenever there is a lack of awareness of how the metaphors are controlling their responses [Postman, 1976, p. 132].

It is impossible to exaggerate how important it is for people to have some interpretive framework—an intelligible "story"—within which to fit the news of the day, especially when the news is mostly bad and when it affects our lives directly and urgently [Yankelovich, 1982, p. 8].

The media don't have to endorse "the system" in any overt way or say anything particularly nice about it at all. Conversely, we don't have to like or believe anything the media may say—so long as we don't have access continuously and pervasively to models which describe *in detail* a completely different kind of life. The only thing that's not permitted is the possibility of negating this social system by describing another one so completely that we could vividly imagine what life would be like in it, hence to desire it and then, perhaps, to demand it [Youngblood, 1977–1978, p. 13].

SUGGESTED READINGS

GARDNER, H. "Strange Loops of the Mind." *Psychology Today*, March 1980, pp. 72–85. (A good article on *Goedel, Escher, Bach,* with a careful discussion of the process of metaphor.)

———. "Gifted Worldmakers." *Psychology Today*, September 1980, pp. 92–96. (A comparison of the "realistic" view of the world—that we see it as it is—and the "constructivist" view, that we construct what we perceive.)

———. and E. WINNER. "The Child Is Father to the Metaphor." *Psychology Today*, May 1979, pp. 81–91. (Discussion of children's difficulties with metaphors.)

KINSLEY, M. "The Easy Chair: Waiting for Lenny." *Harper's*, March 1982, pp. 8–11.

NIMMO, D., and J. E. COMBS. *Subliminal Politics: Myths and Myth-makers in America*. Englewood Cliffs, N.J.: Prentice-Hall, Inc., 1980. (See quotation above.)

ODIORNE, G. S. *The Change Resisters: How They Prevent Progress and What Managers Can Do about Them*. Englewood Cliffs, N.J.: Prentice-Hall, Inc., 1981. (Directed at managers, but applies to any situation in which you need to convince others to change and are faced by stubborn resistance. Highly recommended.)

POSTMAN, N. *Crazy Talk, Stupid Talk: How We Defeat Ourselves by the Way We Talk—and What to Do about It*. New York: Dell Publishing Co., 1976. (See quotation above.)

SHARP, D. "Aristotle's Garage. *Harper's*, March 1981, pp. 91–93. (An example of an extended metaphor, in which the acts and decisions of an automobile mechanic are carefully fit into a point-by-point match with those of a philosopher, among other things.)

SNYDER, M. "The Many Me's of the Self-Monitor." *Psychology Today*, March 1980, pp. 33–40, 92. (A discussion of what Snyder calls "impression management," a deliberate modifying of one's language and nonverbal communication to create particular impressions.)

TRENT, J. D., et al., eds. *Concepts in Communication*. Boston: Allyn & Bacon, Inc., 1973. (An excellent handbook presenting basic concepts and supporting research on the theory and practice of communication. Good summaries of the effects, or noneffects, of such things as logic and order of presentation. Highly recommended.)

WILLS, G. "Feminists and Other Useful Fanatics." *Harper's*, June 1976, pp. 35–42.

YANKELOVICH, D. "Reagan and the National Psyche." *Psychology Today*, January 1982, pp. 5–8. (See quotation above.)

YOUNGBLOOD, G. "The Mass Media and the Future of Desire." *Co-Evolution Quarterly* No. 16 (Winter 1977–78), pp. 6–17. (See quotation above.)

8

Body Language

The term *body language* is not the exact term, not the perfect term, for the subject of this chapter. If you read the literature you will find many other terms being used to refer to the field or to parts of it—for example, *paralanguage, proxemics, chronemics, pragmatics, kinesics.* I will stay with *body language* as a cover term because it is no more or less imprecise than the others, but I want to define it carefully here.

By *body language* I mean *every part* of the communication act that is not the actual spoken or written words used. This includes gestures, facial expressions, postures, intonation (the melody of the voice as it carries the word, and the symbols we use to indicate that melody roughly in writing), the way the body is located in space and time within a communication situation, the messages carried by clothing and the decoration of the body, and so on.

This is a much broader use of the term than you will find in most writing on the subject, either popular or scholarly. I have run into objections that this definition makes all human be-havior, including silence, into language. I am perfectly willing to accept that. So far as I can see, there are no human behaviors under the voluntary control of human beings that can be clearly defined as *not* part of language. But you need not agree with me on this, even partially, to make use of this material. Just keep it in mind, so that you will not misunderstand what I say because we are using different definitions of *body language*.

Researchers trying to find out exactly how much of any message is carried by the body rather than by the words themselves have had a variety of results. You will see claims that 90 percent of all information communicated is carried by body language. The precise figure is not crucial for us, however, because even the lowest figure cited—a claim for 65 percent—shows that well over one half of all information is on the body language channel, and that makes it a matter of major importance.

LEARNING ABOUT
BODY LANGUAGE

You'll find many books on body language written for the mass market; the two most widely distributed are Julius Fast's *Body Language* and *How to Read a Person Like a Book*, by Gerard Nierenberg and Henry Calero. A brief quotation from the second book will give you the general tone of such works: "Pinching the Bridge of the Nose. ... This gesture, usually accompanied with closed eyes, communicates great thought and concern about the decision to be made. [page 65]." Nierenberg and Calero provide a catalog of body gestures, postures, and facial expressions, each with a line drawing to make it more clear. The book states what each item in the catalog is supposed to mean and provides anecdotes about businesspeople, lawyers, housewives, and various nationalities as examples of the items.

I am sure that these books, and the many others like them, can be valuable to the student of verbal self-defense. They contain much interesting information, in a general sense, and are well worth reading. But the impression given by their titles and their covers, even when the authors try to counteract it occasionally inside the books, is very misleading.

In the first place, the information offered is valid in the strict sense of the word *only* for white middle-class Americans. And I would not be at all reluctant to restrict that even further and state that it is valid only for white middle-class American *males*, because the information regarding women is dubious at best.

In the second place, there are no items of body language that can be relied on independent of the context in which they occur. Take any unit of body language that can be easily identified. It will mean one thing when used with eyebrows raised, another when the eyes are fixed on the floor, another when it occurs at the same time as a clenched fist, and so on for all the multitude of possible combinations. Identical clusters of body language units will mean one thing in conjunction with one topic of conversation and quite a different thing in conjunction with another. You may be pinching the bridge of your nose not because you are expressing "great thought and concern about the decision to be made" but because your glasses are too tight or your sinuses hurt.

I don't think that the authors of these books intend to imply that the lists they give of body language units with corresponding "meanings" are to be relied on in anything but a rough way. But unfortunately, cautious scholarship doesn't sell millions of copies of books, and their disclaimers and qualifications are forgotten in the barrage of hype—just think of the title *How to Read a Person Like a Book* for a perfect example.

In the third place, the entire premise of the books is wrong. They have as underlying framework the claim that you can read the books, memorize the information, and use it to interpret the body language of others around you. It's amusing to me that the authors base this assumption on the success of their seminars and workshops around the country. Certainly people have learned to use the information through those workshops—but they have learned it because they were able to *observe demonstrated body language*. When you see someone standing before you demonstrating a particular combination of body language units, you will always—unless you have a compelling reason to resist—take on that posture yourself. You will *model* the body language you are watching.

It's not your eyes that are doing the learning, but your whole body. And it's not what you see that teaches you. Seeing is only the tool that you use for obtaining the information. What you learn from is the feedback you get from your own body as you try to match the body language being demonstrated. You can't learn this from a book, and that includes *this* book. No set of detailed written instructions will replace the feedback you get from your body as you try to follow someone's instructions—right before your eyes—to "hold your hand like this."

Unfortunately, teachers of body language are not easily found. Where they do exist, they are too expensive for most of us. And you can't go around copying the body language of other people and asking them what their postures and gestures mean. You need a self-teaching program, but where are you to find it?

Unless you are very unusual, you have available to you an excellent teaching machine for this purpose—your television set. Unlike people, who would find your behavior annoying, the television set is completely indifferent to your body language. Use it like this.

Turn on a program that has people talking, and turn off the sound. Now watch, carefully, until you see a particular set of body language units that you recognize *as* a set. Try to model that set. Match it as closely as you can, given the fact that the speaker will not hold it for very long. Hold that position (whether the person you were modeling has moved or not) and ask yourself: "How do I feel when my body is like this? What do I mean by holding my body this way?" Each such body set that

203

you isolate and recognize should then be recorded for your future reference.

EXAMPLE

You see someone draw his eyebrows together over his nose, firm his mouth, and grasp his chin between his thumb and index finger. His body is bent slightly forward in his chair. Assume the same "configuration" as far as you can—draw your eyebrows together, firm your mouth, and so on. Hold it!

Now, ask yourself—"How do I feel? What emotional labels would I attach to myself in this posture? What sort of situation would I be likely to be involved in when I did this?"

And ask "What other body language units go *with* this set? How am I holding my shoulders? Is my head tilted? What am I doing with my legs and feet? Are my eyes wide or slightly closed? What else is happening with my body?"

You will find that so long as you and the person you were watching are of the same approximate culture you will know the answers to these questions. Your body knows all the "grammar rules" of its language, although most of the information is not accessible to your conscious mind without deliberate effort. One or two body language units from any set will usually be enough to allow your own internalized nonverbal grammar to take over and provide the rest of the units that go with the ones you picked out. And you will know the meaning of the position when you have taken it yourself. Furthermore, unlike information you have read in a book, you will *remember* it.

There is no way any book could record all the minute details of a given body language set. The human eye cannot record all those details in the fraction of time that the set is held. Even with the technology of the modern camera, which can freeze a body language set and keep it before your eyes for as long as you want to look at it, you are able to see only some of the necessary information. But this doesn't matter, because your body *knows* all that information. All you are doing when you work with this technique is bringing what you already know into conscious awareness so that you can make deliberate use of it.

When you look at the letter *m* on a page you are reading aloud, you have no conscious awareness of how to form an English *m*. You don't know how many millimeters your lips must move, or how much muscle tension they must exert to hold themselves together, or how much air must be released from your diaphragm through your vocal tract. You have no idea what maneuvers your body has to carry out to cause the little flap of tissue that is closed during nonnasal sounds to drop open in the back of your throat and let air excape through your nose as well as your mouth. You don't "know" any of this unless you have taken an advanced course in phonetics, speech pathology, or some related discipline, and even then you won't know everything there is to know. But your body, fortunately, *does* know how to make an *m*, down to the most infinitesimal detail—and knows it so well that you don't even have to think about it when you do it.

Exactly the same is true for body language. When you open your eyes wide, raise your eyebrows, and put your spread fingers over a slightly opened mouth, your conscious mind has no idea what the rest of your body should be doing at the same time—but your body does know and can be relied on to do it. You can therefore trust your body to provide you with the necessary information for your self-teaching project using the silenced television set. All you have to do is let your body function and pay attention to what it does, making notes if you feel that is helpful.[1]

This is a slow project, by the way, especially in its early stages. If you set aside thirty minutes for it, and do it properly,

[1]If your preferred mode is eye or ear, you may find this more difficult than the person who strongly prefers the sensory mode of touch will. But you can do it. It will just take you longer.

you should expect that each session will allow you to add perhaps two new body sets to your store of conscious information. If you are very good at it, you might add three. However, as you go along you'll begin to spot certain general rules that will save you time. You will begin to be able to identify a body set more quickly and to arrive at the meaning it has for you more efficiently. And you should then begin to check your work by turning up the sound to find out if the words being spoken on television match the meaning you have assigned to the body language you were modeling.

Some people are so highly skilled in their command of body language that they can use their bodies to lie with—our great actors are perhaps the most obvious examples. They are trained to present body language that they don't personally feel, even body language that is repulsive to them as individuals, and to do it so well that it is completely believable. That is why most of our teachers of body language are found in acting classes and studios.

But this is unusual. Most people are not great actors. Most of the time, for most people, no matter how the words may lie the body will tell the truth. When there is conflict between the message of the words and the message of the body, you can ordinarily rely on the body. (Not that one message is more important than the other—it's very important to know what lie is being told—but you need to be able to tell them apart.) Because this is true, you shouldn't necessarily decide that you've made a mistake if you predicted one meaning for a body language set you saw on television and modeled and then when you turned up the sound the words were in conflict with your prediction. Unless the person you are watching is a professional actor, the words being said might not represent the speaker's feelings, and the body is betraying that fact to the viewer.

Think of what happens when you are frightened and you're trying not to let people know that. Your mouth may be saying "Oh, I'm fine" or "There's nothing to worry about." But if you are shivering, your lips are trembling, and your muscles are tense, people watching you will understand that the words are false. The speaker who punctuates "I love you with all my heart" with the steady pounding of his or her fist on a table is demonstrating a conflict, whether or not that conflict is consciously understood. And it is probably the fist that can be relied on.

Body language often carries messages that make the whole communication a double bind. If the words being used urge the listener to make one choice while the body language urges another, that constitutes a double bind. The listener cannot follow either choice without refusing the other one, and therefore nothing that he or she does is going to be right.

If you tell a child to kiss you, but make it clear by your body language that you don't want to be kissed, you have put that child in a double bind—especially because, as an adult, you are in a dominant position. When everything about the body language of a dominant person gives one consistent message, but everything that the person says or writes gives a consistent contradiction of that message, the subordinate person is in a double bind.

After you've spent a good deal of time practicing observation and modeling and self-interpretation of body language with the television, you will be able to start practicing with people around you. You will then have the entire context available to you for checking—that is, if the body language you see communicates a negative emotion while the words you hear convey a positive one, you will probably know things about the speaker and the situation that will help you understand why the conflict exists. You should only move on to this after you have become skilled enough to do body language modeling without being obvious, however. Take your time. You've spent your whole life without conscious awareness of body language grammar, and you have functioned capably nonetheless. If it takes you a year or two to make enough of your knowledge conscious to put it to effective use, that is quite all right. Very few things worth knowing can be mastered in less time than that. And every little bit that you learn will be a help to you.

SEX AND POWER DIFFERENCES AND BODY LANGUAGE

What about sex differences and body language? If you are a woman, you will be wondering whether you should observe only women; if you are a man, you will be wondering if your self-teaching should be confined to males. The question is reasonable, given the publicity over the past ten years or so about "women's language." If you feel that you've been reading and hearing about a specific speech used by women, with characteristics that identify it and differentiate it from the speech of men, you are right. The problem is that the research on which the reports you heard and read were based has turned out to be *wrong*. (If you wonder why scholars and researchers sometimes hesitate to report their findings, this may help explain it. It's very hard to take back an error and get out a correction to the public, especially when your original reports caught the attention of the media and were widely featured on news broadcasts, talk shows, and the like.)

The researchers studying women's language behavior were misled by a kind of social accident. They noted a set of characteristics that appeared consistently in the language of women and were usually absent from the language of men. They then concluded that the difference was directly correlated with sexual gender, which was an error. When they looked further— for example, at language interactions between lawyers and witnesses, doctors and patients, police and suspects—they realized that regardless of gender the same characteristics that had identified "women's speech" turned up in the speech of the witnesses, the patients, and the suspects. Those characteristics were absent from the speech of the lawyers, doctors, and police, whether they were male or female.

What they had seen was the identifying characteristics of the language of *subordinates*. Because in any man-woman interaction it is so often the man who is dominant and the woman who is subordinate, the overpowering majority of people exhibiting those characteristics had been women—leading the researchers to conclude that they were observing "women's speech." What they were really seeing was subordinate speech—there is no evidence for any such thing in English as "women's speech" (or "men's speech") as such.

It is true that a massive amount of research shows that women are far better at observing body language and using it effectively than men are. But we have no idea whether this is true because they are women. It appears that way because they are so rarely dominant in interaction with males, and it may be only that any subordinate group is better skilled at body language. Even if as grown women today they are lawyers, surgeons, or senators, as children and adolescents they were subordinates. Little girls and young girls almost never have dominant roles—those are reserved for the males. As a result, American females grow up with the body language skills characteristic of subordinates. If the social situation should change radically and a generation of little girls grow up without spending all their preadult lives in subordination, we would be able to see whether the seeming "gender difference" would disappear or not. At the moment, the prospects for such a change do not impress me.

In terms of your self-teaching, this means that you need not worry about whether you are observing males or females on your television or in your environment. There are no body language sets reserved exclusively for either gender except in the sense dictated by actual physiology. If you don't *have* a penis or a beard, you obviously cannot carry out body language that requires the use of either one. But with such minor (and obvious) exceptions, both sexes have the same body parts, and this is not a major difficulty for body language study. The differing physiology of the female pelvis will make a woman's walk differ from a man's—that will be obvious, and you should exclude the walk of a member of the opposite sex from your attempts at language modeling. Common sense will prove a reliable guide in such matters.

A man who becomes a suspect under interrogation by several police officers of either sex will, in that context, use the body language characteristic of subordinates. A woman lawyer who is interrogating a witness, male or female, will show body language characteristic of dominance. Both types of body language will be used by both genders, depending on the context. You can safely observe and learn from individuals of your own cultural group without worrying about their sexual gender as models.

A good example of the way popular information about body language can cause trouble is what happens when a woman tries deliberately to use a set of body language units that she has heard or read is considered "male." If she is relying on written information or an oral description without demonstration, this never works.

Assume a woman has been told that one of the "male" items of body language is arms folded across the chest with each hand firmly grasping the opposite forearm. She has also been informed that she will be more effective in her role as manager, professor, financial consultant, or any other dominant, high-status role if she appears more male. She proceeds to use the folded arms posture, deliberately, as a strategy for increasing her perceived dominance. However, not only is the rest of her body not doing what the "male" body does when that posture is used, it is in actual *conflict* with it. Unless she *feels* dominant, she will insert the crossed arms body language unit right into the middle of an otherwise subordinate body language set. The effect is not something you'd want to strive for, even if nobody present understands why things are as they are. It is directly comparable to the effect she would achieve by wearing a football helmet with a traditional bridal gown—ridiculous.

If you feel you know very little about the body language of dominance, watch some dominant males. Watch the television anchormen—and the term is not meant to include females. Watch cowboys, sheriffs, policemen, and military officers. When they cross their arms over their chests, look carefully: what are they doing with their legs and feet? How do they hold their shoulders and heads? How do their faces look? Observe the whole body and try to match it, paying attention to what the rest of *your* body does. When you feel comfortable with it, you might begin using it as a tool for achieving dominance in your interactions—but only after you've gone through this procedure.

Chances are good that if you are a woman who has never had an opportunity to participate in the roles of dominance professionally, you have several children requiring your attention. In this case, think of a situation when those children are defying you and you are insisting that they obey. Keep the situation firmly in your head—imagine it as completely as you can. *Now* fold your arms over your chest and grasp each forearm with the opposite hand! You will find that your body knows exactly what to do with all the rest of its parts and that the posture is a part of your grammar after all. You will then have identified the set and made yourself consciously aware of it; now it will be available to you for future deliberate use.

I don't recommend any hasty attempts to incorporate particular body language sets into your own behavior. This takes time, study, and careful practice. But there is no reason why you can't—speedily—eliminate undesirable sets. Consider the characteristic "teacher–drill instructor" gesture in which the hand is made into a fist and the index finger is extended, and then that fist and finger are shaken at the listener. This is a threatening body language set and one that becomes an absurd habit. There's no reason why you can't decide *not* to do this. Whenever you catch yourself doing it you can stop, until you break yourself of it. Ask people to let you know if you're doing it, if you can't trust yourself to notice and if you can trust them to be reasonable.

Remember that when you don't use one set you will be forced to substitute something else for it. Your safest course is to choose some very neutral position and substitute that until you no longer are tempted to use the set you're trying to get rid of. (I tell my students and clients, and especially my teacher trainees who are trying to dump that finger-and-fist gesture, to clasp their hands loosely behind their backs for a while instead. This may not be an ideal body language set, but it's easily done, easily remembered, and much less threatening than the other one.)

BODY LANGUAGE
ACROSS CULTURES

Outside your own culture, you are *not* safe trying to learn body language on your own. If you are an Anglo and you manage to train yourself to model the body language of blacks that you observe, however flawlessly, you will have acquired nothing but a rather hazardous trick—because you will not know what you *mean* by that language. It's as if you did what classical singers used to do and memorized the lyrics of songs in foreign languages without having any idea what the words meant—it can be done, but it's not useful, and the possibilities for unpleasant errors are awesome.

To learn the body language of another culture, you have to have the help of a native speaker (native "mover," if you prefer) of that body language. The native speaker can assume the body language set the two of you see on the television screen, ask himself or herself the questions listed on page 204, and then tell you the answers. But that is a task for experts and can get you into a great deal of trouble. In the same way that an American who can manage a near-flawless Cockney accent risks anger from

Cockney natives when using it because they think they are being made fun of, it can be extremely offensive to one cultural group to encounter someone from another culture using their body language. This is probably even more true for the very obvious body language units, the ones that are easiest to observe and copy, than for the subtle ones—because the obvious ones are nearer to conscious awareness in the native speaker as well. I strongly recommend that you resist the temptation to try this kind of cross-cultural communication unless you really do know what you're doing.

If you are fortunate enough to have native or fluent control of several body language systems, be grateful. Most of the contemporary books on communication mention that it was possible to tell whether former New York Mayor Fiorello La Guardia was speaking English or Italian in films even with no sound by watching his body language. He had native control of both systems. And it is common to hear from bilingual individuals statements like this: "I am a different person when I am speaking Spanish [Laotian, German, Navaho, or whatever]." The person who speaks another language fluently, making no mistakes of grammar or pronunciation but with the body language of his or her native tongue, can always be spotted as a foreigner.

Because of the way the American educational system deals with foreign-language teaching—reserving it until after puberty despite the fact that the ability to learn languages begins to decay *at* puberty—Americans tend not to be fluent in any language but English. They "learn" French, German, Russian, or Swahili, perhaps; but while their lips speak that language the rest of their bodies go right on speaking American English. And so long as that is true they will always "look" American, no matter what language they happen to be speaking. If you have full command of more than one body language grammar, it is probable that you learned both before you were more than eleven or twelve years old.

BODY LANGUAGE
AND WRITING

The fact that the grammar of the body is not readily available to people has far-reaching effects. It's difficult for beginning writers to write natural-sounding dialogue, as I have mentioned before. It's harder, *much* harder, for them to write down the little bits of body language description that go with the dialogue. When you read page after page of dialogue followed only by "he said" and "she said," you are probably reading dialogue written by someone uncertain of body language and uncertain what to do about it. I write fiction myself, and the only way I can set down the body language is to say the dialogue out loud and pay careful attention to what my body does as I say it. Then I can record that information in words. But I can't answer the question "What body language goes with this sentence?" if I am required to hold still. I have to go through the act of speaking the words, and moving with them, to find out what my body already knows about the accompanying postures, gestures, and expressions. I know no writer for whom this isn't true, although after years of practice you will remember a large vocabulary of body language units because you've worked them out before. And whether you write or not, you should try this out for yourself. Choose any brief sentence and then sit as motionless as possible—hold your hands absolutely still, and your face as well. And *think*. What words would you use to describe the way someone used his or her body while saying that sentence? Can you do it, without acting it out for yourself first? If you can you are very unusual.

It's lucky for the writers of those "graded reader" sets that they are allowed to set up their dialogue without any kind of comment on body language. Because there *is* no body language that you can use with a dialogue like this one:

X: Oh, oh, oh! See, see, see!
Y: Jump, Tweedledee, jump!

X: Oh, oh, oh! I can jump!

Y: Jump, jump, jump!

If little children cannot read such stuff aloud with any sort of natural intonation, it is not because their reading skills are poor. Try reading it out loud yourself, and see.

BODY LANGUAGE SYNCHRONIZATION

So far, we've been talking about the most directly observable level of body language, for the most part. It takes no special equipment or training to notice the clenched fist, the crossed legs, the hunched shoulders, the arched eyebrows. It simply takes an investment of time, careful observation, and a willingness to participate in the learning process. Your body knows how to do the fine tuning that is beyond your conscious control.

There is, however, another level of body language, an even more inaccessible level, and this one can only be observed if you have available to you advanced photographic equipment that will break movement down into fractions of seconds and freeze it. Such equipment has existed only recently, and therefore much of what we know about this level is relatively new—not to mention surprising.

First it was discovered that speakers' body language was synchronized with their own speech. Willett Kempton (1980) says that "during speech, various parts of the speaker's body move in time with each other and with the articulation of his speech. Although different body parts move at different speeds and in different directions, they tend to change direction at the same time." This is called *self-synchrony,* and it can be observed by the naked eye at the level of the spoken phrase, if you are concentrating on watching for it. But that's not all. Kempton goes on:

The hearer's behavior is also organized self-synchronously, follow-ing the same principles as that of the speaker. ... The units of the hearer's behavior are usually formed by different body parts moving or the same body parts moving in directions different from those of a speaker, but they sustain direction of movement as the speakers sustain direction of movement and change when the speakers change. Interactional synchrony is defined by this isomorphism of pattern of change between the speaker (and) hearer. This isomorphism is difficult to detect at the normal speed of body motion [Kempton, 1980, p. 68].

(*Isomorphism* is point-for-point matching, like the match be-tween the English alphabet and the cryptogram alphabet in Chapter Seven.) And Kempton adds, "It may not be too surprising that a speaker coordinates the muscular activity of his speech production with his other muscular activity, but the finding that a listener also synchronizes with that speech (to within at least 50 milliseconds) is quite remarkable."

I found it even more extraordinary when it was discovered that this shared dance of language is present in human infants from the *first day of life,* regardless of the language that is being spoken to the infant. The failure to show this synchronization with speech is a sign of trouble—autistic children, for example, do not body-synchronize with language as do nonautistic chil-dren. Their response comes later than it should, or they respond as if a sound had been repeated a number of times rather than only once, or they do both of these things. Something is interfering with their ability to self-synchronize with the speech they hear.

Watching stop-frame films of a large audience "hanging on every word" of a skillful speaker is like watching an exceedingly slow motion ballet, because every member of the audience is body-syncing with the language of the speaker.

It requires a deliberate effort on the part of the normal listener *not* to participate in these shared patterns. When someone who doesn't want to listen to you insists on reading, staring at the ceiling, or watching the television screen while you talk, that person is demonstrating their knowledge of the effort required not to listen. It's very hard to pay close attention to the words of a speaker, to watch his or her body language with scrupulous care, and still refrain from body-syncing. When it happens, it requires a sort of self-hypnosis—you suddenly realize, after a passage of time, that not only have you not heard a word the speaker said, you have not heard *anything*. When you say, "I'm sorry, my mind was a million miles away," you are expressing the situation well—if your mind were not far away, you couldn't do it. You have in effect lost the time that has passed while you were not-listening and not-participating.

The sounds that make up the sound system of all human languages come from a shared set of around seventy possible sounds. No language has a sound pronounced by putting the lower teeth against the upper lip, although that's easily done. It just isn't on the list of possible human language sounds. And an infant is able to produce *all* the sounds in the potential inventory, even if they aren't part of his or her language. American infants in the babbling stage will be heard saying the *r* of French, the *q* of Arabic, and so on through the full range of possibilities. Gradually, as the infant hears a language spoken, it eliminates all those sounds that aren't useful because they are not part of the language or languages that will be native to it.

In the same way, the human infant is able to synchronize its body with any language whatsoever. An infant of Chinese parents adopted shortly after birth into a household where only Swahili is spoken will body-sync flawlessly with Swahili. Then, as the language is mastered, the body language of other tongues is gradually eliminated from the child's repertoire.

We know that adults have a hard time learning to pronounce sounds of foreign languages that are very unlike their own, and that the ability they had to do so as infants is little use to them. We don't have much information yet about the ability of adults to body-sync with foreign languages, and we don't know if that ability is lost in the same way that the ability to pronounce nonnative sounds is. It would be logical and not surprising if this were true—but it can't be taken for granted. I look forward to the research studies that will settle the question. And while I am waiting, I will assume tentatively that one of the reasons it is so hard to listen to someone speaking a language you don't understand is because you are unable to synchronize with it properly.

The more closely you attend to another person's speech, the more closely you will be body synchronized with that person's speech. And the more closely you are synchronized, the more the other person will enjoy speaking—because you will be perceived as truly interested and truly caring.[2] Women, as subordinate groups, appear to do more of this careful attending in American society than men do. But any person who has a good reason to be subordinate—for example, a man who is being physically threatened by someone who is armed—will quickly muster up the same kind of scrupulous attention.

The good public speaker helps the audience to attend by providing strong rhythmic patterns in the language used, much as a conductor provides a strong beat of the baton for the orchestra to follow, to keep them together. We'll discuss this further in a later chapter, along with the physical signs that let you know you are losing your audience (even if it is an audience of one). For now, the best way I know for you to study this sort of verbal "conducting" of an audience is to watch one of the television evangelist preachers in action. Watch first with the sound turned off to become familiar with the body language; then turn the sound back on and listen as you watch. If you have access to a videotape recorder, watch the same sermon a number of times so that you can become thoroughly familiar with it. These ministers are virtuosos of the use of language to maintain

[2]Another listening technique involves not just synchronizing your body movement to that of the speaker but actually matching those movements *exactly*. This is called various things by various writers—*mirroring, shadowing, pacing, modeling,* and so on. Unless you are exceptionally good at it, you will be noticed doing it, and the speaker will think you are mocking him or her. It's not a good idea for ordinary language interaction.

attention, and careful observation of their performance can teach you things that don't appear in any book about the subject.

If you have a videotape recorder available, you have a ready-made and convenient tool for body language training right at hand. Make yourself a tape of ten minutes or so of each of several compelling speakers and write down the words from the tape. Now try to say the words along with—*not after*—the speaker as you play back the videotape. Repeat this until you can match the speaker's delivery with little or no difficulty. Then, turn your attention to the body language you are using—notice the ways in which it is different from the body language you use in your own conversation.

The reason for taping several different speakers is that you don't want to train yourself to be an exact imitation of some one of them. Being able to do Walter Cronkite imitations (or imitations of anybody else) is of limited usefulness unless you are desperate for something to amuse people with at parties or plan a career as an impersonator. Be certain that you have chosen *compelling* speakers, because it's just as easy to train yourself to be boring as to be interesting—if you're not certain, get a second opinion. If the speaker is saying things you agree with, you're running the risk of perceiving him or her as an excellent speaker for only that reason—what you learn from practicing such language behavior will be effective only with other people who agree with what he or she is saying.[3]

SUPPLEMENTARY QUOTATIONS

A listener provides the speaker with almost constant feedback that he is attending, including information about the level of that attending. The body of the listener moves in time and intensity with the speech of the speaker [Condon, 1980, p. 58].

[3]For a complete explanation of the use of audio tape recording to improve the quality of your voice and intonation, see *The Gentle Art of Verbal Self-Defense* (Book One).

Allen Ivey and Eugene Oetting describe the results of attending in a college psychology course. They trained six students in attending behavior. [Bolton defines *attending* as "listening with the whole body."] Then a session, taught by a visiting professor, was videotaped. The students started out in typical student nonattending classroom behavior. The professor lectured, unaware of the students' prearranged plan. His presentation was centered on his notes. He used no gestures, spoke in a monotone, and paid little attention to the students. At a prearranged signal, however, the students began deliberately to physically attend. Within a half a minute, the lecturer gestured for the first time, his verbal rate increased, and a lively classroom session was born. Simple attending had changed the whole picture. At another signal, the students stopped attending, and the speaker, after awkwardly seeking continued response, resumed the unengaging lecture with which he began the class [Bolton, 1979, pp. 33–34].

If the person you're talking to keeps moving closer to you, making you feel a little crowded, assume that that person needs a smaller personal space than you do for conversation, and *hold still*. If he or she then stops moving in on you, you've made the right decision, and things will go better, provided that you can master your own feeling of being hemmed in. Conversely, if the person you're talking to keeps backing up, assume that he or she needs a bigger personal space than you require, and stop trying to get closer. If you're right, again things will improve. Notice that in both cases the remedy is to hold still and let the other person set the limits of the space for your conversation [Elgin, 1980, p. 204].

SUGGESTED READINGS

BIRDWHISTELL, R. L. *Kinesics and Context*. Philadelphia: University of Pennsylvania Press, 1970. (A scholarly book, but not overly technical; the classic text in the field of body language.)

BOLTON, R. *People Skills: How to Assert Yourself, Listen to Others, and Resolve Conflicts*. Englewood Cliffs, N.J.: Prentice-Hall, Inc., 1979, pp. 29–113. (See quotation above.)

HENLEY, N. *Body Politics: Power, Sex, and Nonverbal Communication.* Englewood Cliffs, N.J.: Prentice-Hall, Inc., 1977. (Valuable especially for its brief reports of research studies that apply to theoretical claims in body language and kinesics.)

KEY, M. R., ed. *The Relationship of Verbal and Nonverbal Communication,* student edition. The Hague: Mouton Publishers, 1980. (A collection of articles, some quite technical, but all very useful to the student of verbal self-defense.)

GELDARD, F. A. "Body English." *Psychology Today,* December 1968, pp. 43–47. (An excellent discussion of research on the sensory capabilities of the skin and the sense of touch.)

SCHEFLEN, A. E., and A. SCHEFLEN. *Body Language and the Social Order: Communication as Behavioral Control.* Englewood Cliffs, N.J.: Prentice-Hall, Inc., 1972. (One of the best books on body language; thorough and nontechnical. Especially valuable because it illustrates body language sets with photographs from real interactions, rather than by line drawings or *posed* pictures. Highly recommended.)

In addition, three books written by Edward T. Hall take up body language in its broadest aspect and with particular reference to cross-cultural differences. Things change so rapidly today that some of the information is now out of date, but the basic principles remain accurate, and the books themselves make fascinating reading. (All three are also available in paperback editions.)

HALL, E. T. *The Silent Language.* New York: Doubleday, 1959.

———. *The Hidden Dimension.* New York: Doubleday, 1966.

———. *Beyond Culture.* New York: Doubleday, 1976.

9
Supplementary Techniques

Our specific focus up to this point has been on the language of direct interactions, face-to-face encounters with one or more people. (And perhaps ear-to-ear encounters, considering that a good deal of the material is applicable to telephone conversations.) Written language has been mentioned only in passing. This is reasonable and efficient because oral language in direct interaction is the largest area of your language environment for potential conflict. It deserves the lion's share of your efforts. By no means, however, is it the only sort of language you need to be able to deal with. In this chapter we will also take up some of the language situations, which—because they are beyond the boundaries of the ordinary business and home—may require verbal self-defense techniques for use in indirect language interactions.

STRESS
FROM VERBAL POLLUTION

Your body has a number of adjustable settings, much like thermostats, that were appropriate when human beings were obliged to spend their lives fleeing, hiding, and doing hand-to-hand combat with wolves and tigers. You are a bundle of thermostats and rheostats for such things as the speed of your heartbeat, the quantity of your sweat, the acidity of your stomach fluids, the tenseness of your muscles, the rate of processing of your wastes, and so on. All these settings are on automatic, in the sense that they are ordinarily beyond your conscious control. And if the stresses in your life that ready you for "flight or fight" were still saber-tooth tigers, all this apparatus would be useful. Unfortunately, that's not the way it is, and the persistent line taken by so many social scientists and health scientists—that the words of others can't hurt you, only *you* can hurt you—comes directly from this set of facts.

When your boss chews you out unjustly in front of your colleagues, your body reacts with the same sort of violent stepped-up activity that it would need for mortal combat or a ten-mile run. The immediate reaction is hard on you physically and emotionally. Worse yet is the strong tendency to keep going over and over the words that so upset you, in your head, thinking about what the boss said and what you said and what you *wish* you had said. You react to each mental replay of the encounter with the same bodily overload you gave to the real thing.

Gradually, particularly if you have encounters every day that bring on this kind of reaction—with your mechanic, your plumber, your spouse, your parents, your students, your doctor, your dentist, your friends—your body can no longer handle the constant state of high tuning. If you keep tightening the strings on a guitar, they are going to break; if you keep winding your *self* tighter and tighter, something will have to give. You pay for that

223

state of tension—with asthma, ulcers, skin disorders, heart attacks, depression, and a multitude of other miseries.

In the sense that it is your *reaction* to the encounters that triggers the state of bodily stress, it is true that you are hurting yourself. But that is relevant only if you believe that controlling the reactions of your body to outside stimuli is something everyone can do if they really put their backs into it. I don't believe that. Furthermore, if you have been convinced that you *would* have that control of yourself if you were a really well put together person, you are going to add a load of guilt, shame, and embarrassment to the load already imposed by the hurtful language behavior. It is cruel to dump all that on other human beings; they have trouble enough in this world without having to be ashamed that they are human.

The verbal self-defense techniques discussed in this book so far have all been ways to reduce the quantity of hurtful language coming at you, as well as the quantity of hurtful language you aim at other people. But other people, present-in-the-flesh other people, are only one source of the pollution in your language environment. Another major source is the language of what we will call "the Absent X," for convenience. This pollution enters your life when:

- you would be willing or eager to interact verbally with the Absent X, but Absent X won't see you or won't talk to you.
- whether the Absent X would see you or talk to you is irrelevant, because you're scared to try it.
- the Absent X is someone you will never know, never meet, and have no means to approach directly.
- the Absent X is a gigantic entity or abstraction—such as Violence in the Streets, or the Pentagon.
- the Absent X is media pollution—such as television commercials or pornographic or violent movies.

For an excellent example of an Absent X using language that creates a feeling of distress and guilt, take a look if you can at the campaign of magazine advertisements in the early 1980s by the Health Insurance Companies in America. (It appeared in almost every major national publication.)

These ads showed patients allegedly abusing the medical system. For example, one page would show an apparently healthy but overweight middle-aged woman in a hospital bed, surrounded by magazines, gobbling chocolates as she talked on the telephone, while an attractive young nurse arranging her vase of flowers gave her a look of knowing disgust. The slogan with the illustration said, "There should be a word for people who take up hospital space they don't really need."

The "word" was provided on the facing page, in much smaller type—it was *Outpatients*. It was followed by a rational presentation of the reasons why health-care costs mean that people should not go into the hospital if they can avoid it. But the damage was already done by the photograph and its big-print slogan. Just as saying "Now, don't think about elephants!" is a certain method to make you think about elephants, the "There should be a word . . ." line made the reader think of a variety of negative words to apply to the woman in the picture. *Outpatients* took the insurance companies off the hook legally, but all the unpleasant words were presupposed by the combined language and the photographed context. The ad was fiendishly clever.

In these situations, your inability to "get it off your chest" creates a stress situation that is extremely unhealthy. Precisely because you feel that you have no way to express your feelings, you are highly likely either to brood about the problem to an extent that interferes with the rest of your life or to bury what you feel so deeply that it lies there and festers.

Whether the Absent X involved is your sister-in-law, General Motors, the feminine hygiene industry, your senator, or any one of thousands of other possibilities doesn't matter. What matters is that you find a way to respond to this verbal-abuse-once-removed so that it doesn't harm you, so that you don't find yourself constantly fretting about what you would do if you only had the chance.

One way to deal with such situations is to take up one or more of the practices called *stress-management techniques.* Yoga, for example. Biofeedback. Transcendental Meditation. Autohypnosis (also called self-hypnosis). Visualization. Neurolinguistic programming. There is a brand for every taste and every metaphor.

I think these techniques are valuable, although many of the manuals, training institutes, and practitioners marketing them approach their task with a cavalier carelessness that gives me cold chills. Properly learned—which includes "properly taught"—they can free you from many of the effects of stress in your life. But they are not the universal remedies they are often made out to be.

They aren't suited for everyone, to begin with. Many people do not have the time or the money necessary to become proficient in these techniques. Many people are uneasy with them because those available in their personal situations are in direct or indirect conflict with their life metaphors. The person who is highly conservative and attempts to meet all situations with cold logic and common sense may have access only to systems that seem pervaded with mysticism and "occult nonsense." Others who would find *those* systems appealing may have access only to such completely nonmystical systems as Benson's "relaxation response." Many individuals find it as hard to muster the discipline necessary to use such techniques as they do to pursue a regular regime of traditional calisthenics or to practice a musical instrument daily.

You cannot relax and reduce stress using a method that makes you feel tense, uncomfortable, self-conscious, and out of place. Worse yet, if you are a highly competitive person, you may turn any technique for stress management into a kind of contest—"Hey, my trance is deeper than your trance!" And I am inclined to suspect that resorting to meditation because you had a disagreement with your electrician may be a waste of meditation time. It is just as much a verbal attack for someone to say to you "Well, if you *really* wanted to get over your allergies, you'd study *yo*ga" as it is to use any of the other attacks described in this book. I would like to suggest some other things that you can do, which involve language directly for the most part and which can be very efficient at "managing" stress. If these fail you, you always have the smorgasbord of other techniques to fall back on.

You have two choices when your language environment has become stressful because of the Absent X and you want to act on the situation rather than bury it. First, you can do something public—when the point is actually to respond, even if it must be from a distance. Second, you can do something private—when the point is not to respond but to get rid of the frustration caused by having no outlet for response available to you. We'll begin with the private options.

PRIVATE RESPONSES
TO THE ABSENT X

The Letter You Don't Mail

Sit down and write a letter to the Absent X, but don't mail it. This is so simple that it may impress you as simpleminded—but it should not be underestimated, because it has advantages that go beyond simplicity. You don't have to worry about spelling, grammar, your handwriting, or your typing skills. You don't have to worry about the possible consequences, such as anger or a lawsuit. You can say anything at all that you want to say, no matter how excessive, no matter how garbled. You can say the same thing over and over. You can underline the parts that you mean the most. If there's no word for exactly what you want to say, you can make one up—if you can't think of something that looks real to you, substitute *xxxx* wherever the unavailable word would go. You can let go and absolutely give the Absent X seventy-five different kinds of flaming hell, in complete safety.

When you hear your congressional representative explaining that he or she is entitled to completely free health care on demand and you yourself are going down for the third time in a sea of medical bills you can't pay, write down exactly what you would like to be able to say on that subject. When your doctor insists that your pain is all in your head and suggests that you take up tennis—and you couldn't afford to take up tennis even if you agreed with her—write your doctor a letter you don't mail. When your relatives insist that Congress is *not* entitled to free health care and it is your firm conviction that members of Congress must be protected from ordinary annoyances of daily life (like medical bills) so that they can devote their full attention to national problems—but you don't dare alienate your relatives because they loaned you the down payment on your house— write them a letter.

You'll find that these letters are a magnificent semantic garbage disposal system. When you do nothing but brood over the distress Absent X's words are causing you, the distress doesn't go away. You keep coming back to it the way you keep worrying at a sore tooth with your tongue until you make *it* sore, too. But if you put down on paper all those things you can't or won't say to Absent X directly, you'll discover that that's the end of it. The amount of energy that goes into the letter is just enough to let you dump the whole thing. You may still be just as outraged at your senator or your surgeon, but you won't be torturing yourself with a perpetual tape in your head that plays the same sorry scenario over and over again.

It doen't *matter* if somebody has convinced you that you "can't write." Nobody is going to see your letter but you. Go ahead and write it, and never mind.

The Diary or Journal

When you write a letter not to be mailed, you behave as if you were face to face with Absent X. You say, "Professor Blah, I think you are completely without principles, and so on." Another way to dump the distress is to put your response in a diary or journal, where you talk *about* Absent X rather than *to* Absent X. So far as I know, *diary* and *journal* are equivalent terms, but for many people *diary* has a bit of extra meaning associated with childhood or genteel ladies out of history—I will therefore use *journal* here.

My own favorite form for a journal is a loose-leaf notebook and plenty of the ruled paper you used in school. I can fill up a notebook like that, write the time period it covers on the outside, and put it on the shelf, and start a new one. A cardboard box on my closet floor and the blank backs of all the junk letters that come in my mail would do just as well except for a bit more difficulty if I wanted to read what I had written later. But it may be that for the journal to seem real to you it needs to have a more impressive form—if so, and if you can manage the expense, buy the kind with a leather cover, thick white pages, and a sturdy lock. The journal isn't going to help if you are not at ease with it; if casual scribbling doesn't do the job, get the finest volume you can afford to buy. Later, after you are more used to journal keeping, you can always switch to notebook paper or scrap.

In a journal, as in the unmailed letter, you need not be concerned with the mechanics of writing. Spelling, punctuation, and composition skills have nothing to do with the act of eliminating stress from your language environment. Forget about them. If you're writing a journal because you hope it will be published after your death, making you famous and your heirs wealthy, you have a different purpose entirely. That is not verbal self-defense, that's literature. Our purpose here is to let the journal serve as a way of responding to the irritation that is doing you harm.

People sometimes complain to me that journal keeping takes too much time. This usually means that they've learned a rule somewhere along the way, like the rule about always coloring inside the lines; and the rule says that if they have a journal they have to write in it every day and if they start a page they have to *fill* that page. They may have had a parent who checked their five-year diary from Woolworth's to be sure that no pages had been skipped. I can solve that problem by pointing out to them that they are grown up now and under no obligation to write any more often or for any longer than they need to.

If your problem with journal writing is not this phony rule, but really is that writing is so stressful for you that you perceive it as requiring large amounts of your time and energy, I suggest you choose some other private response instead.

Role Playing

For role playing you need only privacy. ("Only privacy," she says, and you with five children in a two-bedroom apartment. I know. But I'm doing the best I can here.) You may want to have a friend helping you, but that's not necessary; it depends on your own preferences.

If you are doing this with a friend, it works just like a play. Let your friend be your dentist, or the head of General Motors. You be yourself. And just let Absent X—in the person of your friend—have it, as long and as hard as is necessary to get rid of all the hurt. Your friend doesn't have to say anything, you see— an occasional "You have a lot of nerve" or "Really!" will do it. On the other hand, your friend may be interested in playing Head of General Motors to the maximum. If this gets out of hand—that is, if your friend starts causing you as much distress as the original Absent X—get a different friend. Or switch to Solitaire Role Playing, as follows:

Don't talk to a living human being, who can interfere with your garbage disposal by answering you back. Instead, use something inanimate as a substitute. One of those Styrofoam heads for wigs, with a properly anonymous unisex face drawn on with anything that marks, is inexpensive and works well for many people. A cardboard cutout of a person, with a label like "Head of Maytag" taped on for the occasion and changed as needed, is useful for others. I know one woman who swears by (and at) a very tall rubber plant that she always hated anyway; so far, it has shown no ill effects from its participation. It is not strictly inanimate but has the one essential characteristic—it does not answer back.

I do think you need some concrete *thing* to direct your words at. However foolish you may feel at first, talking to a Styrofoam head or an African violet, trying to talk to nothing at all is too much like setting up the repeating tape in your head, and too likely to turn into *exactly* that. It doesn't work because there is nothing outside you to help you get the verbal toxin outside as well.

There are cultures that pick out one tree at the edge of town and name it "The Cussing Tree" or something similar. People in those cultures routinely march out to the Cussing Tree and dump all their linguistic garbage under its branches. They can even kick it, if they feel the need to do that, and be quite sure that it will hurt their toe worse than it hurts the tree. This is a sensible practice, and if you are fortunate enough to have outdoor privacy available to you, you might consider picking out a sturdy tree on your back forty to play roles with you.

Role playing will let you say all the things you wanted to say and get rid of them, without any fear of consequences or any concern about the skill with which you speak. Don't hold anything back that will hang around to torment you later. If writing is a stressful activity for you but talking is easy, this technique is useful and effective.

The Fantasy Dialogue

Long ago, when a person wanted to get some information to the public, a common form of the information was the written dialogue. A scientist eager to tell the world of a new discovery would let Zeus, Mercury, Diana, and Athena do the talking and then publish the results. The dialogue was like a play without stage instructions. And dialogues have turned up again recently (in *Goedel, Escher, Bach*) with Achilles, a Crab, and a Tortoise as the speakers. I expect to see them become popular again now that Hofstadter has broken the ice with his book.

There is a lot of healthy satisfaction to be gained from tackling your Absent X in a fantasy dialogue. You set this up just as I've set up the interactions in this book.

FANTASY DIALOGUE

Payroll Clerk: Sorry, you can't have your check until Friday.

Me: You idiot! You hair-brained, incompetent, arrogant, conceited, callous, nit-picking ninny! You can't talk to me like that!

Payroll Clerk: Oh, I'm so sorry!

Me: I should hope to *Hannah* you're sorry! Now you go get my check! (*And so on*)

This would never work in real life—if it would, you'd have no need for verbal self-defense techniques. But the fantasy dialogue will let you say exactly what you want to say to Absent X without any worries. You can forget about matching realities and watching for presuppositions. You can forget about what other people present might think. You have all the power in your fantasy, and you should let go and enjoy it. You can say all the things that in real life would put you in jail or a doctor's office and still come out of it with whatever you wanted—including an apology from Absent X, which you can make as abject as you care to.

Again, I don't care at all if you "can't write." (I hear this so often that I am convinced it worries many people more than they realize.) This is not being written for the CBS television network or your English teacher. It takes a certain investment of time and energy to get it all out of your system, which is what makes the dumping effect permanent. It does *not* take a professional writing style or a fancy vocabulary. I recommend it, because it will allow you to manage half a dozen Absent Xs at a time if that's appropriate.

The Collage

Some people are not comfortable with words, either spoken or written, as a mechanism for relaxation. The American culture is constructed to guarantee such people misery, because it either neglects their needs entirely or does its best to stamp them out. People who have a strong preference for touch as their sensory mode often fit into this category.

Ideally, such people would just turn their hands to painting, sculpture, the dance, or something of that kind. If you can do that, fine. Draw a picture of the head of General Motors being fired. Make a statue of the film star who does the tackiest commercial that pollutes your living room, and smash it with a hammer. Turn your nausea at the latest outrageous remark from your economics professor into a piano concerto. Get out in the middle of the floor and *dance* your precise opinion of the lady at the hospital who wouldn't let you in until you filled out the forms, even when your labor contractions were only two minutes apart. I approve of all these things.

But what if you can't do any of them well enough to serve as a garbage disposal system for language pollution? This is not exactly like the conviction that you "can't write." People who tell you you can't write ordinarily mean that the way you write doesn't meet the set of arbitrary standards used to determine who gets a B or better in English classes. They mean that your writing doesn't remind them of the published work of professional writers, scholars, and college professors.

If you speak your language, know its alphabet, and do not have severe physical handicaps, you can carry out the act of writing well enough for your private use, no matter how crude the product might appear to an editor. You've been using your language all your life long, and you are completely in control of its grammar and of the mechanisms for putting it on paper.

This is distinctly not true of what are called "the arts." For every "natural" like Grandma Moses, there are thousands of people who cannot draw or paint even a recognizable stick figure. The tools and materials of most arts and crafts are expensive, and it's not likely that you'd know what to do with molten bronze even if it were free. You don't observe others all around you composing at the piano or tackling blocks of marble with hammer and chisel. Dance requires years of intensive training and practice. The "folk" arts, such as quilting and basketmaking, are as foreign to the average American as the "fine" arts. This entire channel of expression is unavailable to all but a privileged few.

There is one "art" technique, however, that you can approach in the same way that you approach writing the unmailed letter: the collage. If words feel entirely useless to you for expressing your distress, you can make collages with almost no investment for materials and with no training beyond the cut-and-glue skills you mastered as a child.

When I am sick of words, or when I feel that words aren't available for what I want to say, I make collages. I keep old pieces of cardboard, old boxes, old wrapping paper. I especially keep the round pieces of cardboard that come with frozen pizzas and other exotic shapes. And I keep a box full of things cut out from the magazines, newspapers, and greeting cards, as well as the junk catalogs, brochures, and advertisements that fill my mailbox. I keep feathers, scraps of cloth, those small samples of materials that come to me unordered to convince me I need to buy things—anything that is clean and has an interesting feel to its surface. And when I want to make a collage, the only thing I need in addition is a jar of rubber cement, so that when I glue things down they won't wrinkle and pucker and streak—the rubber cement is my total investment of money.

I can't draw or sculpt a monster attacking a city and leaping from building to building above innocent victims, if that happens to be how I feel about the local chemical plant or the political party that's not the party of my choice. But I can certainly cut out the pieces and glue them on cardboard to say precisely that; advertisements are full of suitable monsters. And it makes no difference to me that nobody would want to hang the result on the wall. The point is that this lets me get a lot of unpleasant emotion out of my system at a time when for one reason or another words aren't adequate for my needs.

I have never met anyone who didn't have materials readily available for collages, because the best material is usually what everyone else is busy throwing away. And if you can get your doctor to give you old medical magazines, or promotional literature from drug companies, grab it. Some of the most beautiful and spectacular photography to be found anywhere (and some of the best representations of Absent Xs) are in advertisements for drugs.

The Sonnet

This one may surprise you. If you've always heard of sonnets only in school, you will associate them with Shakespeare, Milton, and similar luminaries. You will be inclined to tell me that you are as unable to write a sonnet as you are to sculpt a Greek goddess, and for the same reasons.

I understand where you got that idea, but I'd like to disabuse you of it. The materials necessary for the sonnet are a pencil and any piece of paper at all, including the backs of junk mail already mentioned. Use the backs of bills. The craft of the sonnet is merely the arrangement of words—plain ordinary words, the vocabulary of your native language—in a simple pattern. Your sonnet is a private act and doesn't have to please anyone but yourself. I know few methods for discharging intense hurt or anger that are as wholly satisfying and permanent as writing a sonnet—it's like sculpture made with words, you see.

At one time in my life, I went to the Denver Zoo. It had been remodeled as one of the new zoos where animals had been released from the old-fashioned cages and were able to roam free in open areas, with moats and other natural barriers instead of bars. But the zoo had an old polar bear that had been there long before the remodeling took place, and he had gone completely blind while still caged. This meant that although he now was not shut up behind bars, he didn't know that; and he spent his days pacing back and forth in the same tiny space his cage had occupied. He had no idea that he was now more free.

I found this heartbreaking. It was an Absent X of considerable size and caused me much pain. But there was no one to complain to, because the zoo officials were on my side in the matter. They were just as upset as I was, and so far as any of us knew this was one of those situations where nothing can be done and the proper course is to "put it out of your mind." As a way of doing that, a way of freeing myself from the hurtful repeating tape in my head that was wasting my time and energy without helping the bear in any way, I wrote the following sonnet:

DENVERBEAR

This brave new zoo discarded bars
and spread broad space and stone about,
with dens and caves and demi-lakes
and moats to keep the people out.
They have a bear there, large and white,
that paces on a great grey rock,
ten feet forward, ten feet back,
within a cage without a lock.
There was a time when he was caged,
there was a time when he could see,
but then his eyes went bad on him
before they came and set him free.
Blind to the rock he moves upon,
he does not know the bars are gone.

Now I think it's important for you to notice the vocabulary of that sonnet, because it's the ordinary vocabulary of daily life. The longest word in it is *discarded,* and that's no hifalutin item. The only "arty" word I used was *demi-lakes,* and I regret that now. The problem was that "little lakes" sounded wrong and I couldn't think of a better way to describe the miniature bodies of water that were provided for these animals. And it doesn't *matter,* you see. When I had written the sonnet, which took me a couple of hours spread over two or three days, I still felt sorrowful about that blind old bear—but I no longer tormented myself about it. I was able to give it up.

The sonnet is no harder to do than a crossword puzzle and just as much fun. It is a way of writing down one experience, one big thought, and making something out of that material. It uses the natural rhythms of the English language. It is just long enough to let you move around a bit, and just short enough to keep you from spoiling the whole thing by going on too long. It does *not* have to rhyme—I like to rhyme my sonnets for the same reason I like to work puzzles, because it's more sport that way. But it's not required.

A sonnet is fourteen lines long, in any arrangement you like. The one about the bear is three groups of four followed by a pair of lines that wind it up. The rhythm of the lines is easy to master—there are fancy variations, but the basic form is a pattern that lets you hear or feel four or five (rarely, six) beats to the line, for example:

| *They HAVE* | *a BEAR* | *there, LARGE* | *and WHITE* | (four beats) |
| *and MOATS* | *to KEEP* | *the PEOP-* | *le OUT* | (four beats) |

Sometimes the first two syllables in the line are turned around, with the strong beat coming before the weak one, like this.

| *BLIND to* | *the ROCK* | *he MOVES* | *upON* | (four beats) |

If I'd wanted five strong beats in my line instead of four, I could have done this:

| *This BRAVE* | *new ZOO* | *dis-CARD-* | *ed BARS* | *and GATES* |

And to make it six, the maximum allowed, I would have done this:

This BRAVE | *new ZOO* | *disCARD-* | *ed BARS* | *and GATES* | *and WALLS*

It does no good to try to make lines contain more than six strong beats in English. Someone hearing a seven-beat line automatically divides it into a three-beat line and a four-beat line. Hearing an eight-beat line, you make it into two four-beat lines, and so on. Six strong beats is as far as your ear is willing to go before concluding, "That's a finished chunk of poem and now something new is coming."

Unless writing itself is stressful for you, you can write sonnets. Usually what will get you started is a single line—perhaps a sentence that you really wish you could say to Absent X, or the words that distressed you in the first place. That line may end up anywhere in the fourteen final ones. Here are a few sonnet lines that have come my way lately; I've made a note of them because they bother me:

> *"The senators lunch on crab meat, subsidized ..."*
> *"We shall not sacrifice the safety net ..."*
> *"The welfare cheat is a national disgrace ..."*
> *"When unemployment goes to 10 percent ..."*

Technical rules explain why sometimes two English syllables can count as only one beat, as in *senators* or *is a*. But you don't need the rules to write the lines. Your own ear, because you speak English, will tell you when you can wrap up two syllables as one in that way. You would never read the third line above like this:

The WEL- | *fare CHEAT* | *is A* | *naTION-* | *al DIS-*
                                                    (with *grace* left over)

You can depend on your ear to carry you through. When you write a line, say it out loud and ask yourself: If I were holding a mug of beer, or root beer, and swinging it in time, when and where would I *swing*? And you can rely on that. Furthermore, it is not important if your lines have mistakes in rhythm, any more than if they have mistakes in spelling. You are writing for your health, not the *New Yorker* magazine.

The sonnet is just enough of a pattern to keep you from flailing about helplessly and wasting all your energy. It's the difference between swimming in the ocean and swimming in a pool or pond; the Atlantic is best left to experts, but we can all manage in the smaller waters where we always know which way we're going and there's an edge nearby to head for. Leave the big and seemingly formless poetry to the professionals if you don't feel comfortable with it. But we can all write the sonnet. And after you write one, you'll feel a lot better.

PUBLIC RESPONSES
TO THE ABSENT X

If you don't want to confine your activities to a private response, your situation changes. You have no way to interact directly with your Absent X, but you feel that a public response of some kind is necessary. Then what?

The rules are different, of course. If you want your response to be read or listened to, you're going to have to be concerned about such things as vocabulary, punctuation, and neatness. You'll have restrictions of time and space. You will have to consider possible consequences—from a family member's hurt feelings to the lawsuit for libel or slander. If, nevertheless, you choose to make a public response, so be it; as in any other action, it helps if you know a little bit about what you're doing.

Five public response situations are likely to be available to you: the informal speech, the formal speech, the panel or debate, the letter (mailed this time), and the letter to the editor. You can take courses in most of these skills from experts, and you can read whole books about how to do each of them. I won't try here to compete with either courses or complete books, but I will offer you a brief outline that will let you decide if you want to investigate further.

The Informal Speech

Two things make a speech a speech, rather than just a violation of the rules about turn-taking in conversation. First, those rules are suspended by agreement of both speaker and listener or listeners for the duration of the speech—you, the speechmaker, have the floor all to yourself, and if anyone interrupts it is called "heckling." Second, a speech is intended specifically to *persuade* other people—that you are right, that they are wrong, that there is something they ought to do or not do, that they should trust you. Formal speeches will usually be longer, and perhaps more elaborate, than informal ones; but both types will have these two characteristics.

If you are going to make a speech, whether it is within your home, at your workplace, or in a public forum, you have a certain responsibility. Well-mannered people who are present at the time are going to feel that they have to listen to you—you are therefore obligated to say something worth hearing. Never mind whether you are being paid money for your speech or not; you are *always* being paid in your listeners' time. They could be doing something else instead of listening to you. You owe them.

You know that the first rule of persuasion is that you must enter the reality of your listeners at some point (and detailed instructions for doing so are the subject of Chapter Seven of this book). You know that logic and rational argument are little, if any, use to you. What else should you know?

First, choose either Leveler or Computer as your Satir Mode. Leveling is always best if it is suitable for the occasion and if you feel safe doing that. If not, Computer is your only possible alternative. Nobody is going to sit still and listen to Blaming, Placating, or Distracting from a speaker. Even if you have sufficient power to force them to do so, you are still wasting your time, because they will neither believe you nor agree with you under such circumstances.[1]

If you know the preferred sensory mode or modes of those you are speaking to, match them when you can. This will go a long way toward keeping your audience comfortable and attentive. If you don't know, or if you have a number of people with different preferences, you have two choices. Use sight vocabulary, visual predicates because they are the most common preference, or avoid sensory vocabulary as much as possible, as a way of remaining neutral. Trying to move from one mode to another to share your speech equally among the modes is very difficult and will sound artificial, especially in the informal speech that has not been written down to be read aloud and has not been memorized for delivery. This doesn't mean that you should worry about the occasional change of modes, of course—everyone shifts from one mode to another at times, and often the most natural phrase will require you to make such a shift. But you can make a deliberate effort to control the majority of your vocabulary choices in this way.

Be extremely careful that your speech doesn't contain any of the verbal attacks discussed in Chapters Five and Six. Keep dangerous words, such as *only, even, each, all, really, nobody, never, nothing, always,* out of your sentences as much as possible. Make sure the pattern of *even* plus a modal doesn't turn up in what you say. And pay attention to the way you stress your words—remember that unusual stresses and heavier than ordinary stresses always signal presuppositions. Be sure you don't drag in meanings you hadn't intended to include.

Framing your speech as a metaphor is your best strategy, if you can find a reasonably good one for your purposes. Even in the very brief at-home attempt to persuade the rest of your family that a vacation in the Ozarks would be better than a vacation in the Bahamas, the use of a metaphor will help your

---

[1]It's true that Werner Erhard's *est* trainers accomplish this, in spite of locking people up and subjecting them to extreme verbal violence. But they need *many hours* to bring it off.

cause. Informally, you say "This situation reminds me of . . ." and then you put your metaphor there.

Watch your body language. If you're angry and hostile but your message isn't supposed to show that, know that your body is going to give you away. You're much better off admitting what cannot be hidden. Say "I know that I'm angry, and upset, and hostile about this, and I'm sorry. If I could keep from feeling that way, I would—but I can't. I'll try to talk about it reasonably all the same." Then the inevitable anger communicated by your body language in combination with your unangry words won't make you appear a liar. If you feel that you really don't dare be honest, try to assume a Computer stance that is at least aimed at neutrality; your best choice is probably hands clasped—loosely, now!—behind your back or in your lap. That will keep quite a lot of your body out of trouble. If your hands are out of sight to your listeners, you can touch your thumbs to the tip of one of your fingers and maintain that; it requires just enough of your attention to be useful as a way of keeping you from slipping into hostile body language without realizing it.

And keep it brief. An informal speech is made by reason of the tolerance of your listeners. They can withdraw that tolerance at any time. Three minutes is long enough; five minutes is the *absolute upper limit*. (If that horrifies you, you can be certain that you have acquired the habit of talking too long.) Anything longer than five minutes is wasted time, because your audience will resent you. Pay attention to the body language of your listeners—if they fidget, yawn, or stare at the ceiling, that's *your* problem and should serve as a good indication that you are not as fascinating to listen to as you may have thought you were. In that situation, nothing is less useful than "Pay attention! I'm *talking* to you!" They know that already. But they are not under any obligation to pay attention to you. *You* are the one attempting to persuade, and you are obligated to be sufficiently interesting that they'll want to hear what you have to say.

Within the brief time you have available, try to structure your words so that they will be easy to remember and attend to.

That means taking advantage of the ancient verbal strategy called *parallelism*.

English has many different ways to frame the same or approximately the same meaning. I'm going to discuss just one set of patterns available to you as a way of showing you what I mean about parallelism: the *embedded* sentence serving as the subject of a larger sentence. Look at the following set of examples:

1a. "That you are so extravagant upsets me."
 b. "For you to be so extravagant upsets me."
 c. "Your being so extravagant upsets me."
 d. "Your extravagance upsets me."

(The first three patterns will always be possible; the fourth will sometimes not be, because there may not be a special word like *extravagance* for what you want to say.)

All the sentences in Example 1 contain a form of the statement "You are so extravagant." And that statement is serving as the subject of the predicate "upsets me." Now, what if you have several objections to the behavior of the Absent X, at which your response is aimed? Perhaps you dislike the way that they leave their belongings strung all over your house, the way that they are so untidy. Perhaps you object to the fact that they don't remember to turn off the water faucets, they throw matches and cigarettes that aren't always out into wastebaskets and onto grass, and they neglect to lock the door when they leave. You object to the way they are so careless. That makes three objections. If you keep the predicate "upsets me" throughout, there are a number of ways to put this all together, including:

A. "That you are so extravagant upsets me. For you to be so untidy upsets me. Your being so careless upsets me, too."
B. "That you are so extravagant upsets me. That you are so untidy upsets me. That you are so careless upsets me, too."
C. For you to be so extravagant upsets me. For you to be so untidy upsets me. For you to be so careless upsets me, too."

243

D. "Your being so extravagant upsets me. Your being so untidy upsets me. Your being so careless upsets me, too."

E. "Your extravagance upsets me. Your untidiness upsets me. Your carelessness upsets me, too."

You could choose among these different patterns for a variety of reasons. For example, the last one, with its possessives and its nominalizations by special word endings, carries the most powerful presupposition that your claims are *true*. But whatever your choice, the weakest will be the first example—because it doesn't have parallelism. The use of parallel structure makes it possible for you to set up a pattern, in both word order and rhythm, that helps your listeners synchronize with your speech—thus, they can attend more easily. It helps them remember what you say because the structure itself is predictable, and they can devote more of their attention to what the structure contains. Parallelism is always worth the trouble.

Assume that the Absent X is made up of one interfering friend and a big chunk of media pollution. Your family is living on a modest income and has always done so. But the local television station has been pushing a heavy advertising campaign for a travel package to the Bahamas for almost a month. And the spouse of a successful lawyer from a family that has been wealthy for several generations has made an obvious point of urging *your* family to take advantage of this opportunity to see the islands. You don't want to accuse your friend of deliberately trying to make trouble and you know there's no point in explaining to your local TV bosses that most of their viewers can't afford the Bahamas tour and are being unfairly tempted by the commercials—if that weren't true, they wouldn't be pushing it so hard. How do you proceed?

INFORMAL SPEECH 1

I know that you want us to take our vacation in the Bahamas this year—and I understand that. The Bahamas are beautiful, and

244

fun, and a new experience. But for us, going on vacation to the Bahamas is like going to the Yacht Club in a rowboat. We don't have enough money to pay for the trip. We wouldn't be comfortable in those fancy hotels and expensive restaurants. And we wouldn't know how to enjoy ourselves after we got there. We get exactly one vacation a year, remember—are you sure we want to spend it being the only little old rowboat in a whole row of luxury yachts?

This is just long enough. It mentions a few plain truths, but it's completely nonthreatening and unaggressive. It avoids sensory predicates, because the various family members have different preferences. It uses parallelism to set out three characteristics of the Bahamas as a vacation site and at the same time anticipates what the family members would say if they were speaking. It acknowledges that they are *right* about those three characteristics. It uses a metaphor—the little rowboat in a slip at the yacht club surrounded by fancy yachts—and it sets that metaphor up using parallel structure. All three sentences offering objections to the Bahamas vacation are formed according to the same pattern. Finally, the last sentence begins with a fact about which there is no question—only one vacation a year—and ends with a question that brings the metaphor in again.

Compare this with the following losing effort.

INFORMAL SPEECH 2

I know, *I* know! All of you want to go to the Bahamas for our vacation! That figures. You don't even *care* if we spend the rest of the year eating macaroni because we blew our whole budget traipsing off to some island ... and why *should* you? *You* don't have to earn the money to pay for it, do you? You never con*sid*er what it might be like to have to come up with the cash for your crazy ideas. You just say you want this, you want that—and *I'm* supposed to find the money somewhere! Well, let me tell *you*, it's not going to work this time. *This* time, you're going to do something sensible or you're not going to do anything at all. Has *everybody got that straight?*

Well? Has everybody got that straight? If that's your idea of effective persuasion, I suggest you take up some other line of work. It will only make your family hate you, even if you are absolutely 100 percent correct in every word you say. They will perceive you as stingy, mean, abusive, irrational, and horrible in every way, not to mention being a constant whiner. If that really is how you'd like to be perceived by your family, then the speech just quoted is a guaranteed way to achieve your goal.

In both cases you're going to overrule your family and oblige them to do what you want instead of what they want. But the first speech will allow them to give in without appearing to be the terrified slaves of a brutal bully. And your metaphor about the way the rowboat looks all alone among the yachts will get across the unpleasant facts without forcing you to lay out each and every detail about not being able to afford the vacation. They may complain. They may have a few words to say about wishing things were different. But they can give in without losing any serious amount of face. And you have whipped both your interfering wealthy friend and the indifferent television station.

The Formal Speeech

The formal speech will include everything that I said above under the informal speech heading, for starters. The formal speech does *not* differ from the informal simply because it is longer. People are so deathly tired of listening to long speeches, even *good* long speeches! If you can provide a good five-minute speech, it will be ten times as effective as an equally good thirty-minute one. (And you'll find yourself in demand as a public speaker. The person who can provide good short speeches is a rare commodity, and much treasured.)

Don't—please don't—try to do a formal speech off the top of your head. If you are a superb extemporaneous speaker, fine—you know that already, and you go right ahead. But I have been making speeches and listening to speeches a good percentage of my time for the past thirty years, and I think you should be aware that in all that time I have heard *only one* good speaker who could just stand up and wing it. And even that person was much more effective when the speech had been prepared in advance.

There's an unfortunate tendency in American society to set up a sort of rule for ourselves that prices speeches in the way surgery or auto mechanics are priced. The professor who would never think of talking off the top of her head if she were getting a $500 lecture fee goes off to the Kiwanis Club's monthly meeting as a featured—and unpaid—speaker, with nothing to go by but a couple of notes scribbled on a three-by-five card. The lawyer who would never go into court without blocking out half a dozen legal pads of careful strategy thinks nothing of standing up to present his neighborhood's objections to videogame machines in the grocery store without a note to his name. This is a serious mistake and is precisely why the private response is often preferable.

When people listen to you talk on a subject of your choice they are giving up their time to you. Time, in American culture, *is* money. They are entitled to hear the best you've got to give them in return. Furthermore, a good speech is never wasted. When you write your speeches and keep them, you can use them again, to respond to the same Absent X or to other ones of the same kind. Gradually you will build up a repertoire of talks that can, with only a little tailoring to the occasion, be used any time you are invited to speak. Each time you present such a talk you are being given a chance to improve it, to try it out on different people, and to fine-tune it as you watch their response. This is opportunity, and your chances to practice and hone your speeches are gifts given to you. It's foolish to waste them by presenting whatever unorganized drivel happens to be running through your head on the spur of the moment.

At a normal rate of oral speech, a typed double-spaced page or its equivalent in your own handwriting takes about three minutes to deliver. (If you're not sure how long it takes you to read one of your handwritten pages aloud, write one, read it aloud, and time it. You need to know.) If I'm asked to do a ten-minute talk, I know that means three pages—three and a half at the very most—and I can plan for that.

Write your speech down, keeping it to the length that you know will fill the time you have. If you can, say it aloud into a tape recorder. The cheapest recorder and tape are more than adequate, because you're not after high fidelity. And then, listen to that tape carefully.

How do you sound? Are there things you should change? Do you bore yourself? Are there sequences that looked good on the page but sound awkward or are difficult to say without stumbling?

It's helpful to have somebody else listen to your speech and give you a second opinion. But don't choose someone who (a) will listen to the speech when you finally give it in public, or (b) thinks every word that falls from your lips is priceless. You need someone who has a little objectivity and who won't pay for his or her help by having to listen to you after already having heard you do it once.

If the speech is too long, *cut it*. Under no circumstances can you fix that problem by talking a bit faster. Cut the speech until it is the length it's supposed to be. And don't practice it to death—that's as bad as not practicing it at all. If you've done the speech fifty times in the week before you give it, you'll be tired of it, and your tiredness will show in your delivery. If you're not tired of it by then, that's a danger signal—you are probably too fond of the sound of your own voice to be a good judge of what you say. Do it as many times as it takes to get it right, then do it two or three times for polish if you feel uneasy, and then quit.

Except in the most trivial of public speeches, there is one device that is worth everything it costs. You want to be listened to. You want to be remembered. You want people to be comfortable as they attend to your speech. You want the speech to stand as a *memorable* response to your Absent X, not as a service and a gift. One of the most useful things you can do to ensure these goals is provide your audience with a *handout*.

To prepare a handout, type or print clearly on a page the major points you want to make, with any supporting statistics or quotations you have room for, and then have enough copies of that page made to go around. At the bottom of the page you'll want your name and the date, and—if you have no objections— an address or telephone number where you can be reached for more information. Ideally, get a friend or helper to pass out the materials, and leave extra copies at the back of the room for people who come in late; if you can't manage this, put all copies near the entrance door and announce a few minutes before you start talking that they are there. People will ordinarily take care of the distribution problem without your having to call for volunteers.

This is particularly important if you're going to be using technical terms unfamiliar to your audience or if you're going to be using example sentences, charts, or graphs. You probably have a blackboard or other writing surface at hand when you give a formal speech, but putting material on that board takes time from your delivery. The lights ordinarily make it hard for anyone to read what you've written there in advance, and anything you write as you go along forces people to watch you writing, which isn't interesting. If you don't have a prepared handout *or* a blackboard, people must rely entirely on their memories, and they probably won't remember what you say. Or they will have to take notes—which will mean that they miss a lot of what you say and misunderstand what they don't miss.

By all means, provide a handout, to organize your speech for the listeners and give them a way to see how the talk will be paced. If I had been doing this chapter as a talk, I would have typed up a handout like the following:

RESPONSES FOR
INDIRECT COMMUNICATION

I. In private
  A. The letter you don't mail
  B. The diary or journal
  C. Role playing
  D. The fantasy dialogue
  E. The collage
  F. The sonnet

II. In public
  A. The informal speech
  B. The formal speech
  C. The panel or debate
  D. The letter you do mail
  E. The letter to the editor

Dr. Suzette Haden Elgin
Route 4, Box 192-E
Huntsville, AR 72740

With that piece of paper in hand, a person who came in late for my speech could find out how much had been missed and orient himself or herself to what I was then saying. A person who wasn't sure that he or she could stay for the entire talk could decide at what point it would be appropriate to leave. And everyone would have a verbal security blanket to help them remember and understand. This is not condescension, it is courtesy.

When you give a formal speech, whatever the situation, watch your audience carefully. Scan the rows of people from front to back and from one side of the room to the other. Watch their body language, because by the time someone has begun talking to his or her neighbor instead of listening to you, it's *too late*. The danger signal with American Anglo audiences is a slight forward hunching of both shoulders—this happens at least thirty seconds before the person doing it becomes sufficiently aware of boredom to start talking, reading, doodling, or walking out on you.[2] When you see that shoulder movement, *then* you know it's time to do something. At that moment you must bring in a colorful example, an anecdote, a change of subject, anything to get back the attention of the audience. If you never let one of these signals pass without reacting, your listeners won't become aware that you almost lost them. And if all else fails, if I can think of nothing whatever to say as a way of restoring attention, I simply Level. I say, "You're restless out there—am I boring you, am I unclear, or are you just double parked?" This, in a pinch, will serve.

Most of us don't often make formal speeches or even informal *public* speeches. This may lead us to try making a speech as fancy as possible, because of an assumption that fancy speeches are expected of us and are necessary to impress audiences. I think this is a mistake in almost all cases. Anything you understand well enough to justify your talking about it publicly can be said simply and in ordinary language. The public speaker who talks over the heads of the audience, like the supercilious speaker who obviously talks *down* to the audience, is inexcusable. Don't join that club. If you can't avoid using a technical term or two—for example, I almost never can avoid using the word *presupposition*—be sure that you have a clear definition ready for each one, made up of ordinary English words. And put that definition on your handout so that people don't have to struggle to remember it.

[2]I wish I could give you a corresponding signal for other cultural groups, but I can't. Giving a formal speech before people from another culture can be a crushing experience. For one thing, you have trouble interpreting their facial expressions, so it's hard for you to tell if they are interested, annoyed, or something else entirely. For another, it may not be a rule of their culture that a speaker has to have the undivided silent attention of the audience. They may therefore talk to one another quite freely while you are giving your speech. This can be more than somewhat alarming for an Anglo American speaker who hasn't been warned. If you're scheduled to talk to another cultural group or to an audience of mixed cultural groups, try to discuss this in advance with someone who *does* know what you should expect to run into—you'll save yourself a lot of grief that way. And if you must go ahead with no information, be prepared for surprises and mysterious feedback.

Finally, the best way I know to get a feeling for the formal speech is to copy half a dozen really fine ones out by hand. (I use the phrase "get a feeling for" deliberately here; it is exactly what I mean.) Long ago people learned to write English prose by copying out a classic novel or two from start to finish in longhand—the method is not used today, but it's lost none of its effectiveness.

The point of copying good prose, or good speeches, by hand is that when you do that you expose all your senses to a display of useful data from which you can learn. Your body, your perceptual systems, your cognitive systems, and your emotional systems, all work *within* that set of data, and you *learn* from that. Go to your public library and check out a book of classic speeches by experts or make copies of a few. I recommend Abraham Lincoln, Franklin D. Roosevelt, Winston Churchill, John F. Kennedy, and Martin Luther King as models. Pick out a few of their shorter speeches, and write them out by hand, word for word. It will take time, certainly, but it will repay you many times over.[3] You will learn more that way than you could ever learn simply from a book on speechwriting. You are getting reinforcement for the patterns of good speechmaking through your eyes as you read, through your touch as you write, and in a whole-body mode for which I know no separate word; you may also be getting ear reinforcement, if you are inclined to "hear" what you are reading in your head. And supplementing the training for your ears is the easiest of all—because your library will have tapes and records of speeches that you can listen to and try to read along with, matching your phrasing and intonation to the speech you are using as an information source.

The Panel or Debate

Sometimes you don't want to be alone in your response to Absent X. Let's say that your community has been chosen as the

---

[3]The reason you can't type the speeches instead of copying them in longhand is that if you type at all well you have no awareness of what you are typing. Typing amounts

location for a big new waste water treatment plant, and you feel that your neighbors would dislike the idea as much as you do if they only knew as much about it as you do. You could give a speech on the subject, of course. But it might be more effective, and build more support for your views, if you set up a panel discussion or an informal debate. (*Formal* debates are as rigidly structured as ballets and appeal only to specialists—I am using the term here in a much looser sense.)

You can usually get one of your local clubs, schools, or churches to let you use a room for a purpose like this. And then you choose your participants. If you are holding a debate you need only yourself—the person who will argue against the treatment plant—and someone else who is strongly *for* it, to argue against you. The two of you take turns presenting your views, with a plan roughly like the following:

- Your opponent gives a ten-minute speech for the plant.
- You give a ten-minute speech against it.
- Your opponent gives a five-minute reply (called a *rebuttal*) to what you said.
- You give a five-minute reply to what your opponent said.
- The debate is thrown open for questions from the audience, with both you and your opponent allowed to give a one- or two-minute response to each question. The person asking the question from the audience will specify who is to answer first.

A panel is made up of three or more persons, preferably each responsible for a separate part of the discussion. In the water treatment plant situation, you would need someone who could present the history of the issue, someone else to present the case for the plant, yourself to present the case against it, and an expert or two on the possible effects—perhaps one person to discuss effects on the environment and another to discuss effects

---

to data going in your eyes and right out your fingers, without being processed as language on the way at all. Longhand isn't like that, not any more.

on the economy. (A panel of more than about five is too cumbersome to be effective.)

The structure for a panel presentation is to let each member talk for at maximum ten minutes, with the individual responsible for the history going first in the sequence to provide a background. After everyone finishes the initial presentation, each panel member is given a very brief time—at most two minutes—to respond to anything in the other presentations that seems to require comment. Then the floor is opened to the audience for questions much as it would be in a debate, except that for panels it is not required that every panel member be allowed to answer every question from the floor.

Both panels and debates have to include a moderator (who can be one of the panel participants if necessary). And the moderator absolutely must be a person with guts and determination. The moderator's function is not to "orchestrate" the event. The moderator's function—let us be honest—is to *see to it that the time limits are observed*. To let people go over allotted time is not "being polite." It cheats the other speakers of their time, and it cheats the audience of the opportunity to hear the other speakers. Anyone who can't muster up sufficient "bad manners" to cut off speakers who run over their time limit is not suitable for the role of moderator—get somebody else. Then give the moderator four slips of cardboard with the following messages in large letters: YOU HAVE FIVE MINUTES; YOU HAVE TWO MINUTES; YOU HAVE THIRTY SECONDS; YOUR TIME IS UP. Be sure the moderator also has a reliable watch. This is how it's done, and there's nothing rude about it—your audience has a right to an organized and fair presentation, and unless they're willing to listen for a weekend you have no other way to grant them that right.

As for the content of a panelist or debater's presentation— use exactly the same rules that you use for speeches, adapting them to the situation. (Roughly, a debate is more like a formal speech and a panel is more like an informal speech.) If you're going to respond to the remarks of other people you can't work that out entirely in advance as you can your own remarks. But you should be able to anticipate the most probable arguments that will be raised against you, and you should have already written out and rehearsed your answers to those probable arguments.

When someone comes up with an argument that you were totally unprepared for and you don't feel that you were able to put an effective response together as you listened to it, it's time to choose one of two strategies. If you can do it comfortably, go to Leveler mode. Say, "I wasn't expecting that argument and I haven't had time to prepare an adequate response to it—I'm sorry about that. But I'm going to tell you how I *feel* about it, and ask you to bear with me if I'm not at my best." If you can't do that convincingly, go to Computer Mode and say as little as possible, as neutrally as possible.

I once had to go before a committee to request approval for a new course to be taught at my university. I'd expected to hear that the course was too easy for undergraduates, and I'd prepared a set of things to say that would convince the committee members that the course was in fact difficult enough to justify its number. The one thing I had never anticipated was what actually did happen—the committee's complaint was that the course was too *hard* for an undergraduate class. This was such a stunning surprise to me that I could think of nothing sensible to say, and it taught me a lesson. I have always, since that dreadful afternoon, prepared myself to respond to both of the possible extreme positions in such a situation, just in case. And that afternoon I did my stalling in Computer Mode.

Don't ever let being caught off guard trick you into Blaming or Placating. As for the panic of Distracting, if that's what you find yourself doing, pretend that you have been taken suddenly by appendicitis. It's safer.

People who appear in panels and debates need to have with them a page of solid facts—dates, names, places, and figures. You don't need to memorize the information, but you need to be very familiar with what you have on that page and where each particular item is located—and don't be afraid to look carefully at the page before you answer the question. You're not required to have all the answers on the tip of your tongue and may be resented by the audience if you do. But it makes a bad impression and shakes the confidence of your listeners if you have to search through a stack of materials hunting for the answer to their question. In fact, if you're not sure you can find what they want to know quickly, you're probably better off saying frankly, "I'm sorry, I don't know the answer to your question. I wish I did." Being human is something an audience forgives easily; being arrogant is not. And when you keep a roomful of people waiting while you scrabble about for information that they feel you should have ready to hand, you are being arrogant.

I am sometimes asked how to choose between speeches and panels or debates. I think it's safe to say that it depends on the skill of the participants. A skillful and experienced speaker who can hold an audience is always a good choice. But even a mediocre panel is better than a boring or hostile speaker, or one who can't be bothered to prepare for the talk. When a panel begins to flounder the moderator can always bring things quickly to an end, but a genuinely bad speaker can only be endured. If you're in doubt, choose the panel or debate and get the best speakers for it that you can.

The Letter, To Be Mailed This Time

I strongly recommend that your first step, if you decide to write to Absent X, be writing a letter that you *don't* intend to mail. Put everything in that you need to get off your chest, and get rid of it. Only after you've done this and have lowered your emotional tension about the situation should you set about writing a letter that you *will* mail. It's awful to realize the day after you've sent off a letter that you desperately wish you hadn't done it—the

United States Post Office has no interest in helping you with that problem.

Most people that I talk to tell me it does no good to write letters to corporations, politicians, and all the disembodied powerful Absent Xs out there. It's useless, they tell me, so they don't waste their time that way.

I'm sorry; they're wrong. Precisely because the art of letter writing has fallen off under the influence of the telephone, the computer, and the jet plane, a well-written letter of protest, support, or information has a respectable impact. This is provided it is to be read by a human being. If the letter you write goes to Blue Cross/Blue Shield's computer, it can be the greatest epistolary masterpiece since the letters of St. Paul to the Corinthians—it won't make a bit of difference. If you want to send a letter anywhere that is computer dominant, get on the phone and get the full name and title of the highest-up-the-pecking-order human being you can find there. And address your letter directly and explicitly to that person. This isn't guaranteed, but it does improve your chances.

When I get rotten service or inedible food in a motel, hotel, or on public transportation, I make a note of the precise details. And as soon as I get back to my typewriter I look up the head person in the situation and send off a careful letter of complaint to him or her. I strongly recommend for this purpose one of the national directories of addresses and phone numbers; you will find the one I use listed at the end of this chapter. You don't want to invest time and effort in a letter and then have it come straight back to you undelivered because of an inadequate or outdated address.

If your problem involves one of a chain of businesses or groups, send your letter to the head of the chain at the home office, with a carbon copy to the individual heading up the actual location where you were done wrong. That is, send an original of your letter to the public relations manager of Zanadoo Inns, or to the president, with a carbon to the manager at the Zanadoo Inn where you stayed.

I have never written a letter of this kind without receiving a full apology in return, along with a note good for one free meal (or whatever fit the situation). And if enough people make the effort to protest formally nd specifically in this manner, something will eventually be done about the problem. I promise you. Even those Absent Xs know that they cannot function without the acceptance of the public they claim to serve.

The bigger and more unwieldy the Absent X, the longer it will take and the more people will be required to write before you see results, of course. One does not take on AT&T, or the Pentagon, or the Social Security Administration, with the idea that there will be a speedy response and swift changes made.

When your Absent X is one of those monster bureaucracies or corporations—especially one that has no competition and therefore no incentive to please you—sending a letter is useful in only two ways. It puts your objections on record, and that's the first step in that journey of ten thousand miles that you've been hearing about all your life. More important, it allows you to rid your language environment of the toxic wastes caused by your feeling that you are cut off from all avenues of response to Absent X, and that is the primary function of all the techniques in this chapter. Choose something else as a way of actually budging the monolith, if you're determined to do so—your letter is intended only to short-circuit the hurtful repeating tape in your head that comes from doing nothing at all.

I want to add that I am just as quick to send letters praising the unusually good as attacking the usually and unusually bad, and I consider this very important. When the language you hear or read seems to improve rather than pollute your environment, it's worth letting the source of the language know that you have noticed and appreciate it. The encouragement may be sorely needed and hard to come by.

Don't worry if your letter has a flaw or two in mechanics and content, as long as your facts are accurate. Those very flaws are what let Absent X know that your letter is a genuine home-wrought letter and not something cranked out by the hundreds on a clever computer.

The Letter to the Editor

Letters written to the letter columns of newspapers and magazines are an extremely effective public mechanism for response. People and groups in power pay considerable attention to such columns, because they are a kind of miniature poll on the issues they address and because the letters are a useful item to pin up on a bulletin board, read into the *Congressional Record,* or include in speeches and newsletters and other published materials.

It isn't easy to break into one of these columns, but it's not impossible, either. Someone does have to supply the columns with material or they couldn't stay in existence; and you rarely have to compete with professional writers for space, because professional writers have to be paid for their words and rarely donate them. You can start with a local weekly newspaper and work your way up to the Los Angeles *Times* or the Washington *Post*—nothing obliges you to go the other direction.

As with the letter you send directly to Absent X, you will want to begin by writing a letter that you won't mail, as a way of getting rid of all the things you mustn't get carried away and include in your mailed letter. That's essential.

Then write *about* Absent X rather than to him or her or it. Be sure you follow the directions for such letters given in the newspaper or magazine, being very careful to do such things as send two copies or include your telephone number or whatever else is specified. If you don't do those things—which are checked for first when your letter arrives—the letter won't even be read.

You will want to try for three, or at most four, effective paragraphs. Use every device you have learned for effective language. Your goal is approximately a short formal speech

259

written down, but you must use the resources of written language to make up for what you lose in not being there to provide body language. Here is a sample letter for your examination.

LETTER TO THE EDITOR

Dear Editor:

I have been watching with great interest the recent controversy in your pages over the proposed new English requirements for university students. And I find myself thinking of the sick man who—having taken one hundred pills that did him no good at all—is about to be required by law to take fifty more of them.

Students entering our universities today have ordinarily had at least six years of "language arts" in elementary school, two more in junior high, and two to three at the high-school level, under a variety of labels. Nonetheless, they arrive at college without having mastered the archaic written style demanded of them for academic success. Because the style is utterly different from their normal language mode, and is required of them nowhere else *except* in the academic environment, this is not particularly surprising.

I am impressed by the good sense of those who are unwilling to impose yet one more year of something that almost never works in the first place, has little or no relationship to the real world, and creates in the students nothing more than a counterproductive distaste for both reading and writing.

> Sincerely,
> Suzette Haden Elgin

The letter begins with a metaphor and sets up points at which the two structures match. The English student who cannot pass standardized tests in writing is like the man who cannot pass standardized tests in medicine. The many courses in language arts that do the student no good are like the many pills that do the sick man no good. Giving the students still more such courses is like giving the sick man still more of the same pills. I can count on people who read the newspaper and are interested enough in the issue to read my letter—they will know that the label *sick* matches the label *remedial* in education. They may even know that the student who fails something called a "competency" exam at once attaches to himself or herself the label "incompetent," because that is how the English language works. I do not have to present the entire medical model of education in my letter, because my metaphor brings in enough of it to allow the reader to construct the missing portions.

The second paragraph supports the metaphor with a logical argument: Because all the years of language arts that students have already "taken" as they would take medication have done no good, requiring still another year of what has proved to be useless makes no sense. It is important for this chunk of logic to *follow* the metaphor. It would have been just as logical if it had been the first paragraph of the letter, but it would not have been as persuasive. If the reader has already accepted the metaphor, the logic *fits into* it, and it then becomes useful.

The third paragraph uses parallel structure, presupposes all sorts of things I want to say by putting them inside nominalizations, and takes the essential step of appealing to the common individual (and complimenting him or her for good sense).

You may have no interest at all in being a professional writer and may have always thought that the only thing that might damage an Absent X of any size is one of those massive reports from an investigating commission. As it happens in the real world, however, almost nobody reads the reports, those who do read them forget them in a day or two, and the process has become a kind of joke. If you are faced with a serious problem and want to be perceived as concerned and willing to *do* something about it—but you really don't want to do anything about it—you appoint a commission to investigate it and write a report. You know, of course, that the report will serve no purpose except as a symbol of your concern, allowing you to say "Whaddaya *mean*, I don't even care? I appointed a commission."

A good letter to the editor, on the other hand, is read by many people and is remembered. It goes up on bulletin boards, where it is read by many more people, including people who would not read the newspaper itself. It gets mailed to the Absent X that it is about and may well turn up on Absent *X's* bulletin boards. When it is good enough, it often brings Absent X right out of the woodwork and into the letter columns! That is, although if you wrote directly to a giant bureaucracy or corporation you would be lucky to get a form letter in reply, your published letter will often result in a countering letter from a high official in that bureaucracy or corporation. And that is very satisfying indeed. It means that you have managed to achieve a language interaction with Absent X *despite* the vast distance between you—and, furthermore, you have managed to alert large numbers of other people to the exchange. It is definitely worth the effort.

No matter which of these techniques you decide to use, keep in mind their *purpose*. They are intended to give you a way to get rid of language that would otherwise cause you harm. You use them instead of setting up an endless self-tormenting tape in your head about what X said or wrote and what you would like to say or write in response. They are meant to serve as lightning rods do, draining off surplus energy harmlessly. If you become wound up in trying to "do them right"—worrying about whether your journal is correctly punctuated or not, fretting over the selection of colors in your collage—they will only be one more source of stress. Keep their intended function *firmly* in mind, and don't lose track of it.

SUPPLEMENTARY QUOTATIONS

In general, the genesis of a stress disorder is as follows. A person is confronted with a situation that is extremely difficult to resolve or avoid. This situation becomes overwhelming and he sees no respite from it. As a result he makes an unconscious choice that allows him a means of coping with this irresolvable situation; often the choice is to develop a symptom. Once this course of action proves successful, the person will unwittingly tend to repeat this same pattern in response to stress ... so that finally the person suffers from a maneuver that was originally to bring him relief.

Since the decision that leads to the development of disease in response to stress is made at an unconscious level, the person is at a loss to undo the decision that brought on his problem [Pelletier, 1977, p. 36].

It makes more sense to think of various versions of the world that individuals may entertain, various characterizations of reality that might be presented in words, pictures, diagrams, logical propositions, or even musical compositions. Each of these symbol systems captures different kinds of information and hence presents different versions of reality [Gardner, 1980, p. 94].

SUGGESTED READINGS

BLACK, D. "Medicine and the Mind." *Playboy*, February 1980, pp. 121–22, 211–22. (A very extensive discussion of the major figures in health care who put responsibility for illness on emotional stress—including Simonton, Ellerbroek, Pelletier, and Menninger, among others.)

COOPER, C. L., ed. *Improving Interpersonal Relations: A Guide to Social Skill Development for Managers and Group Leaders*. Englewood Cliffs, N.J.: Prentice-Hall, Inc., 1982. (Contains one chapter each presenting transactional analysis, interaction analysis, assertiveness training, and "the T-group approach," by various experts. Cooper provides an introduction and a concluding chapter which compares and contrasts the four theories.)

FINCHER, J. "Inside an Intensive Journal Workshop." *Medical Self-Care* No. 4 (1978), pp. 6–10. (Personal report on a journal workshop with Ira Progoff. The same issue has an interview with

Progoff by editor Tom Ferguson, as well as a review of Progoff's book *At a Journal Workshop*, which includes a set of index tabs for your own "intensive journal." Highly recommended.)

GARDNER, H. "Gifted Worldmakers." *Psychology Today*, September 1980, pp. 92–96. (See quotation above.)

GOLEMAN, D. "Meditation without Mystery." *Psychology Today*, March 1977, pp. 55–67, 88. (A brief description of each of the traditional primary systems of meditation—does not take up such contemporary systems as Transcendental Meditation.)

GOSHGARIAN, G., ed. *Exploring Language*. Boston: Little, Brown & Co., 1977. (A collection of articles offering much useful information on a variety of sources of semantic pollution. In particular, the following articles: "How to Write Potent Copy," by David Ogilvy, pp. 266–73; "The Semantic Environment in the Age of Advertising," by Henryk Skolimowski, pp. 275–83; and "Doctor Johnson, Glenn Miller and the Seven Deadly Sins," by David Bernstein, pp. 284–92.)

JAMES, M. "The OK Boss in All of Us." *Psychology Today*, February 1976, pp. 31–37. (Very fine brief summary of Transactional Analysis, with many useful items of information for verbal self-defense.)

KAISER, R. B. "The Way of the Journal." *Psychology Today*, March 1981, pp. 64–76. (Thorough discussion of the journal method developed by psychologist Ira Progoff, and a good supplement to the articles listed above under Fincher 1978.)

LAPHAM, L. H. "Gilding the News." *Harper's*, July 1981, pp. 31–39. (Fine discussion of newspapers, books, and magazines as sources of pollution in the linguistic environment.)

LAZARUS, R. S. "Little Hassles Can Be Hazardous to Health." *Psychology Today*, July 1981, pp. 58–61. (Discussion of the fact that it doesn't require a major life crisis to create health-damaging stress.)

LOOMIS, K. S., ed. *National Directory of Addresses and Telephone Numbers*. New York: Concord Reference Books, Inc., 1982. (*My* source for names and addresses of Absent Xs. It comes from 14 Park Road, Tinton Falls, N.J. 07724.)

PELLETIER, K. R. "Mind as Healer, Mind as Slayer." *Psychology Today,* February 1977, pp. 35–40, 82–83. (A discussion of "medical and psychological problems caused by stress" with recommendations for coping with them.)

RICE, B. "Can Companies Kill?" *Psychology Today,* June 1981, pp. 78–85. (A discussion of physical and/or emotional illnesses alleged to be the result of stress in the workplace, and legal decisions made in a number of such cases.)

ROSENBAUM, R. "The Body's Inner Voices." *New Times,* June 26, 1978, pp. 45–57. (Discusses the theory that any bodily function for which clear feedback information can be provided can be made subject to the voluntary control of the individual.)

SCARF, M. "Images That Heal: A Doubtful Idea Whose Time Has Come." *Psychology Today,* September 1980, pp. 32–45. (A discussion of the idea that negative emotions are a primary cause of cancer, and of the technique of "imaging" developed by Dr. O. Carl Simonton to combat cancer. Begins with a reference to Arnold A. Hutschnecker's claim in his 1951 book *The Will to Live* that human beings choose not only when they will get sick, but also which diseases they will get and how badly they will have them.)

SLANSKY, P. "Presidential Speechwriting in Thirteen Easy Lessons." *New Times,* October 26, 1975, pp. 32–33. (A humorous but most revealing list of the thirteen basic ingredients of presidential speeches.)

STAFF. *Medical Self-Care No. 5* (1978). (Special issue on stress and various methods of dealing with it, including much information in the form of book reviews and discussions of organizations.)

VONNEGUT, K. "A Truly Modern Hero." *Psychology Today,* August 1981, pp. 9–10. (From a speech given by Vonnegut at Southampton College. Worth careful study for its rhetorical structure and its examination of language as semantic toxin.)

Appendix:
A Verbal Self-Defense
Survival Kit

A GLOSSARY OF TERMS

AUDITORY (EAR, HEARING, AURAL) MODE: One of the sensory modes; typical utterances for this mode include "I hear what you're saying." "That sounds good to me." "I can't believe my ears."

BLAMER, BLAMING: One of the Satir Modes; a pattern of language behavior that has anger as its nonverbal impression. Typical Blaming utterances include "*Why* do you always spoil everything?" "*Why* don't you ever consider anyone else's feelings but your own?" "You *always* act like that!"

COMPUTER, COMPUTING: One of the Satir Modes; a pattern of language behavior that has the absence of emotion as its nonverbal impression. Typical Computing utterances include "One would think that . . ." "It can safely be assumed that . . ." "Obviously, there is no cause for alarm."

DISTRACTER, DISTRACTING: One of the Satir Modes; a pattern of language behavior that has panic as its nonverbal impression. The Distracter has no single typical utterance type because he or she cycles rapidly among all the Satir Modes, seemingly at random.

For example, "*Why* do you always blame me for everything? Not that *I* care if you do or not . . . you know me, *I* don't care! Why should *I* care? However, it would appear obvious that blaming a single individual for all events is illogical. Don't you think so?"

INTERACTION: Any contact between two or more human beings in which language is used as a medium of communication; this includes conversations, lectures, interviews, interrogations, arguments, debates, conferences, and so on.

INTONATION: That part of the sound system of language that refers not to the words used but to the melody of the voice *as* they are used. It includes tone of voice, voice quality, pitch, volume, stress, and the like. Punctuation is the system used for writing down intonation.

LEVELER, LEVELING: One of the Satir Modes; a pattern of language behavior in which the nonverbal message, the verbal one, and the inner feelings all match. There are no typical Leveler utterances; they vary with the situation.

METAPHOR: An organization of symbols and/or statements that compares one thing to another by demonstrating that they share a relationship between pairs of items or characteristics, as in "Language is a tree." You could use a tree as a metaphor for a language by comparing sentences to branches, words to twigs, and letters or sounds to leaves. It isn't necessary for every characteristic in one half of a metaphor to match every characteristic in the other half, which is extremely rare in the real world.

NATIVE SPEAKER: Someone who has acquired a language natively, almost always as an infant or very small child, and who speaks and understands it with total fluency. It is very rare for adults to be able to achieve native fluency in a language.

PLACATER, PLACATING: One of the Satir Modes; a pattern of language behavior that has anxiety as its nonverbal impression. Typical Placating utterances include "Oh, you know me, *I* don't care!" "Whatever you want is okay with *me!*"

PRESUPPOSITION: Anything that a native speaker of a language knows is part of the meaning of a sequence of that language, even if it isn't overtly present in the surface form (usually, the words) of that sequence.

SATIR MODE(S): Five terms developed by Dr. Virginia Satir to classify language behavior: Blaming, Placating, Computing, Distracting, and Leveling (see individual entries).

SENSORY MODE(S): The way information from within yourself and from the outside world is perceived, interpreted, and expressed, in terms of a particular sense. The sensory modes include the eyes (visual, sight); the ears (auditory, hearing, aural); touch (tactile, feeling, kinesthetic); smell (olfactory); and taste (gustatory) (see individual entries). There may be additional sensory modes, but at this time there is no evidence for them as expressed in language.

SMELL (OLFACTORY) MODE: One of the sensory modes; typical utterances for this mode include "I don't like the smell of this at all." "That smells fishy to me." "You're just sniffing around the problem."

STRESS: A phenomenon from the sound system of a language that is heard as slightly louder volume and higher pitch on a word or part of a word; stress is very important to meaning in English. (NOTE: The word also appears in this book with the meaning "strain, tension," as in "She was under a great deal of stress.")

TACTILE (TOUCH) MODE: One of the sensory modes; typical utterances for this mode include "I get your point." "That feels right to me." "I can't seem to grasp what you're saying." "I think I can handle that."

TASTE (GUSTATORY) MODE: One of the sensory modes; typical utterances for this mode include "That's a sweet thing to say." "She makes me sick at my stomach." "What a rotten way to talk!" "This gives me a bad taste in my mouth."

UTTERANCE: Any sequence of words, either spoken or quoted; an utterance can be a nonsentence or a sequence of connected sentences. It is typical for an utterance to contain meaningful noises (such as *uh* or *mmm*) that are not strictly words at all.

VERBAL SELF-DEFENSE (VSD): A systematic method for using language as a means for defense against verbal abuse and as a means for preventing such abuse. VSD is a linguistic equivalent for the physical "martial arts" and is entirely nonviolent.

VISUAL (EYE, SEEING, SIGHT) MODE: One of the sensory modes; typical utterances for this mode include "I see what you mean." "That looks good to me." "I can't believe my eyes."

ATTACK PATTERNS FROM THE VERBAL VIOLENCE OCTAGON

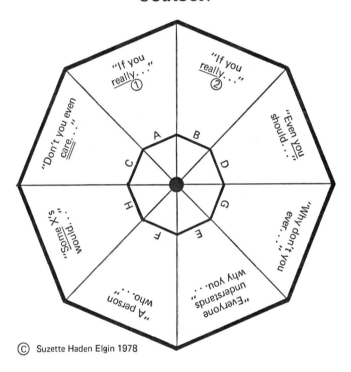

SECTION A:
"If you *really* loved me, you wouldn't leave."
>*Presupposition:*
>You don't love me.

269

SECTION B:

"If you *really* loved me, you wouldn't *want* to leave."
> *Presuppositions:*
> You don't love me.
> You have the power to control your feelings if you choose to.

SECTION C:

"Don't you even *care* about your weight?"
> *Presuppositions:*
> You don't care about your weight.
> You should care—it's wrong not to.
> You should feel guilty and rotten.

SECTION D:

"Even a *man* should be able to understand *math.*"
> *Presuppositions:*
> There's something wrong with being a man.
> It doesn't take much to understand math.
> You should feel guilty and stupid.

SECTION E:

"Everybody under*stands* why you can't get along with other people!"
> *Presuppositions:*
> You can't get along with other people.
> The reason you can't get along with other people is pretty unsavory.
> Everybody knows what that reason is—no point in your trying to hide it.

SECTION F:

"A person who *really* wanted to save money would spend it *care*fully."
> *Presuppositions:*
> You don't want to save money.
> You spend money carelessly.

SECTION G:
"*Why* don't you ever think about my feelings?"
  Presuppositions:
  You never think about my feelings.
  You have a reason for that, and I want to know what it is—tell
me.

SECTION H:
"*Some* husbands would really get mad if you forgot dinner."
  Presuppositions:
  It's wrong of you to forget dinner.
  I'm not like other husbands—I'm unique and superior.
  You should feel very guilty about forgetting dinner.
  You should feel very grateful to me for being so unique and
superior.

NOTE: The heavy stresses (marked in the sample sentences by italics) are extremely important. The same words without those stresses are probably not attacks at all. Sometimes a slightly different pattern may appear; for example, you may hear "If you really *loved* me . . ." instead of "If you *really* loved me. . . ." But you will quickly learn to spot these variations, and the cue that lets you know the utterance is an attack is in the word patterns *plus* heavy stress.

THE BASIC PRINCIPLES
OF VERBAL SELF-DEFENSE

1. KNOW THAT YOU ARE UNDER ATTACK

Some Cues: Use of Blamer Mode.
       Use of an attack pattern.
       Use of *even, really, only, just, ever, never, always,*
       especially with heavy stress.
       Use of threatening posture, gesture, tone of voice,
       or facial expression.

2. KNOW WHAT KIND OF ATTACK YOU ARE FACING.

Some Cues: What Satir Mode is being used?

What sensory mode is being used?

Which verbal attack pattern (if any) is being used?

How intense is the attack?

What power in the real world does your opponent have to harm you or reward you?

3. KNOW HOW TO MAKE YOUR DEFENSE FIT THE ATTACK.

Some Cues: Defend yourself—don't counterattack.

Use only as much force as is absolutely required.

Use your opponent's strength as part of your defense.

If you don't know what to do, *go to Computer Mode and maintain it.*

4. KNOW HOW TO FOLLOW THROUGH.

Some Cues: Remember that verbal self-defense is nonviolent and honorable.

Remember that your goal is to *defuse* confrontations.

Remember that in any martial art you will be awkward at first and will improve with practice.

If you're not accustomed to defending yourself, be prepared to feel guilt and to work through it. But don't let guilt *stop* you.

THE VERBAL SELF-DEFENSE BOOKSHELF

BOLTON, R. *People Skills: How to Assert Yourself, Listen to Others, and Resolve Conflicts.* Englewood Cliffs, N.J.: Prentice-Hall, Inc., 1979.

ELGIN, S. H. *The Gentle Art of Verbal Self-Defense*. Englewood Cliffs, N.J.: Prentice-Hall, Inc., 1980.

ELLUL, J. *Propaganda: The Formation of Men's Attitudes*. New York: Random House (Vintage Books), 1973. (This is a scholarly book, but not difficult to read—and it is remarkably useful with regard to the formation of *women's* attitudes also.)

HENLEY, N. *Body Politics: Power, Sex, and Nonverbal Communication*. Englewood Cliffs, N.J.: Prentice-Hall, Inc., 1977.

MACNEILAGE, L. A., and K. A. ADAMS. *Assertiveness at Work: How to Increase Your Personal Power on the Job*. Englewood Cliffs, N.J.: Prentice-Hall, Inc., 1982.

Here are two otther books not specifically on language, but invaluable for conversations in which everyone talks about things you have never heard of, never read, know nothing about, or have forgotten.

HORNSTEIN, L. H., et al., eds. *The Reader's Companion to World Literature*. New York: New American Library (Mentor Books), 1973.

KOFF, R. M. *How Does It Work?* New York: New American Library (Signet Books), 1968.

And a subscription to two magazines: *Psychology Today* and *Human Behavior*.

Bibliography
and References

ARTICLES

ANDREWS, L. B. "Mind Control in the Courtroom." *Psychology Today*, March 1982, pp. 66–73.

BENDERLY, B. L. "Dancing without Music." *Science 80*, December 1980, pp. 54–59.

BIRDWHISTELL, R. L. *Kinesics and Context*. Philadelphia: University of Pennsylvania Press, 1970.

BLACK, D. "Medicine and the Mind." *Playboy*, February 1980, pp. 121–22, 211–22.

CAIN, W. S. "Educating Your Nose." *Psychology Today*, July 1981, pp. 48–56.

CHARROW, V. R. "Linguistic Theory and the Study of Legal and Bureaucratic Language," in *Exceptional Language and Linguistics*, eds. L. K. Obler and L. Menn. New York: Academic Press, 1982, pp. 81–101. (An excellent article, not overly technical, on the language of law and bureaucracy; includes a useful bibliography on the subject.)

274

COLE, R. A. "Navigating the Slippery Stream of Speech." *Psychology Today,* April 1979, pp. 77–87.

CONDON, W. S. "The Relation of Interactional Synchrony to Cognitive and Emotional Processes," in *The Relationship of Verbal and Nonverbal Communication,* student edition, ed. Mary Ritchie Key. The Hague: Mouton Publishers, 1980, pp. 49–65.

———, and W. D. Ogston. "Speech and Body Motion Synchrony of the Speaker-Hearer," in *Perception of Language,* eds. D. L. Horton and J. J. Jenkins. Columbus, Ohio: Charles E. Merrill, 1971.

COUSINS, N. "Anatomy of an Illness (as Perceived by the Patient)." *Saturday Review,* May 28, 1977, pp. 4–6, 48–51.

———. Cousins, N. "The Mysterious Placebo: How Mind Helps Medicine Work." *Saturday Review,* October 1, 1977, pp. 9–16.

ELLERBROEK, W. C. "Language, Thought, and Disease." *The Co-Evolution Quarterly,* Spring 1978, pp. 30–38.

———. "Language, Emotion and Disease." *Omni,* November 1978a, pp. 93–95, 120.

EWING, D. W. "Canning Directions." *Harper's,* August 1979, pp. 16–18.

FERGUSON, M. "Karl Pribram's Changing Reality." *Human Behavior,* May 1978, pp. 28–33.

FINCHER, J. "The Joy (Grief, Love, Hate, Anger, Sex and Reverence) of Music." *Human Behavior,* April 1977, pp. 25–30.

———. "Inside an Intensive Journal Workshop." *Medical Self-Care,* No. 4 (1978), pp. 6–10.

GARDNER, H. "Strange Loops of the Mind." *Psychology Today,* March 1980, pp. 72–85.

———. "Gifted Worldmakers." *Psychology Today,* September 1980, pp. 92–96.

———, and E. WINNER. "The Child Is Father to the Metaphor." *Psychology Today,* May 1979, pp. 81–91.

GELDARD, F. A. "Body English." *Psychology Today,* December 1968, pp. 43–47.

GOLEMAN, D. "Meditation without Mystery." *Psychology Today,* March 1977, pp. 55–67, 88.

———. "People Who Read People." *Psychology Today,* July 1979, pp. 66–78.

HILGARD, E. R. "Hypnosis Is No Mirage." *Psychology Today*, November 1974, pp. 121–28.

JAMES, M. "The OK Boss in All of Us." *Psychology Today*, February 1976, pp. 31–37.

JONAS, G. "Manfred Clynes and the Science of Sentics." *Saturday Review*, May 13, 1972, pp. 42–51.

————. Review of *Sentics: The Touch of Emotions* by Manfred Clynes (New York: Doubleday, 1977). *Psychology Today*, February 1977, pp. 98–99.

KAISER, R. B. "The Way of the Journal." *Psychology Today*, March 1981, pp. 64–76.

KEMPTON, W. "The Rhythmic Basis of Interactional Micro-Synchrony," in *The Relationship of Verbal and Nonverbal Communication*, student edition, ed. Mary Ritchie Key. The Hague: Mouton Publishers, 1980, pp. 67–75.

KIMURA, D. "The Asymmetry of the Human Brain." *Scientific American*, March 1973, pp. 2–9.

KINSBOURNE, M. "Why Is the Brain Biased?" *Psychology Today*, May 1979, p. 150.

————. "Sad Hemisphere, Happy Hemisphere." *Psychology Today*, May 1981, p. 92.

KINSLEY, M. "The Easy Chair: Waiting for Lenny." *Harper's*, March 1982, pp. 8–11.

KOTKER, Z. "The 'Feminine' Behavior of Powerless People." *Savvy*, March 1980, pp. 36–42.

LAKOFF, G. "Hedges: A Study in Meaning Criteria and the Logic of Fuzzy Concepts," in *Papers from the Eighth Regional Meeting of the Chicago Linguistic Society* (CLS-8), eds. P. Peranteau et al., 1972, pp. 183–228.

LAKOFF, R. "Linguistic Theory and the Real World." *Language Learning* 25, No. 2, 1976, pp. 309–38.

LANDEFELD, J. "Speaking Therapeutically." *Human Behavior*, September 1975, pp. 56–99.

LAPHAM, L. H. "Gilding the News." *Harper's*, July 1981, pp. 31–39.

LAZARUS, R. S. "Little Hassles Can Be Hazardous to Health." *Psychology Today*, July 1981, pp. 58–61.

LEHRER, A. "Critical Communication: Wine and Therapy," in *Exceptional Language and Linguistics*, eds. L. K. Obler and L. Menn. New York: Academic Press, 1982, pp. 67–80.

LEONARD, G. "Language and Reality." *Harper's*, November 1974, pp. 46–52.

LOFTUS, E. "Words That Could Save Your Life." *Psychology Today*, November 1979, pp. 102–10.

MARIN, P. "The New Narcissism." *Harper's*, October 1975, pp. 45–56.

MILLER, G., and E. HALL."Giving Away Psychology in the 80's." (Interview.) *Psychology Today*, January 1980, pp. 38–50, 97–98.

MILLER, J. "A Message Center for Mental Health ..." *Human Behavior*, July 1977, pp. 25–36.

PAPCUN, G., et al. "Is the Left Hemisphere Specialized for Speech, Language and/or Something Else?" *Journal of the Acoustical Society of America* 55, No. 2 (February 1974), pp. 319–27.

PARLEE, M. B. "Conversational Politics." *Psychology Today*, May 1979, pp. 48–56.

PELLETIER, K. R. "Mind as Healer, Mind as Slayer." *Psychology Today*, February 1977, pp. 35–40, 82–83.

PERT, A. "The Body's Own Tranquilizers." *Psychology Today*, September 1981, p. 100.

PHILIPS, S. U. "Sex Differences and Language." *Annual Review of Anthropology* No. 9, (1980), pp. 523–44.

REICH, W. "The Force of Diagnosis: Opportune Uses of Psychiatry." *Harper's*, May 1980, pp. 20–32.

RESTAK, R. "The Brain Makes Its Own Narcotics!" *Saturday Review*, March 5, 1977, pp. 7–11.

RICE, B. "Can Companies Kill?" *Psychology Today*, June 1981, pp. 78–85.

_____. "Between the Lines of Threatening Messages." *Psychology Today*, September 1981, pp. 52–64.

ROSENBAUM, R. "The Body's Inner Voices." *New Times*, June 26, 1978, pp. 45–57.

SACKS, H., et al. "A Simplest Systematics for the Organization of Turntaking for Conversation." *Language* 50, No. 4 (December 1974), pp. 696–735.

SCARF, M. "Images That Heal: A Doubtful Idea Whose Time Has Come." *Psychology Today,* September 1980, pp. 32–45.

SHARP, D. "Aristotle's Garage." *Harper's,* March 1981, pp. 91–93.

SHUY, R. W. "The Medical Interview: Problems in Communication." *Primary Care* 3, No. 3 (September 1976), pp. 365–86.

SLANSKY, P. "Presidential Speechwriting in Thirteen Easy Lessons." *New Times,* October 26, 1975, pp. 32–33.

SNYDER, M. "The Many Me's of the Self-Monitor." *Psychology Today,* March 1980, pp. 33–40, 92.

SPERRY, R. W. "Left-Brain, Right-Brain." *Saturday Review,* August 9, 1975, pp. 30–33.

STAFF. *Medical Self-Care,* No. 5 (1978). (Special issue on stress.)

STAFF. "Psychiatry on the Couch." *Time,* April 2, 1979, pp. 74–82.

VENDLER, Z. Review of *Pragmatics* by Peter Cole (New York: Academic Press, 1978). *Language* 56, No. 1 (January 1980), pp. 209–11.

VONNEGUT, K. "A Truly Modern Hero." *Psychology Today,* August 1981, pp. 9–10.

WILLS, G. "Feminists and Other Useful Fanatics." *Harper's,* June 1976, pp. 35–42.

YANKELOVICH, D. "Reagan and the National Psyche." *Psychology Today,* January 1982, pp. 5–8.

YOUNGBLOOD, G. "The Mass Media and the Future of Desire." *Co-Evolution Quarterly* No. 16, (Winter 1977–78), pp. 6–17.

BOOKS

ADDEO, E. G., and R. E. BURGER. *EgoSpeak: Why No One Listens to You.* New York: Bantam Books, Inc., 1973.

BOGARD, M. R. *The Manager's Style Book: Communication Skills to Improve Your Performance.* Englewood Cliffs, N.J.: Prentice-Hall, Inc., 1979.

BOLTON, R. *People Skills: How to Assert Yourself, Listen to Others and Resolve Conflicts.* Englewood Cliffs, N.J.: Prentice-Hall, Inc., 1979.

CLARK, V. P., et al., eds. *Language: Introductory Readings,* third edition. New York: St. Martin's Press, 1981.

COOPER, C. L., ed. *Improving Interpersonal Relations: A Guide to Social Skill Development for Managers and Group Leaders.* Englewood Cliffs, N.J.: Prentice-Hall, Inc., 1982.

DOIG, I., and C. DOIG. *News: A Consumer's Guide.* Englewood Cliffs, N.J.: Prentice-Hall, Inc., 1972.

EDWARDS, B. *Drawing on the Right Side of the Brain.* Los Angeles: J. P. Tarcher, Inc., 1979.

ELGIN, S. H. *Pouring Down Words.* Englewood Cliffs, N.J.: Prentice-Hall, Inc., 1975.

———. *The Gentle Art of Verbal Self-Defense.* Englewood Cliffs, N.J.: Prentice-Hall, Inc., 1980.

———. *What Is Linguistics?* second edition. Englewood Cliffs, N.J.: Prentice-Hall, Inc., 1980a.

ELLUL, J. *Propaganda: The Formation of Men's Attitudes.* New York: Vintage Books, 1976.

FAST, J. *Body Language.* Philadelphia: M. Evans & Company, Inc., 1970.

FELBER, S. B., and A. KOCH. *What Did You Say? A Guide to the Communication Skills,* second edition. Englewood Cliffs, N.J.: Prentice-Hall, Inc., 1978.

GOSHGARIAN, G., ed. *Exploring Language.* Boston: Little, Brown & Co., 1977.

GRINDER, J., and R. BANDLER. *The Structure of Magic: II.* Palo Alto, Calif.: Science and Behavior Books, Inc., 1976.

HALL, E. T. *The Silent Language.* New York: Doubleday, 1959.

———. *The Hidden Dimension.* New York: Doubleday, 1969.

———. *Beyond Culture.* New York: Doubleday, 1976.

HENLEY, N. *Body Politics: Power, Sex, and Nonverbal Communication.* Englewood Cliffs, N.J.: Prentice-Hall, Inc., 1977.

HORNSTEIN, L. H., et al., eds. *The Reader's Companion to World Literature.* New York: New American Library (Mentor Books), 1973.

HUNSAKER, P. L., and A. J. ALLESSANDRA. *The Art of Managing People.* Englewood Cliffs, N.J.: Prentice-Hall, Inc., 1980.

KEY, M. R.,, ed. *The Relationship of Verbal and Nonverbal Communication*, student edition. The Hague: Mouton Publishers, 1980.

KOFF, R. M. *How Does It Work?* New York: New American Library (Signet Books), 1968.

LOOMIS, K. S., ed. *National Director of Addresses and Telephone Numbers*. New York: Concord Reference Books, Inc., 1982.

MACNEILAGE, L. A., and K. A. ADAMS. *Assertiveness at Work: How to Increase Your Personal Power on the Job.* Englewood Cliffs, N.J.: Prentice-Hall, Inc., 1982.

MILLER, G. A. *The Psychology of Communication.* New York: Basic Books, Inc., 1975.

MILLER, M. *Where to Go for What: How to Research, Organize, and Present Your Information.* Englewood Cliffs, N.J.: Prentice-Hall, Inc., 1981.

NIERENBERG, G. I., and H. H. CALERO. *How to Read a Person Like a Book.* New York: Pocket Books, 1971.

NIMMO, D., and J. E. COMBS. *Subliminal Politics: Myths and Mythmakers in America.* Englewood Cliffs, N.J.: Prentice-Hall, Inc., 1980.

OBLER, L. K., and L. MENN, eds. *Exceptional Language and Linguistics.* New York: Academic Press, 1982.

ODIORNE, G. S. *The Change Resisters: How They Prevent Progress and What Managers Can Do about Them.* Englewood Cliffs, N.J.: Prentice-Hall, Inc., 1981.

POSTMAN, N. *Crazy Talk, Stupid Talk: How We Defeat Ourselves by the Way We Talk—and What to Do about It.* New York: Dell Publishing Co., 1976.

SATIR, VIRGINIA. *Conjoint Family Therapy.* Palo Alto, Calif.: Science and Behavior Books, Inc., 1964.

———. *Peoplemaking.* Palo Alto, Calif.: Science and Behavior Books, Inc., 1972.

SCHEFLEN, A. E., and A. SCHEFLEN. *Body Language and the Social Order: Communication as Behavioral Control.* Englewood Cliffs, N.J.: Prentice-Hall, Inc., 1972.

SONTAG, S. *Illness as Metaphor.* New York: Vintage Books, 1979.

TRENT, J. D., et al., eds. *Concepts in Communication.* Boston:Allyn & Bacon, Inc., 1973.

Index